Troy
From Homer's *Iliad* to Hollywood Epic

Troy
From Homer's *Iliad* to Hollywood Epic

Edited by

Martin M. Winkler

Blackwell
Publishing

© 2007 by Blackwell Publishing Ltd

BLACKWELL PUBLISHING
350 Main Street, Malden, MA 02148-5020, USA
9600 Garsington Road, Oxford OX4 2DQ, UK
550 Swanston Street, Carlton, Victoria 3053, Australia

The right of Martin M. Winkler to be identified as the Author of the Editorial
Material in this Work has been asserted in accordance with the UK Copyright,
Designs, and Patents Act 1988.

First published 2007 by Blackwell Publishing Ltd

1   2007

Library of Congress Cataloging-in-Publication Data

Troy : from Homer's Iliad to Hollywood epic / edited by Martin M. Winkler.
    p.   cm.
  Includes bibliographical references and index.
  ISBN-13: 978-1-4051-3182-7 (hardcover : alk. paper)
  ISBN-10: 1-4051-3182-9 (hardcover : alk. paper)
  ISBN-13: 978-1-4051-3183-4 (pbk. : alk. paper)
  ISBN-10: 1-4051-3183-7 (pbk. : alk. paper)
  1. Troy (Motion picture)   2. Trojan War.   3. Trojan War—Motion
pictures and the war.   I. Winkler, Martin M.
  PN1997.2.T78 2007
  791.43'72—dc22
                                                        2005030974

A catalogue record for this title is available from the British Library.

Set in 10/12.5pt Photina
by Graphicraft Limited, Hong Kong
Printed and bound in Singapore
by C.O.S. Printers Pte Ltd

The publisher's policy is to use permanent paper from mills that operate a
sustainable forestry policy, and which has been manufactured from pulp
processed using acid-free and elementary chlorine-free practices. Furthermore,
the publisher ensures that the text paper and cover board used have met
acceptable environmental accreditation standards.

For further information on
Blackwell Publishing, visit our website:
www.blackwellpublishing.com

Contents

List of Plates

Notes on Contributors

FREDERICK AHL is Professor of Classics and Comparative Literature and Stephen H. Weiss Presidential Fellow at Cornell University. He is the author of *Lucan: An Introduction*, *Metaformations: Soundplay and Wordplay in Ovid and Other Classical Poets*, *Sophocles' Oedipus: Evidence and Self-Conviction*, *The Odyssey Re-Formed* (with Hanna M. Roisman), and of articles on Greek music, Homeric narrative, ancient rhetoric, and Roman imperial poetry. He has also translated Seneca's tragedies and Virgil's *Aeneid*.

ALENA ALLEN is Instructor of Latin at Cathedral High School in San Diego, California. She wrote her graduate thesis on Ovid's use of Homeric characters in the *Heroides* and frequently lectures on Ovid and Homer.

MONICA S. CYRINO is Associate Professor of Classics at the University of New Mexico. She is the author of *In Pandora's Jar: Lovesickness in Early Greek Poetry* and *Big-Screen Rome* and has published articles on Greek poetry, mythology, and classics and cinema. She frequently lectures on and teaches courses in classics, film, and popular culture.

GEORG DANEK is Associate Professor of Classics at the University of Vienna. His interests include Homeric studies, comparative epic studies

(South Slavic heroic songs), and the performance of Greek poetry and music, especially a reconstruction of the technique of Homeric performance. His books are *Studien zur Dolonie*, *Epos und Zitat: Studien zu den Quellen der Odyssee*, and *Bosnische Heldenepen* (a German translation of selected Bosnian epics, including one by Avdo Medjedovic, the "Yugoslavian Homer").

J. LESLEY FITTON is curator in the Department of Greek and Roman Antiquities at the British Museum, for which she organized the exhibition *Troy Retold* in 2004. Her books include *The Discovery of the Greek Bronze Age* and *Minoans*.

MANFRED O. KORFMANN, Professor of Prehistoric and Protohistoric Archaeology at the University of Tübingen and director of the excavations at Troy-Hisarlık since 1988, died in 2005. He was the author of more than 150 publications in international archaeological journals. From 1991 he was the editor of *Studia Troica*, a series of annual excavation reports. He received several international awards for his archaeological work.

JOACHIM LATACZ is Professor Emeritus of Greek Language and Literature at the University of Basel. He is the author of several books and numerous essays on Homer. Two of his books have appeared in English translation: *Homer: His Art and His World* and *Troy and Homer: Towards a Solution of an Old Mystery*. He is the founder and director of the *Basler Homer-Kommentar*, an international multi-volume project of textual edition, translation, and commentary on the *Iliad*. He has published articles on early Greek lyric poetry, Greek tragedy, Roman literature, and linguistics and is co-editor of *Studia Troica*. He was co-organizer of a large-scale exhibition on Troy that attracted 850,000 visitors in Germany during 2001 and 2002.

ROBERT J. RABEL is Professor of Classics at the University of Kentucky. He is the author of *Plot and Point of View in the Iliad* and the editor of *Approaches to Homer, Ancient and Modern*. He has published articles on Homer, on Greek and Roman literature, and on classics and cinema.

STEPHEN SCULLY is Associate Professor of Classics at Boston University and the author of *Homer and the Sacred City*. He has published on Virgil and Greek tragedy and translated Euripides' *The Suppliant Women* (with Rosanna Warren) and Plato's *Phaedrus*.

KIM SHAHABUDIN is a sessional lecturer at the University of Reading. She has published articles on aspects of the ancient world on film and gives lectures on and teaches courses in the representation of Greece and Rome in the cinema.

JON SOLOMON is Robert D. Novak Professor of Western Civilization and Culture and Professor of Cinema Studies at the University of Illinois. He is the author of *The Ancient World in the Cinema* and the editor of two collections of essays, *Accessing Antiquity: The Computerization of Classical Studies* and *Apollo: Origins and Influences*. He has also published a translation, with commentary, of Ptolemy's *Harmonics*.

MARTIN M. WINKLER is Professor of Classics at George Mason University. His books are *The Persona in Three Satires of Juvenal*, *Der lateinische Eulenspiegel des Ioannes Nemius*, and the anthology *Juvenal in English*. He is also the editor of *Classical Myth and Culture in the Cinema*, a revised edition of *Classics and Cinema*, the first collection of scholarly essays on the subject of antiquity and film. More recently he has edited the essay collection *Gladiator: Film and History*. He has published articles on Roman literature, on the classical tradition, and on classical and medieval culture and mythology in the cinema.

Editor's Introduction

Harry Cohn heard there was a good story, *The Iliad*, written by somebody named Homer, and thought it might have picture possibilities. He called his writers together and said, "Now, boys, I want a one-page treatment of it by tomorrow." So a team of Columbia writers worked all night, and the next morning, blurry-eyed, they handed Harry a one-page synopsis. Cohn read it, but looked doubtful: "There are an awful lot of Greeks in it."[1]

Too many Greeks for the American public? The head of Columbia Pictures and *enfant terrible* among Hollywood moguls may have thought so, but ancient Greeks, especially Homer's heroes, have been long prominent in the cultural and popular history of the United States, if not to the extent that the Romans have been. The early history of America readily lent itself to providing analogies to classical history or myth.[2] The tradition of referring to the *Iliad* became prominent at several moments in nineteenth-century America, as at the revolution of Texas from Mexico that culminated in the 1836 siege of the Alamo and in flare-ups

---

1 Paul F. Boller and Ronald L. Davis, *Hollywood Anecdotes* (New York: Morrow, 1987), 68–69, from a 1986 interview with actress Dolly Haas.
2 On this see John P. McWilliams, Jr., *The American Epic: Transforming a Genre, 1770–1860* (Cambridge: Cambridge University Press, 1989), especially chapters 4 ("A White Achilles for the West?") and 5 ("Red Achilles, Red Satan").

of frontier violence, most famously the 1881 gunfight at the OK Corral.[3] In between, the American Civil War (1861–1865) provided ample opportunities for references to the *Iliad*.[4]

The American tendency to draw ancient and specifically Homeric parallels to modern war has seen a resurgence in recent years in connection with World War II, the Korean War, and the wars in Vietnam and Iraq. Here are only a few examples, intended to indicate the broad range that such analogies may take. A recent translation of the *Iliad* has a photograph of the American D-Day landing for its cover illustration.[5] Christopher Logue makes specific allusions to World War II in his free poetic retellings of the *Iliad*.[6] A novel on the Korean War was hailed as an "epic story worthy of the ancient Greeks" by television journalist Dan Rather and characterized by novelist Kurt Vonnegut, Jr., with the statement: "The Korean War now has its own *Iliad*."[7] Concerning Vietnam, the best-known analogy to the Trojan War is developed in psychiatrist Jonathan Shay's book *Achilles in Vietnam*; Shay compares the psychological effects of Achilles' killings on himself to post-traumatic

---

3   On these two episodes see Stephen L. Hardin, *Texian Iliad: A Military History of the Texas Revolution, 1835–1836* (Austin: University of Texas Press, 1994), and Walter Noble Burns, *Tombstone – An Iliad of the Southwest* (Garden City: Doubleday, Page, 1927).

4   Cf. the title of Charles Pierce Roland, *An American Iliad: The Story of the Civil War*, 2nd edn (Lexington: University of Kentucky Press, 2004). *The Civil War* (1990), an eleven-hour documentary film by Ken Burns, was frequently compared to Homer's epic. A review of Jay Winik, *April 1865: The Month That Saved America* (New York: HarperCollins, 2001), sees in the burning of Richmond, the Confederate capital, an analogy to that of Troy and in Ulysses S. Grant and Robert E. Lee analogies to Achilles and Hector: Max Byrd, "The Month That Was," *The New York Times Book Review* (April 22, 2001), 25. Larry McMurtry, "His True Love Is Politics" (review of Bill Clinton, *My Life* [New York: Knopf, 2004; rpt. 2005]), *The New York Times Book Review* (July 4, 2004), 1 and 8–9, refers to Grant's autobiography as "an Iliad, with the gracious Robert E. Lee as Hector and Grant himself the murderous Achilles" (8). Thematically comparable is the perspective expressed in a speech elaborately entitled "The Soldier's Faith: An Address Delivered on Memorial Day, May 30, 1895, at a Meeting Called by the Graduating Class of Harvard University" by Oliver Wendell Holmes, best accessible in *The Collected Works of Justice Holmes: Complete Public Writings and Selected Judicial Opinions of Oliver Wendell Holmes*, ed. Sheldon M. Novick; The Holmes Devise Memorial Edition, vol. 3 (Chicago: University of Chicago Press, 1995), 486–491.

5   *Homer: Iliad*, tr. Stanley Lombardo (Indianapolis: Hackett, 1997).

6   See especially Christopher Logue, *All Day Permanent Red: The First Battle Scenes of Homer's Iliad* (New York: Farrar, Straus and Giroux, 2003).

7   James Brady, *The Marines of Autumn: A Novel of the Korean War* (New York: St. Martin's, 2000). The two quotations appeared in a full-page advertisement of the novel in *The New York Times Book Review* (July 23, 2000), 5.

stress disorder (PTSD) in Vietnam veterans.[8] Since the beginning of the second war in Iraq, waged chiefly by the United States and its ally the United Kingdom, more or less loose analogies to the Trojan War and specifically the *Iliad* have become commonplace in political comment-aries and elsewhere.[9]

American popular culture, too, and especially the cinema, has long been aware of the *Iliad* and the *Odyssey*, chiefly in retellings of the story of the Trojan War from the abduction of Helen by Paris to the fall of Troy and the return of Odysseus.[10] Large-scale adaptations have attempted to bring the Homeric and heroic past to life in glorious color and on the wide screen associated with epic subjects since the early 1950s. Some of the cinematic spectacles based on Homer are discussed in the following chapters in connection with *Troy* (2004), the most recent big-screen adaptation of the Trojan War myth and the film on which the present book focuses. *Troy* was written by a young American screenwriter, David Benioff, and produced by Warner Brothers at a cost of about 180 million dollars. (Published figures vary.) The film was directed by Wolfgang Petersen, a German filmmaker with a successful Hollywood career. So two questions immediately arise: Why *Troy* now? And why Petersen as its director?

The first question is relatively easy to answer. As Petersen himself has said, the gigantic and wholly unsuspected worldwide success of Ridley Scott's *Gladiator* (2000), the first big-screen ancient epic since the demise of large-scale historical works in the early to mid-1960s, made *Troy* possible.[11] In Petersen's words: " 'Gladiator' was a big surprise for

8   Jonathan Shay, *Achilles in Vietnam: Combat Trauma and the Undoing of Character* (New York: Atheneum, 1994). Richard J. McNally, *Remembering Trauma* (Cambridge: Belknap Press/Harvard University Press, 2003), provides a recent critique of PTSD and related psychological issues. Cf. also Shay, "Achilles: Paragon, Flawed Character, or Tragic Soldier Figure?" *The Classical Bulletin*, 71 (1995), 117–124. Ernst A. Schmidt, "Achill," in *Antike Mythen in der europäischen Tradition*, ed. Heinz Hofmann (Tübingen: Attempto, 1999), 91–125, surveys the influence of Homer's Achilles from antiquity to today, with special attention to Shay's book. On modern war, its artistic heritage, and the *Iliad* see also James Tatum, *The Mourner's Song: War and Remembrance from the* Iliad *to Vietnam* (Chicago: University of Chicago Press, 2003).

9   Edward Rothstein, "To Homer, Iraq Would Be More of Same," *The New York Times* (June 5, 2004), Section B (*Arts and Ideas*), 9, is just one example of an article in the mainstream media connecting *Troy*, the *Iliad*, and the contemporary war. An internet search for "Homer," "*Iliad*," and "Iraq" is instructive.

10   A list of American and European film and television adaptations appears below in Chapter 13.

11   M. E. Russell, "Helmer of Troy," *In Focus*, 4 no. 5 (May, 2004); quoted from the complete interview at http://www.infocusmag.com/04may/petersenuncut.htm.

the industry, for the audience, for all of us – because, as you know, it sort of connected again to a kind of film we hadn't seen for decades. It became so successful that all of a sudden these projects were popping up that dealt with the times of 2,000 years ago – 3,000 years ago, in our case." *Gladiator* inaugurated a veritable renaissance of classical antiquity on American and European cinema and television screens.[12] In addition, *Gladiator* revealed more about the spirit of contemporary America at the beginning of the third millennium A.D. than about the history of the Roman Empire in the second half of the second century. *Troy* also contains current political and military analogies.[13]

The answer to the second question is more complex and, for the context of the present book, more important. On the most basic level, Petersen is an experienced commercial Hollywood director whose films have almost invariably proven successful at the box office. He is also a highly versatile craftsman in the tradition of the studio directors who had made Hollywood's Golden Age possible. Petersen is at ease directing films on different subjects in a variety of genres, especially action films, and has complete mastery of his craft. His craftsmanship almost single-handedly revived the flagging careers of Clint Eastwood and Dustin Hoffman when they starred in his films *In the Line of Fire* (1993) and *Outbreak* (1995). Today, Petersen is one of only a few filmmakers in Hollywood who have final cut on their films, a sign of respect not easily attained. It is also an achievement that justifies our consideration of *Troy* as primarily Petersen's and not Benioff's or the studio's product. While he is not one of the great directors who decisively shaped or are shaping the history of cinema as a popular and artistic medium, Petersen may always be relied on to deliver a solid product. Many of his films reward repeated viewings. If this were not the case, he could not have

12   Works include Antoine Fuqua's *King Arthur* (2004), written by the principal screenwriter of *Gladiator* and despite its title as much a Roman as a medieval film, and Oliver Stone's *Alexander* (2004), both made for the big screen. The small screen preceded *Troy* with John Kent Harrison's *Helen of Troy* (2003) and followed it with *Imperium: Augustus* and *Imperium: Nero* (2003–2004), the first installments of an ongoing series, and with two other multi-part series, *Rome* and *Empire* (both 2005). All films were made at considerable expense and relied on the financial successes of *Gladiator*, *Troy*, or both.

13   On the cinema as a kind of cultural seismograph in general see my brief comments in the "Introduction" to *Classical Myth and Culture in the Cinema*, ed. Martin M. Winkler (New York: Oxford University Press, 2001), 3–22, at 8 (examples there in note 7). On this aspect of *Gladiator* in particular cf. Monica S. Cyrino, "*Gladiator* and Contemporary American Society," and Peter S. Rose, "The Politics of *Gladiator*," both in *Gladiator: Film and History*, ed. Martin M. Winkler (Oxford: Blackwell, 2004), 124–149 and 150–172. Regarding this side of *Troy* cf. Petersen's comments below.

expected to be granted the assignment to direct as expensive, techno-logically complex, and logistically demanding a project as *Troy*.

More important for the content and style of *Troy*, however, is Petersen's background in classical antiquity and epic filmmaking. The former goes back to his high-school education at the Johanneum, an elite *Gymnasium* in Hamburg, dedicated like all the country's traditional high schools to humanist education. Petersen attended it for the entire nine years of the regular German high-school curriculum. He studied Latin for all of those years and classical Greek for six. Reading and trans-lating excerpts from the Homeric epics was part of the Greek curric-ulum. Like most teenagers, Petersen was not particularly fascinated by his Greek and Latin courses, but on his high-school diploma his grade in Greek was the second highest possible, the equivalent of an American "B." Petersen enjoyed reading Homer in the original:

> we had to learn to write and read in ancient Greek . . . I actually learned to speak it. I can still kind of write it. At school, we were reading the Iliad in Greek. I always hated these Greek and Latin lessons – but the Iliad was always fun . . . I heard that Warner Brothers was developing a film inspired by the Iliad and I flashed back right away to schooltime.[14]

Looking back on Petersen's body of work from the vantage point of *Troy*, we can trace a line of development from his earliest films to his Homeric epic despite the variety of his output.[15] After film school, Petersen started honing his craft in 1970, chiefly directing feature-length and occasion-ally longer films for German public television. He had developed his pas-sion for cinema as a teenager and directed his television films as if for the big screen.[16] He specialized in crime thrillers for the popular and still

14   Quoted from Russell, "Helmer of Troy." Cf. Petersen's comment in Wolfgang Petersen with Ulrich Greiwe, *"Ich liebe die grossen Geschichten": Vom "Tatort" bis nach Hollywood* (Cologne: Kiepenheuer and Witsch, 1997), 57. The internet site of the Johanneum lists Petersen among its "famous alumni." I am grateful to Joachim Latacz for some of this information.

15   On Petersen's continuing affinity to Germany and his awareness of the country's importance for the archaeology of Troy cf. his comments in an interview in which he mentions Heinrich Schliemann and Manfred Korfmann: Peter Zander, "Deutscher Härtetest: Wolfgang Petersen hat 'Troja' verfilmt – und fand in den Sagen Parallelen zu George W. Bush," *Berliner Morgenpost* (May 12, 2004), at http://morgenpost.berlin1.de/archiv2004/040512/feuilleton/story677622.html.

16   As he emphasizes in Petersen and Greiwe, *"Ich liebe die grossen Geschichten"*, 315. Prominent among the directors whom he admires most are John Ford and François Truffaut.

continuing series *Tatort* ("Scene of the Crime") and in films of political criticism.[17] Even his thrillers tended to address topical social issues. Particularly significant in this regard is *Die Konsequenz* (*The Consequence*, 1977), a film about a homo-erotic love affair that is still remarkable for the open-mindedness with which it treated an almost taboo subject. The film was highly controversial but found wide resonance.

Such serious, sometimes large-scale, explorations of topical or controversial subject matter with tragic overtones prepared Petersen for his first true epic, *Das Boot* (1980–1981), a five-hour television film about the dangerous journey of a German submarine in World War II. "When the Hunters Become the Hunted" and "The Other Side of World War 2" were slogans used to advertise the film. Released theatrically in a version shortened to half its original length, the film established Petersen's international reputation and made his move to Hollywood possible.[18] Describing the reception at its American premiere, Petersen himself has best summarized the impact on foreign audiences of a film in which the enemy is portrayed with a human face:

> We were all full of suspense. This was the first test [of the film] before an audience outside Germany, in Los Angeles, before many viewers, also many Jewish viewers. There were about 1,500 people in the theater. At the beginning of the film the statement appears that of about 40,000 Germans on board the U-Boats 30,000 did not return. During this sentence gigantic applause erupted, sending chills down our spines. I thought: This is going to be a catastrophe! When the deaths of 30,000 people are met with applause, you know what to expect. But it was weird: in the following 150 minutes, the film turned the audience completely around. I'll never forget it: at the end, I went up on the stage to thundering applause and discussed [the film] with the audience.[19]

17   Noteworthy are *Smog* (1972), on the effects of pollution; *Stadt im Tal* ("City in the Valley," 1974), a two-part psychological and political portrait of a small town; *Stellenweise Glatteis* ("Spots of Ice," 1974–1975), a two-part film on corruption and electronic surveillance in an industrial concern; and *Planübung* ("Scheduled Drill," 1976–1977), an apocalyptic vision of World War III.

18   *Das Boot* was nominated for six Academy Awards, including Best Director. It is now available on DVD as *Das Boot – The Director's Cut* (209 mins.), with an audio commentary by Petersen, and *Das Boot – The Original Uncut Version* (293 mins.). On the film's production and early critical reception see the chapter in Petersen and Greiwe, *"Ich liebe die grossen Geschichten"*, 151–183, especially 155 and 165–166 (Petersen on Fascism and its fascination).

19   Quoted from Petersen and Greiwe, *"Ich liebe die grossen Geschichten"*, 174. Here and below, quotations from this book appear in my translation.

Das Boot is the first of Petersen's films with clear analogies to the *Iliad*. Petersen's words about his approach to the subject of war, heroism and its seductive appeal, and death and destruction may remind us of some of the themes and passages of Homer's epic:

> The film shows [all] this quite strongly, especially at the beginning . . . The film contains all of that. It shows first what fogged up the minds of the young generation and then the wretched reality . . . Quite simply, the film was intended to show what war really means – especially to young people, for they are the ones whose lives are wasted in war . . . "A Journey to the Limits of Reason" was the [film's] subtitle, which was right on the mark. From below a glorifying façade there surfaces total insanity.[20]

If Petersen turned to recent history with *Das Boot*, he returned to the roots of his education with *Troy*. In between (and besides several other films) came transitional works like *In the Line of Fire*, *Outbreak*, and *Air Force One* (1997), polished commercial films that dealt with heroism, masculinity, militarism, and politics in ways easily palatable to mass audiences. Much closer to epic and tragic themes was *The Perfect Storm* (2000), a kind of disaster epic and Petersen's last film before *Troy*. Although again a commercial work, it nevertheless addressed the subject of heroism and hubris in unforgettable images. A small fishing vessel's crew faces up to implacable nature when they find themselves engulfed in a huge storm. Almost willfully dismissing its overwhelming power, the captain and his men bring about their own deaths.

Troy brought several of the themes of these films into closer focus. Telling an ancient story, it also addressed contemporary issues, as reviewers and commentators noticed. In several interviews given to German journalists on a promotion tour for *Troy*, Petersen himself explained how a story set over three thousand years ago can express current concerns. His understanding of Homer may not find every scholar's assent but is worth considering:

> Look at the present! What the *Iliad* says about humans and wars is, simply, still true. Power-hungry Agamemnons who want to create a new world order – that is absolutely current.
>
> Of course, we didn't start saying: Let's make a movie about American politics, but [we started] with Homer's epic. But while we were working on it we realized that the parallels to the things that were happening out there were obvious.

20 Quoted from Petersen and Greiwe, *"Ich liebe die grossen Geschichten"*, 166–167.

You develop such a story [for your film], and then almost the identical thing happens when you turn on the television. You can't help thinking that this Homer was a real genius, that he exactly understood us humans who apparently need wars again and again; also that someone like Agamemnon reappears again and again. Still, Homer was never interested in black–white, good–bad. Such a concept doesn't exist in reality. Only in the mind of George W. Bush . . . But this direct connection between Bush's power politics and that of Agamemnon in the *Iliad*, this desire to rule the world, to trample everything underfoot that gets in your way, that became evident only during filming. Only gradually did we realize how important Homer still is today.

Homer's story shows that projects driven by belief and fanaticism often end in disasters. You need only open the newspaper to notice that nothing has changed in this regard.[21]

Why Petersen thinks that nothing in human nature has changed since Homer becomes evident when we consider his views on war and politics in connection with his perspective on cinematic storytelling:

With my camera I want to tell grand stories that touch everybody. I don't want to preach, I don't offer any definite solutions. I want viewers to be able to recognize their personal experiences in a film. What makes grand stories interesting is the feeling that we're part of this story, that something is treated there that forms the endless complexity of our own existence, that my longings, my dreams, or my sorrows are being addressed . . . For me, friendship is one of these grand topics . . . I love grand stories. When a viewer notices that a largely unknown world is being described with genuine curiosity, he'll find what happens on the screen especially credible.[22]

Petersen is not the only contemporary director to believe in the ever-present appeal of myths and other stories, as the very title of *Die unendliche*

21   I have translated these passages from the following sources, listed here in the order in which they are cited: Tobias Kniebe, "Homer ist, wenn man trotzdem lacht: 'Troja'-Regisseur Wolfgang Petersen über die mythischen Wurzeln des Erzählens und den Achilles in uns allen," *Süddeutsche Zeitung* (May 11, 2004), at http://www.sueddeutsche.de/kultur/artikel/607/31576/print.html; Frank Arnold, "Wolfgang Petersen: Keine Welt in Schwarz und Weiss," *Kölner Stadtanzeiger* (May 14, 2004), at http://www.ksta.de/artikel.jsp?id=1084203219381; Zander, "Deutscher Härtetest"; and Tobias Wiethoff, "Interview mit dem Regisseur Wolfgang Petersen: 'Ich gehe dahin, wo der Stoff ist'," *Westdeutsche Zeitung* (May 7, 2004), at http://www.wz-newsline.de/seschat4/200/sro.php?redid=58942.

22   Quoted from Petersen and Greiwe, *"Ich liebe die grossen Geschichten"*, 95, 317, and 330. Years later, Petersen reiterated his love for grand stories (Russell, "Helmer of Troy").

Geschichte (*The Never-Ending Story*, 1984), his film based on a modern German fairy-tale novel, indicates. (The success of the *Star Wars*, *Lord of the Rings*, and *Harry Potter* films points in the same direction.) To Petersen, the *Iliad* is the source of all grand stories in the Western tradition and the best example of the timeless modernity of larger-than-life heroic plots: "I think you can say that Homer's work – for the first time in the history of mankind, in an unbelievable, breathtaking way – describes the brutality and suffering of people in war."[23] But in order to preserve their appeal and importance over millennia, such stories must change – or better: must be changed by their modern tellers, not least when they tell them in a medium different from the original's. Writer Benioff has well summarized this aspect of turning an ancient literary epic into a modern film epic:

> I can't measure up to Homer. His composition has survived for nearly three millennia and remains the world's most beautiful and mournful depiction of war. But the story of the Trojan War does not belong to Homer. The characters he employs were legendary long before he was born. Dozens of different versions of the War have been told, and my script ransacks ideas from several of them. The script is not, truly, an adaptation of *The Iliad*. It is a retelling of the entire Trojan War story. So I'm not worried about desecrating a classic – Homer will survive Hollywood.[24]

Despite the extensive criticisms leveled at *Troy* by reviewers and classical scholars alike for the changes to Greek myth and the *Iliad* that the film contains, Benioff is surely correct about Homer's survival. *Troy* well illustrates, even exemplifies, some of the major aspects of any adaptation or translation of a long textual narrative to a long narrative in images: of an epic or a novel – the latter the logical and legitimate descendant of the former in the age of prose rather than verse narratives – to the screen.[25] Rather than making things easy for ourselves by grumbling about a film's lack of faithful adherence to its literary source or declaring it hopelessly inferior, we may take what Walter Benjamin wrote in 1921 about translation – if only translation from one language to another – as a starting point for a brief consideration of translation from

23   Quoted from Russell, "Helmer of Troy."
24   Quoted from "David Benioff...Web Access" at www.bbc.co.uk/print/films/webaccess/david_benioff_1.shtml.
25   John Kevin Newman, *The Classical Epic Tradition* (Madison: University of Wisconsin Press, 1986), provides a classical scholar's perspective on novel and film as successors to ancient epic.

text to image. Benjamin introduces the concept of "translatability" and comments:

> a specific significance inherent in the original manifests itself in its trans-latability. It is evident that no translation, however good it may be, can have any significance as regards the original. Nonetheless, it does stand in the closest relationship to the original by virtue of the original's trans-latability; in fact, this connection is all the closer since it is no longer of importance to the original . . . a translation issues from the original – not so much from its life as from its afterlife . . . no translation would be possible if in its ultimate essence it strove for likeness to the original. For in its afterlife – which could not be called that if it were not a transformation and a renewal of something living – the original undergoes a change.[26]

Benjamin then turns to two related aspects that are of immediate concern to translators of texts as well as images and to their addressees: "The traditional concepts in any discussion of translation are fidelity and license." After remarking that "traditional usage makes these terms appear as if in constant conflict with each other," he asks a crucial question, one that applies equally to textual translations and text–image translations: "What can fidelity really do for the rendering of meaning?" He answers by concluding that fidelity alone is far from being capable of rendering or preserving the original's meaning. Instead, translators must proceed from a different understanding of their task. For the present purpose, it is not necessary here to trace the entire argument of his essay, but the analogy which he uses to make the point about fidelity as a limited and limiting aspect of translation is worth our attention. Tellingly, Benjamin's analogy resorts to something visual, imparting an aura of immediacy and vividness to his words:

> Fragments of a vessel that are to be glued together must match one another in the smallest details, although they need not be like one another. In the same way a translation, instead of imitating the sense of the original, must lovingly and in detail incorporate the original's way of meaning, thus making both the original and the translation recognizable as frag-ments of a greater language, just as fragments are part of a vessel.

---

26   Walter Benjamin, "The Task of the Translator," tr. Harry Zohn, in *Walter Benjamin: Selected Writings*, vol. 1: *1913–1926*, ed. Marcus Bullock and Michael W. Jennings (Cambridge: Belknap Press/Harvard University Press, 1996), 253–263; quotations at 254, 256, and 259.

The greater language of literature, of narrative texts across different linguistic and stylistic systems, is analogous to the even greater language of visual narratives that cross over from text to image and of visual narratives that have been created and translated within the wide field of cinematic genres and styles. The theoretical foundations of such a view are far older than some film critics or literary scholars may realize. Long ago, linguist Roman Jakobson distinguished among three classes of translation:

> 1) Intralingual translation or *rewording* is an interpretation of verbal signs by means of other signs of the same language. 2) Interlingual translation or *translation proper* is an interpretation of verbal signs by means of some other language. 3) Intersemiotic translation or *transmutation* is an interpretation of verbal signs by means of signs of nonverbal sign systems.[27]

Jakobson's third category includes filmic translations of literary texts. Related to these are remakes of films, both of works based on literature and of originally filmic stories. When Benjamin observes: "Fidelity and freedom in translation have traditionally been regarded as conflicting tendencies," he expresses what even today can cause heated debates in regard to film adaptations of epics, novels, or plays.[28] The fruitlessness of such debates becomes evident when we examine what actually happens when a text becomes a film. George Bluestone's observations in his now classic study of film adaptations of famous novels apply equally to ancient epic when translated to film:

> What happens . . . when the filmist [i.e., filmmaker] undertakes the adaptation of a novel, given the inevitable mutation [from text to image], is that he does not convert the novel at all. What he adapts is a kind of paraphrase of the novel – the novel viewed [!] as raw material. He looks not to the organic novel, whose language is inseparable from its theme, but to characters and incidents which have somehow detached themselves from language and, like the heroes of folk legends, have achieved

---

27   Quoted from Roman Jakobson, "On Linguistic Aspects of Translation," in *Selected Writings*, 2nd edn, vol. 2: *Word and Language* (The Hague: Mouton, 1971), 260–266; quotation at 261. Scholarship on the language and the semiotics of film is extensive; for an introduction and basic bibliography see James Monaco, *How to Read a Film*, 3rd edn: *The World of Movies, Media, and Multimedia: Language, History, Theory* (New York: Oxford University Press, 2000), 150–225 (chapter entitled "The Language of Film: Signs and Syntax") and 607–608.
28   Benjamin, "The Task of the Translator," 260.

a mythic life of their own . . . That is why there is no necessary corres-
pondence between the excellence of a novel and the quality of the film
in which the novel is recorded . . . the filmist becomes not a translator for
an established author, but a new author in his own right.

In this description, we should understand "epic" alongside "novel," as
Bluestone's reference to legendary characters and myth reveals, if rather
unintentionally. The same is true for his conclusion:

> Like two intersecting lines, novel and film meet at a point, then diverge.
> At the intersection, the book and shooting-script are almost indistinguish-
> able. But where the lines diverge, they not only resist conversion; they
> also lose any resemblance to each other. At the farthest remove, novel
> and film, like all exemplary art, have, within the conventions that make
> them comprehensible to a given audience, made maximum use of their
> materials. At this remove, what is particularly filmic and what is particu-
> larly novelistic cannot be converted without destroying an integral part
> of each . . . the filmed novel, in spite of certain resemblances, will inevit-
> ably become a different artistic entity from the novel on which it is based.[29]

The history of cinematic translations from texts to images parallels, at
least in its wide variety and fluctuations, the history of classical myth
within and since antiquity. As Benioff observed, Homer was not the
inventor of the characters or the plots of his *Iliad* and *Odyssey*, and we
should keep the flexibility of myth in mind when we view or judge a
film like Petersen's. The subject is too vast to be dealt with here, but one
classical scholar's voice may be adduced as representative. In a chapter
on the limitations of the structuralist approach to myth, G. S. Kirk comments on the variety of mythical storytelling in antiquity. His words

---

29   Quoted from George Bluestone, *Novels into Film* (1957; rpt. Berkeley: University of
California Press, 1961), 62–64 (in a chapter entitled "The Limits of the Novel and the
Limits of the Film"). The literature on adaptation has become extensive since this book
was published. Representative works are André Bazin, "Adaptation, or the Cinema as
Digest," tr. Alain Piette and Bert Cardullo, in *Bazin at Work: Major Essays and Reviews from
the Forties and Fifties*, ed. Bert Cardullo (New York: Routledge, 1997), 41–51, rpt. in *Film
Adaptation*, ed. James Naremore (New Brunswick: Rutgers University Press, 2000), 19–
27; Neil Sinyard, *Filming Literature: The Art of Screen Adaptation* (New York: St. Martin's,
1986); Brian McFarlane, *Novel to Film: An Introduction to the Theory of Adaptation* (Oxford:
Clarendon Press, 1996); Robert Stam, "Beyond Fidelity: The Dialogics of Adaptation," in
Film Adaptation, 54–76, and "Novel and Film: The Theory and Practice of Adaptation,"
in *La decima musa: il cinema e le altre arte/The Tenth Muse: Cinema and the Other Arts*,
ed. Leonardo Quaresima and Laura Vichi (Udine: Forum, 2001), 441–457.

are also applicable to the history of ancient myths as they are retold in literary and other forms until today:

> If . . . myths are traditional tales, then their telling is subject to the rules of all traditional tales: they will be varied in some degree on virtually every occasion of telling, and the variations will be determined by the whim, the ambition or the particular thematic repertoire of the individual teller, as well as by the receptivity and special requirements of the particular audience. Themes will be suppressed, added, transposed, or replaced by other apparently equivalent themes.

Kirk concludes with a call for open-mindedness that viewers of today's adaptations of classical myths in popular culture, especially on cinema and television screens, might keep in mind if they wish to do justice to the continuing presence of ancient culture in modern mass media. After summarizing the various functions of myth that structuralists point to, Kirk observes:

> The important thing for the modern student of myth, in my opinion, is to be prepared to find any or all of these properties in the myths of any culture; and not to apply generalizing theories *a priori* to a category of human expression and imagination that is likely, after all, to be a broad one.[30]

For "theories" we may also read "fixed opinions," "prejudices," or "dismissive judgments." Awareness of Kirk's exhortation does not, of course, entail our uncritical acceptance of each and any new work. Nor should it. But we ought not simply to condemn a work as inferior or unworthy of serious attention if it deviates from what we believe to be the right, true, and beautiful – qualities we tend to ascribe only to our classical originals whose unique greatness we believe no later work can reach. Rather, we should look for strengths and weaknesses of a particular work, such as a popular film that reaches an audience of millions, on its own terms: What made it the way it ended up being? Why did the creators invent characters or events rather than reproducing what they found in their sources? The chapters in this book exemplify this approach in connection with *Troy*.

If we apply a broad perspective to visual adaptations of literature in general and to Homeric epic in particular, we find ourselves in a long

---

30 Quotations from G. S. Kirk, *Myth: Its Meaning and Function in Ancient and Other Cultures* (Berkeley: University of California Press, 1970; several rpts.), 74 and 83.

tradition of adaptation: from Greek vase paintings and Roman, especially Pompeian, wall paintings based on specific episodes from the *Iliad or Odyssey* and from Greek and Roman stage adaptations of Homeric themes to a never-ending parade of works of textual and visual art since the Middle Ages. In the late nineteenth century, technology brought another dimension to bear on this tradition: narratives in moving images, later accompanied by words, sounds, and music. As is true for the history of ancient textual adaptations of Homer in genres other than epic, the history of visual adaptations exhibits anything but faithfulness to its sources. But there is nothing bad or wrong about the lack of slavish adherence to the model provided by a revered master like Homer. We may compare what Goethe wrote in 1801 after seeing a drawing of Homeric heroes by his friend, the painter Johann Heinrich Wilhelm Tischbein. The visual arts, Goethe commented, should treat mythic-epic subjects not according to Homer but like Homer ("nicht nach dem Homer, sondern wie Homer"). Painters who merely translate a text into images fall short of what is accomplished by those who approach their subjects with the model of Homeric creativity in mind.[31]

Such an approach to visual adaptation is both sensible and necessary, but in an era whose technology has enabled visual artists to advance far beyond canvas, paint, and brush the range of possibilities for adaptations has advanced as well. This is nowhere better seen than in the cinema and its offshoot, television, in particular in fanciful retellings of Greek myth. In principle, such free adaptations are nothing new. Even in antiquity, alternate versions of myths spread far and wide throughout literature and the visual arts, as the works of playwrights, mythographers, and epic and lyrical poets on the one hand and those of sculptors and painters on the other attest. Modern visual media have only taken this tradition further. They have proven especially fertile grounds for reimagining and reinventing classical antiquity. Film director Vittorio Cottafavi, who made several films set in antiquity, aptly called this phenomenon "neo-mythologism."[32]

---

31   For quotation and context see *Goethes Werke* (Weimar Edition), vol. 35 (1892): *Tag- und Jahres-Hefte*, 97; easily accessible in the reprint of this edition (Munich: Deutscher Taschenbuch Verlag, 1987), vol. 40, 97.

32   On Cottafavi and his term "neo-mythologism" see Pierre Leprohon, *The Italian Cinema*, tr. Roger Greaves and Oliver Stallybrass (New York: Praeger, 1972), 174–179. I use Cottafavi's term as the theoretical starting point for "Neo-Mythologism: Apollo and the Muses on the Screen," *International Journal of the Classical Tradition*, 11 (2005), 383–423, with discussion of *Troy* at 418–420.

The most notorious genre of neo-mythological film is that of the muscleman epics made in Italy in the 1950s and 1960s. Most, and the most famous – or, depending on one's view, infamous – of these are loose adaptations of the myths of Heracles (Hercules). These in turn spun off slews of comparable films about assorted ancient or quasi-ancient heroes, a veritable band of Herculean brothers. Some of these films are capable of stretching viewers' patience to the breaking point. *Troy* evidently is an example of neo-mythological cinema. But to those who love both classical epics and epic films, the most severe test of their endurance of the freewheeling liberties that the cinema has taken with classical antiquity is a film that goes considerably further than *Troy* in its radically altered retelling of the Trojan War and the *Iliad*. This film is Manfred S. Noa's *La regina di Sparta* (*The Queen of Sparta*, 1931), made for a small Italian production company in Hollywood. Today it is little-known and not easily accessible. Its neo-mythological plot is instructive – and amusing or infuriating, according to a viewer's temperament. The American Film Institute provides the following summary:

> After the kidnapping of Helen, Queen of Sparta, Priam, the King of Troy, is informed that she must return to her kingdom or war between the Spartans and the Trojans will ensue. While Paris, Prince of Troy, begs his father not to return his beloved, Helen insists on averting warfare by returning to her home. When Priam hears that the Spartans have begun to revolt, he insists on fighting, but Helen begs Paris to stay with her rather than risk his life on the battlefield. Priam's consort, the queen, asks Helen to beg Hector, Paris' brother, not to fight. However, Hector insists on going to battle and takes leave of his wife Andromache and his son despite the former's pleading and her accusations against Helen that Hector is in love with her. Priam enlists Paris to lead the troops against Menelaus, Helen's husband. Meanwhile, at the Spartan camp, a messenger announces the Trojans' approach. When Achilles' request to have the honor of killing Paris and Hector is refused by Menelaus, who desires to do the job himself, Achilles refuses to fight. Paris loses the duel with Menelaus, and Helen, fearing for Paris, orders a chariot and begs Menelaus to throw down his arms, which he does. But Agamemnon, another Spartan, convinces Menelaus to continue the fight and to avenge the kidnapping of Helen. On the Trojan side, Hector gives the command to fight and many Spartans are killed. A messenger announces the Trojans' rapid progress toward the Spartan camp, and in his fury, Achilles strangles the messenger and then tries to distract himself from the urge to do battle by watching acrobats and dancers perform. Back in Troy, Spartan prisoners arrive and Helen begs Priam to spare them, reminding him that she too is

a Spartan. Priam menaces Helen, and Paris in turn menaces Priam, who then orders his son taken away. Patroclus, a Spartan, begs to take Achilles' place as high commander in order to save Sparta. Achilles agrees, calls the men to arms, and then sends Patroclus out, the latter eventually being killed when he engages in combat with Hector. When Patroclus' body is brought back to the camp, Achilles vows to avenge his fallen friend and takes up arms, although the Trojans have already declared victory. Achilles fights with Hector in front of the walls of Troy, but Andromache takes her son to the scene and begs her husband not to fight. As Hector tries to run to his family, Achilles pierces his throat with a sword. Achilles takes the body and announces that Patroclus is avenged. The Trojan women denounce Helen, and a prophet from Athens foretells the death of Paris and Hector and the fall of Troy. Priam has the prophet burned to death. Next, Priam, the queen, and Andromache go to Achilles and beg that Hector's body be returned for a proper burial. Achilles says he will only give the body up if Helen relinquishes her crown and has it placed on Patroclus' tomb. Priam agrees but secretly plans to avenge Hector's death by asking Paris to thrust a poisoned arrow into Achilles' heel. He refuses until Priam threatens to send Helen to do the job. Helen tries to stop Paris, but is too late. He kills Achilles and, ashamed at his father's treachery, tries to attack Priam with the poisoned arrow. Priam has him seized and orders that he be put to death. Agamemnon decides on a plan to destroy Troy: he will declare peace, then send a huge horse filled with Spartan soldiers as a friendship offering. Paris, in prison, is visited by Helen and his mother, the queen. He says he will kill himself if Helen leaves him. As the Trojans rejoice in their victory, the horse is brought in. Helen and Paris are sentenced to death and the queen tries to help them to escape, although the brave Helen wishes to stay and die by Paris' side. They see Menelaus emerge from the horse, and then the Spartan king kills Helen's lover. Priam tries to poison Helen, but when he sees the Spartans, he drinks the poison himself. Menelaus enters and Helen tells him to kill her. He tells her to commit suicide, but then changes his mind and invites her to return with him to Sparta.[33]

This film's ending, with its quasi-Oedipal overtones, exceeds anything that Benioff and Petersen do in *Troy*. Noa's film was released well over seven decades before *Troy*, sufficient proof that neo-mythological narratives have never deterred filmmakers. But the neo-mythologism of *La*

---

33   I have anglicized the Italian names, corrected misspellings of others, and slightly altered some punctuation. Only intrepid readers are urged to view the original at https://afionline.org/members/catalog/AbbrView.aspx?s=1&Movie=2343.

regina di Sparta can be traced even further back. The film is a condensed remake of *Helena* (1924), a grandiose three-and-a-half-hour silent epic in two parts that Noa had directed in Germany. So there is nothing at all unusual if *Troy* follows in the long-established tradition of cinematic neo-mythologism by introducing characters and plot twists that were unknown to the ancients and by revealing its debt to cinema history.

Some of the chapters in this book address a number of analogies and similarities to earlier epic films that *Troy* contains. In both plot and visual style, for instance, *Troy* is reminiscent of the first American widescreen epic on the same subject, Robert Wise's *Helen of Troy* (1956), also produced by Warner Brothers. A particular detail in *Troy*, the custom of placing coins on the eyes of the dead, has elicited justifiable criticism for being anachronistic, for coinage did not exist in the Bronze Age or at the time of Homer. But apparently the custom is familiar at Warner Brothers. In Raoul Walsh's *The Roaring Twenties* (1939), one of the studio's classic gangster films, we hear none other than Humphrey Bogart in the role of an ice-cold racketeer warn an accomplice: "You came into this racket with your eyes open. You learned a lot, and you know a lot. If any of it gets out, you'll go out with your eyes open, only this time they'll have pennies on them."

While conservative classicists can still be shocked by all the non-classical plot elements in *Troy*, familiarity has long inured classical cinephiles. Traditionalists might therefore wish to ponder Petersen's own words on the close connections between Homer and himself as epic storytellers:

> He [Homer] wrote down his story only a few hundred years after it all happened, and you can see clearly that he did everything to make his story gripping for the audience of his time. We tried to do the exact same thing. In this sense he could understand us.[34]

The preceding observations are intended to serve readers as a framework for their encounter with the essays on *Troy* in the present book. Their authors are scholars trained in classical history, archaeology, or literature; all have strong interests in the cinema and its importance for the survival of antiquity today. They examine the film from a number of perspectives, including Bronze-Age archaeology, Homeric studies,

34   Quoted from Kniebe, "Homer ist, wenn man trotzdem lacht."

ancient and modern history, and film history and aesthetics.[35] It will be readily apparent to readers from the various points of criticism being advanced in the different chapters that there is no complete consensus between and among contributors about the artistic qualities of *Troy*. But it will be equally apparent that all of them adhere to the belief that simple dismissal of the film as yet another instance of deviation from a sacred tradition is beside the point. We hope that our readers will join us in this perspective. Such readers are all those who are interested, on the one hand, in classical antiquity, Homeric epic, and the classical tradition and its prominence today and, on the other hand, in cinema and the importance of film for our culture. We also address students and teachers of Greek literature, history, and civilization and those in related areas of the humanities such as Film Studies, Comparative Literature, and Cultural Studies. Our contributions are written in non-specialized English and without academic jargon. We explain all technical terms, and all quotations from Greek and Latin texts appear in translation. If we succeed in persuading readers to think anew about Homer, about ancient and modern culture and their interactions, and about epic cinema, our work will have accomplished its purpose.

As editor of this volume, I owe thanks to a variety of people and institutions. First among them are my contributors, whose co-operation made this book a highly pleasant working experience for their *poimên laôn klassikôn kai philokinêmatographikôn*, if they permit me the use of such a quasi-Homeric epithet. For illustrations of the archaeological site of Troy and for images of ancient vase paintings I am grateful to Peter Jablonka of the Troia Project and to the Antikenmuseum Basel, the British Museum, and the Kunsthistorische Museum Vienna. William Knight

---

35   Scholarship on Homer, archaeology, and early Greek literature is vast. Besides works cited in this book's chapters, the following recent publications provide up-to-date information from first orientation to advanced introduction, with additional bibliographical references: *Homer: Critical Assessments*, ed. Irene J. F. de Jong, 4 vols. (London: Routledge, 1999); Jasper Griffin, *Homer*, 2nd edn (Bristol: Bristol Classical Press, 2001); Michael Silk, *Homer: The Iliad*, 2nd edn (Cambridge: Cambridge University Press, 2004); Gregory Nagy, *Homer's Text and Language* (Urbana: University of Illinois Press, 2004); *The Cambridge Companion to Homer*, ed. Robert Fowler (Cambridge: Cambridge University Press, 2004); Carol G. Thomas and Craig Conant, *The Trojan War* (Westport: Greenwood Press, 2005). Michael Wood, *In Search of the Trojan War*, 2nd edn (Berkeley: University of California Press, 1996; rpt. 1998), is a general introduction that accompanies his television series of the same title, now available on DVD. For basic information on translations of Homer see *Homer in English*, ed. George Steiner (London: Penguin, 1996); Philip H. Young, *The Printed Homer: A 3,000 Year Publishing and Translation History of the* Iliad *and the* Odyssey (Jefferson: McFarland, 2003).

Zewadski, Esq., again graciously allowed me to use a number of images from his unique collection of film stills. I am also greatly indebted to the Society for the Humanities at Cornell University and its director, Brett de Bary, for a fellowship during the academic year 2004–2005 that provided me with a congenial working environment. At Blackwell, Al Bertrand, my commissioning editor, deserves thanks for his generous support of this project from its inception. I also thank Angela Cohen, Annette Abel, and the Blackwell staff who worked with me in efficiently seeing the book through the production process.

POSTSCRIPT. Manfred Korfmann, director of the archaeological excavations at Troy-Hisarlık, unexpectedly died in August, 2005. Publisher, contributors, and editor all mourn his death. His chapter in this book is one of the very last essays written by the "Father of Troy," as he was affectionately called. We hope that it will stand as a reminder of the depth of his commitment to increasing our knowledge and understanding of all things Trojan and as a testimony to the breadth of his scholarship, which included a strong interest in the survival of the past in the present and in its importance for the future.

CHAPTER ONE

Was There a Trojan War? Troy Between Fiction and Archaeological Evidence

Manfred O. Korfmann

To an unusual degree, Wolfgang Petersen's *Troy* has directed public attention to the archaeology of Troy – Hisarlık in modern Turkey – and to the work of its excavators. Although the team of the *Troia-Projekt* ("Project Troy"), which I direct, had nothing to do with the film, news of its production brought us numerous requests for information: Who was Homer? Was there a Trojan War? These and other fundamental questions concerning historical facts and the credibility of the film's story continued well beyond the film's release.

Colleagues and I found *Troy* quite enjoyable, but at the same time we looked at it from a perspective different from that of most viewers. For instance, to us the credibility of a film shot in Mexico and Malta rather than on authentic locations is unavoidably problematic. In *Troy* the sun rises above the horizon from the very direction where we are used to seeing it set. This is rather disconcerting to those familiar with the lay of the land. Specialists are almost always disappointed with modern attempts to revive ancient stories. But *Troy* was not made for specialists. If the filmmakers had wished to involve them, the ensuing debates concerning each and every detail would most likely have postponed its production until this day. And the scholarly obsession with details would have made it a boring film as well. Epic films are made for the largest possible audiences worldwide. Their expectations, not those of scholars, have to be satisfied. This is why experts like ourselves were not consulted.

And we do not mind, for the basic theme of *Troy* turned out to be handled right, or at least not wrong. As did Homer's *Iliad*, *Troy* concerns not so much the Trojan War itself as the conflict of Agamemnon and Achilles, two leaders in the same camp. Homer already realized that this fundamental pattern of individual heroism was popular with audiences, especially if it has an aura of historicity. Homer told about this conflict about 480 years after it was supposed to have occurred; Petersen did so about 3180 years afterwards. Both used their imagination and their storytelling skills. Petersen, who had received a classical education in Germany, knows his source, Homer, but scholars today ask what Homer's source or sources may have been. Only few today believe that the *Iliad* and its background are nothing more than products of his imagination.[1] Nevertheless, it is unlikely that Homer was criticized for putting a number of contemporary aspects into his work, as he did. On the contrary; his audience must have expected no less. Like today's audiences, Homer's listeners wanted a bridge between the distant past and their own present. Art has its own rules and its own truth, and this applies to Petersen, too. The question of what he was allowed or forbidden to do to the *Iliad* is rather quaint. It is certainly unhelpful.

As a part of our culture, the cinema reflects our present concerns and desires. In a world linked by technology, these are now global ones. American films of the 1950s and 1960s that were set in antiquity carried topical messages about freedom and tyranny. Recent ones like Ridley Scott's *Gladiator* (2000), *Troy*, and Oliver Stone's *Alexander* (2004) clearly point to the American wish to learn more about the Near East and the eastern Mediterranean world, an area that is currently of special significance through its wars and conflicts. These films appear to raise their voices against despotism and praise the ideals of a united world. As a result, antiquity and its archaeology have become widely popular. So the questions about ancient history, society, and archaeology that *Troy* has raised could in turn lead to positive results by means of such popular attention. Increased media interest in our own excavations and noticeably larger numbers of national and international tourists visiting the site of Troy have already indicated as much. Such travelers return to the origins of Western culture and civilization, and so, in its own way, does *Troy*. This is a positive situation for classical scholars and archaeologists. The latter are usually not primarily concerned with imagining in every detail what the site on which they are working looked

---

1   On this see now Joachim Latacz, *Troy and Homer: Towards a Solution of an Old Mystery*, tr. Kevin Windle and Rosh Ireland (Oxford: Oxford University Press, 2004).

like in the distant past. But films must show everything in detail. So a film like *Troy* in a way forces even archaeologists to wonder: What was Troy really like? This situation is all for the better.

To professional archaeologists, ancient remains and artifacts are of chief interest as means to reconstruct the life and environment of earlier societies that emerge from an analysis and interpretation of these remains. Three general and important questions arise from this: Where do we come from, where are we today, and where are we likely to go? In this context the metaphor of the balancing scales is instructive about past, present, and future. The more knowledge we can put into the scale that represents the past, the more we are justified to deal with the other scale that represents the future. Of course we must also pay attention to the beam in the middle: the pivot representing our own present. But how can we reconstruct sites of ancient settlements and their geographic environs? How can we describe ancient peoples and their appearances, their daily occupations, tools, households, workshops, palaces? To answer such questions, or at least to strive for an answer, is the archaeologists' duty, all too often neglected. A film can remind them of this duty, even if it puts partially wrong images into the one scale.

A book recently published in German and Turkish addresses this topic. Its title translates as follows: "Troy – How It Really Looked."[2] We would dearly love to know how Troy really looked. The book's authors are experts in their field, and in their introduction they acknowledge that the title more accurately should have been something like "Troy – How It Most Likely Looked According to the Best Knowledge of the Scientists Working There." That is as close as we can get. So Petersen's *Troy* can increase interest in and study of the Bronze Age and can even stimulate an archaeologist to deal with the film, as this essay shows. Both sides can fruitfully interact with each other, especially now that classical education is no longer the basis of our school curriculum. In the future, just as in the past and in the present, Troy and the Homeric landscape will be subjects of fiction and objects of research.

The one question that *Troy* has raised again and again and that is most often addressed to me as the director of excavations at Hisarlık is

---

2   Birgit Brandau, Hartmut Schickert, and Peter Jablonka, *Troia – Wie es wirklich aussah* (Munich: Piper, 2004). Cf. in general the internet sites of the *Troia Projekt* at http://www.uni-tuebingen.de/troia and specifically *Troia Virtual Reality (Troia VR)* at http://www.uni-tuebingen.de/troia/vr/index_html (in English).

this: "Do you think that there ever was a Trojan War, and, if so, why did it take place?" I will answer this question in some detail.[3]

Myths and legends practically demand to be connected to the specific places in which they are set. In our case this is, and has been since antiquity, an area of ancient ruins that in Greco-Roman times had been built on and expanded under the name of Ilion or Ilium. (Coins showing this name were struck there.) Today this place is called Hisarlık. Its connection with myth, the world of imagination and illusion, is the very origin of archaeology as a scientific discipline. But in the course of the past decade major archaeological discoveries have significantly changed our knowledge of Troy. Archaeological research includes the entire history of Troy from its two millennia in the Bronze Age to its Hellenistic-Roman era. This means that archaeology at Troy has never aimed at contributing answers to questions about the *Iliad* or the Trojan War, although many people hold that assumption. As a matter of principle it is best to keep these two areas separate. On the other hand, Homer studies, too, have greatly advanced in recent years, and archaeologists are justified to consider or use those pieces or "splinters" of information contained in the *Iliad* which modern scholarship is debating as deriving from the past: the late Bronze Age. Such information primarily concerns the place in which the story of the *Iliad* is set; that is to say, it concerns the ruins of Troy VI–VIIa, which at the time of Homer and for centuries after must have been highly impressive in their appearance. This is true for the fortified citadel and for the area of the settlement below it.

That the Trojan War did take place is something Homer assumed his audience to have known. His main topic was the anger of Achilles and its consequences. Homer used Troy and the war only as poetic background for a tale about the conflict between and among humans and gods. But for archaeologists the *Iliad* provides a different kind of background. Homer and those from whom he may have derived some of his information are witnesses of what the topographical setting and life in the late eighth century B.C. were like. On the whole, his descriptions of the place and its surroundings must have been accurate for the time around 700 B.C., when the *Iliad* was by and large composed. This means that what Homer said about Troy and its environs could not openly

---

3   A brief answer from the perspectives of different disciplines (archaeology, Homeric studies, Hittitology) appeared in Manfred Korfmann, Joachim Latacz, and David Hawkins, "Was There a Trojan War?" *Archaeology*, 57 no. 3 (May–June, 2004), 36–41.

contradict the reality of that time. Contemporary and later listeners to recitals of the *Iliad*, who came from or were familiar with the area of Troy, were supposed to recognize at least the general features of the place in which the poem's action occurred. That place had to be described in a credible manner. As mentioned, in Homer's time Troy was largely in ruins and probably had already become an object of legends and myths. So when local people of that time climbed up a particular hill, they could imagine the Trojans of the *Iliad* ascending to their sanctuary. Such a sanctuary – a wooden structure dating from at least the early seventh century B.C., i.e., Homer's time – had most likely been built on the very spot that served as a cult place down to the era of the late Roman Empire.

One of the most spectacular discoveries of our recent excavations was an exterior settlement south of the citadel of Troy, a settlement from the seventeenth century B.C. down to the early twelfth, i.e., Troy VI–VIIa. In its late phase it consisted of large stone structures. Considerable remains of the houses of this lower city were found, although they had been covered and so were partially destroyed by the foundations of later Hellenistic and Roman buildings during eight to nine centuries of continuous settlement from the third century B.C. until 500 A.D. Magnetometrical measurings and the annual excavation campaigns since 1993 have revealed that from about 1300 until about 1180 B.C. – that is, toward the very end of Troy VI and during Troy VIIa – this lower city had been encircled by a U-shaped defensive ditch that was about 3.5 meters wide and about two meters deep. The existence of this ditch, cut into the limestone, can be clearly demonstrated over an extent of 700 meters. It formed the lower settlement's boundary in accordance with local topography. The extent to which the lower city had been settled by the late second millennium B.C. is further documented by a cemetery south of and outside this ditch. Systematic excavations, surveys, and other research – yielding, for instance, shards of pottery – corroborate our conclusion that the lower city was fully built up throughout this area, an area terminated in the west as well by a clear boundary line. The conclusion is unavoidable that during the second half of the second millennium B.C. Troy was about fifteen times larger than had been previously assumed, covering more than 300,000 square meters. This Troy had a large residential area below a strongly fortified citadel. As far as we know today, the citadel was unparalleled in its region and in all of southeastern Europe. Nevertheless, several phases in which new fortifications were built during this time tell us that this Troy had to defend itself against outside attacks time and again.

Geographically, Troy VIII (Hellenistic Ilion), Troy IX (Roman Ilium), and Troy X (Byzantine Ilion) all belong to Anatolia, an area of western Asia Minor that had been settled by Greeks. American excavator Carl Blegen, among others, considered Troy VI and VIIa to have been Greek settlements, thereby reinforcing a view of Troy established by Heinrich Schliemann, the first excavator at Hisarlık, that Troy closely belonged to Europe historically and culturally. Until the 1930s, when archaeologists began to concern themselves with Bronze-Age Anatolia, there had been little evidence to direct their attention east to Anatolia rather than west to the Greeks, although it is unlikely that Troy in the centuries before Homer had not belonged to Anatolia. Independent evaluation of available evidence now tells us that Troy was integrated far more closely into the culture of Anatolia than into that of the Aegean. Archaeological finds including local ceramics and small works of art, the settlement's layout as a whole, architectural details such as individual palaces or building patterns with brick walls topping stone foundations, and customs like cremation – all these point Troy toward Anatolia during the thirteenth century B.C. The results of recent research on the languages spoken and written at that time corroborate these archaeological findings. Linguistically, Troas, the region surrounding Troy, is Luvian and Old-Anatolian; that is to say, it is Indo-European. Troy or Ilios (or Wilios) is most probably identical with Wilusa or Truwisa, an area or town mentioned in Hittite sources. That even the Egyptians seem to have known of it under the name of Dardanya tells us that Troy was by no means an unimportant settlement. So modern scholarship in Hittite and Homeric studies and other, related, areas of classical studies has complemented our archaeological work.

According to most recent archaeological evidence, Troy VIIa came to its end around 1180 B.C., most likely through a defeat in war. After a hiatus of a few decades new settlers, probably from the eastern Balkans or northwestern Black-Sea area, began to inhabit the ruins. This does not mean that the war in question must have been the Trojan War of legend, although tradition places it at this time. But when modern Homeric scholars present us with a scenario in which details contained in the *Iliad* point to the late Bronze Age for the poem's plot, when scholars of Hittitology tell us that during the thirteenth and early twelfth centuries political and military tensions existed around the area of Wilusa or Ilios-Wilios, and when, in addition, recent years have brought to light evidence of an explosive political situation in western Asia Minor and the Troas around 1200 B.C., then archaeologists have no reason to deny the importance of such non-archaeological findings. Indeed, the archaeologists now working at Troy do not agree with a few traditional scholars who insist that nothing in the archaeological evidence about Troy is connected with Homer at all. These scholars maintain, for instance, that Troy was an insignificant settlement of a size that would not fit a city as large and powerful as Homer describes it. But they fail to take into account recent archaeological discoveries and the new conclusions to which these discoveries lead us.

So where does all this take us regarding the question about the Trojan War? The answer is best expressed in two counter-questions: "Why should or could there not have been a Trojan War?" And: "Why do those who see a measure of historicity in the *Iliad* have to justify their views against any doubters?" Given today's level of knowledge, the burden of proof that there was no such war must rest on the doubters' shoulders. How, for instance, do they propose to reconcile their view of Troy as a third-rate settlement with the modern archaeological evidence concerning the thirteenth and especially the early twelfth centuries? Whether the wars or war-like conflicts of that time, in whole or in part, gave rise to the later legend of the Trojan War, or whether there had been among those wars or campaigns an especially remarkable one that was thought to be worthy of preservation first in memory and legend and then in heroic poetry – all this is yet unknown. But at the moment everything indicates that we ought to take Homer seriously about the background information of a war between Trojans and Greeks that his epic provides. Future research and the evaluation of current and yet-to-be-discovered evidence must take such information into consideration. According to the current state of our knowledge, the story told in the *Iliad* most likely contains a kernel of historical truth or, to put it differently, a historical substrate. Any future discussions about the historicity of the Trojan War only make sense if they ask what exactly we understand this kernel or substrate to be.

Translated by Martin M. Winkler

CHAPTER TWO

From Homer's Troy to Petersen's *Troy*

Joachim Latacz

Not all critics and reviewers of Wolfgang Petersen's film have paid sufficient attention to its title. *Troy* does not mean the same thing as *The Iliad*. Petersen was well aware that his film differs from Homer, as the end credits tell us: it was "inspired" by Homer's *Iliad*, but it is not a retelling of it. Only those who understand what this difference means can appreciate the film. So I will here address two questions to make the difference clear: What does Homer tell about Troy in the *Iliad*, and how does he tell it? And how does Petersen's *Troy* relate to Homer? My answers are intended to provide a fair appraisal of the film in regard to its subject matter.

1. *Homer's Troy*

Troy is not the subject of the *Iliad* but the site of its action. The first line of the poem states the theme: "The wrath do sing, goddess, of Peleus' son Achilles!" This announces not the history of Troy or of the Trojan War but the story of an individual. What the name signified and to what larger context it belonged was known exactly to Homer's first audiences in the late eighth century B.C. as soon as they heard it. Achilles was the greatest hero of the Greeks who once had fought at Troy. To these audiences the name "Troy" immediately conjured up a whole long story: that of a victorious ten-year struggle their ancestors had fought long ago against the Trojans, a struggle with an extensive prehistory and aftermath. As was generally known, that story comprised a very long time. Modern scholarship has calculated a duration of at least forty years: twenty years before and ten years after the war, and a decade for the war itself, as the following outline shows. Italics indicate events occurring or mentioned in the Homeric epics:

THE COMPLETE TALE OF TROY IN ANCIENT LITERATURE
I. PROLOGUE ON MT. OLYMPUS

1. Zeus and Themis confer over the advisability of the Trojan War.
2. Zeus fathers Helen on Nemesis/Leda.
3. *Zeus and Hera force the sea goddess Thetis into marriage to King Peleus.*

II. THE TWENTY-YEAR PERIOD BEFORE THE TROJAN WAR

4. *Zeus' grandson Peleus marries Nereus' daughter Thetis on Mt. Pelion in Thessaly. All gods except Eris (Strife) attend. Peleus' and Thetis' child will be Achilles.*
5. Eris sows discord among Hera, Athena, and Aphrodite over which of them is the most beautiful.
6. *The three goddesses approach Paris (Alexander), son of King Priam and Queen Hecuba of Troy and shepherd on Mt. Ida, as judge. Paris had been exposed there as an infant.*
7. *Judgment of Paris: Aphrodite is the most beautiful. Paris' reward will be Helen, wife of King Menelaus of Sparta.*
8. *Paris sails to Greece and abducts Helen from Sparta.*
9. *The Greeks muster to take revenge. They elect Agamemnon, King of Mycenae and brother of Menelaus, as their leader.*
10. *The Greek fleet departs from Aulis but lands in Mysia, too far south of Troy.*
11. Achilles wounds Telephus, king of Mysia.
12. *The Greek fleet leaves Mysia for Troy but is scattered by a storm.*
13. *The Greek fleet again assembles at Aulis. Agamemnon kills a hart sacred to Artemis and is forced to sacrifice Iphigenia, his daughter by Helen's sister Clytemnestra (Klytaimestra).*
14. Telephus arrives at Aulis and is healed.
15. *Calchas the seer receives an augury that appears to predict the fall of Troy in the tenth year of the war.*

16. *The Greek fleet departs from Aulis again and lands on the islands of Tenedos and Lemnos. Philoctetes is abandoned on Lemnos.*

III. THE TEN YEARS OF THE TROJAN WAR
A.   The First Nine Years

17. *The Greek fleet lands in the Troad. Death of Protesilaus.*
18. *An embassy to the Trojans led by Odysseus and Menelaus to demand Helen and Paris is unsuccessful.*
19. Achilles kills Cycnus.
20. *Achilles conquers 23 mainland and island towns to isolate Troy. Among his captives are Chryseis and Briseis. The former functions as the starting point for the* Iliad.

B.   The Last Year

21. *The plot of the* Iliad *(51 days), a small episode in the entire war, now occurs, with the conflict between Agamemnon and Achilles and its consequences, especially the deaths of Patroclus, Achilles' closest friend, and Hector, son of Priam and Troy's greatest hero.*
22. The Amazon queen Penthesilea arrives and is defeated by Achilles. Thersites abuses Achilles, who kills him. The Ethiopian king Memnon arrives and kills Nestor's son Antilochos, among others.
23. *Paris and Apollo bring about Achilles' death.*
24. Ajax and Odysseus dispute about Achilles' divine armor. Odysseus wins; Ajax is driven to madness and suicide.
25. *Odysseus causes Philoctetes and Achilles' son Neoptolemus to join the army.*
26. *Odysseus' trick with the wooden horse brings about the fall of Troy and the deaths of most of the Trojans, among them Priam.*

IV. THE TEN YEARS OF THE GREEKS' RETURNS

27. *The Greek survivors return home. Agamemnon is killed in Mycenae by Clytemnestra in revenge for Iphigenia's death.*
28. *The plot of the* Odyssey *(40 days): Odysseus returns to his island kingdom of Ithaca after ten years of wanderings. He is reunited with his wife Penelope and his son Telemachus and restored to power after an absence of 20 years.*
29. Further travels of Odysseus; he is killed by Telegonus, his son with Circe.

V.   THE SURVIVAL OF TROY

30.   The plot of Virgil's *Aeneid*: Aeneas, son of Anchises and Aphrodite
      (Venus), journeys to Italy in search of a new home for the surviv-
      ing Trojans, including his son Ascanius. Their descendants found
      the city of Rome. Fusion of Greek myth and Roman history.

The reason why Homer's audiences were closely familiar with this
complex tale is that *aoidoi* ("singers") had already told it in countless
performances to numerous generations. Besides many other such stories such as those about Jason and the Argonauts or the Seven against
Thebes, the story of Troy was part of the standard repertory of these
aoidoi, who formed a kind of professional guild. While the singers told
the familiar stories each in different ways – otherwise they would probably have lost their audiences – certain things remained fixed. They
could not change because the main plot had to remain recognizable.

   One of these unchanging parts was the motif of a quarrel in the Greeks'
own camp. As the old story had it, again and again during the ten-year
siege disagreements had arisen among the leaders allied against Troy.
We may surmise that since long before Homer one of these disagreements in the story was between the most important leaders of the Greek
forces, Agamemnon, king of Argos-Mycenae on the Peloponnesus in
southern Greece and commander-in-chief of the entire military alliance,
and Achilles, prince of Phthia in Achaia Phthiotis (Thessaly), an area
in northern Greece, and commander of the most powerful individual
contingent in the Greek army. We no longer know how large a part this
controversy had played in earlier or contemporary recitals of the *aoidoi*,
but our evidence suggests that it had been rather marginal to the story
of Troy as a whole. Most likely, the *aoidoi* had emphasized the city itself
and the grim nature of the war in their versions – i.e., the outer, action-
driven plot – rather than the inner lives of individual figures, their
emotions and motivations.

   Homer, however, radically turned around audiences' familiar perspective on the story.[1] He did not start with the gigantic panorama of
the mighty Trojan city and country near the Hellespont or with the

---

1   I provide an introduction to Homeric epic in *Homer: His Art and His World*, tr. James P.
Holoka (Ann Arbor: University of Michigan Press, 1996; rpt. 1998). On Homer and his
connections to the history of Troy see now my *Troy and Homer: Towards a Solution of an
Old Mystery*, tr. Kevin Windle and Rosh Ireland (Oxford: Oxford University Press, 2004).
The essay collection *Troia: Traum und Wirklichkeit* (Stuttgart: Theiss, 2001; rpt. 2002) deals
with all aspects of the topic and contains numerous illustrations.

armies of attackers and defenders arranged in battle lines, but he began with something much smaller: an individual hero. Homer did not even take something obvious such as this man's heroic exploits in battle as his point of departure but rather something much more personal, even private: his wrath. For audiences who knew the standard versions of the tale, this beginning must have been utterly new and surprising, conjuring up a feeling of suspense. What was this singer Homer, standing right there before them, getting at? Surely not something soulful or sentimental? Homer's second line at once dispelled any such concerns: "that baneful wrath which brought countless woes upon the Achaeans . . ." So the wrath of an individual hero would only be the starting point of a tale that was going to deal with Troy after all, if from an utterly unusual point of view. The tale was not going to focus on the Trojan War as a real event of the past, nor even on war as such, its struggles, sacrifices, and bloodshed, but on the aftermath that warfare brings to those who fight and suffer in any war. Chief emphasis would be on the Greeks and their alliance: their tensions, dissensions, and, finally, the grievous suffering caused by one man's anger. Homer structured his story as follows; numbers in brackets identify books and lines in the text:

THE TEMPORAL STRUCTURE OF THE *ILIAD*

Prologue (1.1–12a): the poet invokes his Muse and announces his theme

I.   EXPOSITION (21 DAYS)

1. *Day 1* (1.12b–52): Chryses
2. *Days 2–9* (1.53): plague in Greek camp
3. *Day 10* (1.54–476): quarrel between Agamemnon and Achilles, embassy to Chryse
4. *Day 11* (1.477–492): return of embassy, wrath of Achilles
5. *Days 12–20* (1.493): gods visit the Ethiopians
6. *Day 21 and following night* (1.493–2.47): Thetis' plea to Zeus, Agamemnon's dream

II.   MAIN NARRATIVE (6 DAYS)

7. *Day 22 (2.48–7.380): First Day of Fighting*
   - Agamemnon tempts the army
   - catalogues (review of troops)
   - first truce: duel of Menelaus and Paris is to decide outcome of war
   - Helen and Priam look down on Greek army from walls of Troy
   - Pandarus breaks truce

- great deeds of Diomedes
- Hector in Troy
- duel between Hector and Ajax

8.   *Day 23 (7.381–432)*: second truce, burials of the dead
9.   *Day 24 (7.433–482)*: Greeks build walls around their camp
10.   *Day 25 and following night (8.1–10.579): Second Day of Fighting*
- Greeks forced to retreat
- Trojans camp on the plain before Troy
- Greek embassy to Achilles
- Dolon episode

11.   *Day 26 and following night (11.1–18.617): Third Day of Fighting*
- great deeds of Agamemnon
- great deeds of Hector
- Greek leaders wounded
- Achilles sends Patroclus to Nestor
- fighting at the walls of the Greek camp
- Trojans invade Greek camp
- fighting by the Greek ships
- Hera seduces Zeus
- great deeds of Patroclus, his death in a duel with Hector
- Achilles' new armor, description of his shield

12.   *Day 27 and following night (19.1–23.110a): Fourth Day of Fighting*
- settlement of quarrel between Agamemnon and Achilles
- great deeds of Achilles
- duel of Achilles and Hector, Hector's death

III.   CONCLUSION (24 DAYS)

13.   *Day 28 (23.110b–257a)*: funeral of Patroclus
14.   *Day 29 and following night (23.257b–24.21)*: games in honor of Patroclus
15.   *Days 30–40 (24.22–30)*: Achilles abuses Hector's body
16.   *Day 41 and following night (24.31–694)*: Priam visits Achilles and obtains release of Hector's body
17.   *Day 42 (24.695–781)*: Hector brought back to Troy
18.   *Days 43–50 (24.782–784)*: third truce
19.   *Day 51 (24.785–804)*: funeral of Hector

Homer's ultimate subject was how horribly the wrath of a leader, a great personality, could affect a large common undertaking. This was something new and far more gripping than any of the traditional versions of the well-known Trojan War story, for to Homer's audiences this was an urgent problem at that very time.

So Homer's version of the story reflects current concerns about fundamental issues, among them the applicability of traditional values such as honor, rank, devotion to a common cause, and, above all, qualities of leadership. The *Iliad* shows us how discussions or quarrels of such a basic nature may arise between two high-ranking and sharply intelligent leaders through an escalation of emotions that leads to the humiliation and dishonor of one of the antagonists. As a result of his quarrel with Agamemnon, Achilles boycotts the common undertaking. He regards his own dishonor to be a suspension of social and ethical norms. The only way he sees for them to become binding on everybody again is to bring about a situation of extreme danger to his own side. Only this, he believes, will force Agamemnon, now faced with the utter ruin of the alliance he leads, to realize his error, make amends, and beg Achilles to return to the Greek army. In this way Achilles and the social norms that all Greeks had previously adhered to will be rehabilitated.

Indeed, Achilles' calculation leads to the desired effect – but only after insulter and insulted alike and, more importantly, the entire alliance have suffered heavy losses in manpower and prestige and have had to abandon their former innocence regarding human existence. All concerned have to realize that later excuses or remorse among their fellow men or acts of revenge against their enemy cannot undo or even alleviate the losses endured. The military alliance survives; it continues to fight and will eventually be victorious. But it has utterly lost any illusions about the excellence or special quality of its leadership. It has learned a sobering, perhaps useful, lesson, but its old fighting spirit is gone forever. This is the deeper contemporary meaning of Homer's perspective as expressed in the *Iliad*, as his original listeners and the audiences throughout the eighth century B.C. clearly understood.

Evidence of this understanding comes from later epic poems about the matter of Troy that were composed around 600 B.C. At this time Greek culture had made significant advances, brought about mainly by the introduction of writing some 200 years before. Literacy was now almost a matter of course. As a result, people no longer experienced the old stories told orally by *aoidoi* as often as before and so lost their familiarity with the larger framework of their tales. But these tales presupposed audiences' knowledge of their contexts, to which the *aoidoi* constantly alluded; now they ran the risk of being no longer understood. To counteract this growing risk of unfamiliarity, poets began to write down in separate compositions all that the original audiences had spontaneously thought of when listening to the *aoidoi*. These new and written epics told stories "around" the *Iliad*, which by now had also been written down. That is to say, they encircled the *Iliad* with tales of its entire prehistory and aftermath. These cyclical epics, also called the Epic Cycle – after Greek *kyklos*, "cycle, circle" – have been lost, but we possess later prose versions that retell or summarize their content.[2] As a result, we are in a position to reconstruct the entire plot of the Troy story from its earliest beginnings to its ultimate ramifications, as shown in my outline above. From these sources we learn that after the funeral of Hector, with which the *Iliad* closes, the allied Greek armies were indeed unable to take Troy by military force alone. Their vast assembly of originally 1,186 ships and over 100,000 men as calculated in Book 2 of the *Iliad* could win victory only by means of military trickery – a wooden horse! Even worse: after an angry and savage destruction of the city the Greek alliance collapsed. No proud armada returned to the harbors of Greece; no victory parades, celebrations, or speeches for the conquerors upon their arrival. Instead, each king's flotilla sailed home by its own route. The heroes who had survived were driven by storms far off course throughout the Mediterranean and made their way home only years later, quietly and barely noticeably, as was the case with Odysseus. Agamemnon reached home only to be slaughtered that very day by his own wife in the bath. What an end for the glorious conqueror of Troy!

So it is clear that the story which Homer tells is not at all the story of the Trojan War, of its causes and effects. But what kind of story is it, and what does it have to do with Troy?

As mentioned before, Homeric scholarship has made it evident over the past fifteen years or so that the main theme of the *Iliad* can be understood only through the time of its origins. Let us pursue this line of research a bit further. In its present form and under a misleading title added later, the *Iliad* is a product of the second half of the eighth century B.C. For the people of that time the Trojan War, the context of the poem's plot, was a kind of early or pre-history. Today we know that such a war, if it had indeed taken place, must have occurred about 400 years earlier, in the thirteenth century. This is something that Homer's audiences did not know. Since they did not yet possess an exact chronology and so

---

2   On these epics see now Jonathan S. Burgess, *The Tradition of the Trojan War in Homer and the Epic Cycle* (Baltimore: Johns Hopkins University Press, 2001), a recent study with an updated bibliography. For textual editions and translations see *Greek Epic Fragments from the Seventh to the Fifth Centuries* B.C., ed. and tr. M. L. West (Loeb Classical Library; Cambridge: Harvard University Press, 2003). Cf. also Quintus of Smyrna, *The Trojan Epic: Posthomerica*, ed. and tr. Alan James (Baltimore: Johns Hopkins University Press, 2004).

lacked any orderly sense of history, they considered this war to have been an actual event in an era long gone. So the war was only of limited – we might say: historical – interest to them. They had other concerns. To understand the relationship between the epic's narrator and audience in the eighth century, we must turn to the historical conditions then prevalent.

In Greece, the eighth century was a time of departure after a long period of stagnation. Greek tribes had immigrated into the southern Balkan peninsula around 2000 B.C. and had developed a flourishing culture in the area still known as Greece. They had built a sophisticated infrastructure that was administered from palatial centers distributed throughout the region. An early form of syllabic writing, which modern scholars have called Linear B, was used extensively for accounting and governing purposes. It survives on thousands of clay tablets which, together with documents written in other scripts and languages of the time and alongside the vast archaeological finds throughout the Mediterranean, reveal how wide-ranging the Greeks' international diplomatic and economic relations in the second half of the second millennium B.C. had been: with Egyptians in the south; with Hittites, Babylonians, and Assyrians in the east; and with many smaller countries around the Mediterranean. About 1200 B.C., however, an invasion of warlike tribes from the north caused the complete destruction of this culture. The palaces went up in flames, central administration collapsed, and leadership elites, when not killed in defensive battles, fled, mainly to Cyprus. The common people fell back into anarchy, many reverting to the status of nomads.

Still, a few centers survived the catastrophe and provided the impulses for an eventual return to civilization about 450 years later. Among these were Athens, some parts of central Greece, and the island of Euboea. From about 800 B.C. the Greeks sought new contacts with foreign powers. They took over and improved on their neighbors' technical inventions and cultural achievements. Among the latter were the Phoenicians' alphabet, used today in its Latinized form, and long-distance commerce from the Levant via Greece to Italy and from there even to the Baltic Sea. Next came the largest phase of colonization in pre-modern history when Greeks founded cities along all the coasts of the Mediterranean world. Extensive maritime exchanges of goods and information also began. All this amounted to a rapid broadening of the Greeks' geographic and intellectual horizons.

But it did not happen out of the blue. A new leadership class was needed to organize, administer, and direct all commercial, social, and political activities. This new ruling class in part consisted of descendants of those who had been in power before the general collapse. Eighth-century aristocrats provided the impulses for further developments, but at the same time they saw themselves threatened by an all too rapid progress. While the previous aristocracy had enjoyed unchallenged control of leadership, new classes were now rising as a result of increasing colonization, navigation, trade, and productivity and demanded their share of power and influence. So aristocrats became unsure of themselves: How to deal with these developments? What about their traditional cultural norms and ethical values, which before had been followed unquestioningly? Were these to be given up or at least modified? Were honor, dignity, truthfulness, reliability, and responsibility to be adapted to modern times and changing beliefs? Or should they stubbornly adhere to the tried and true? In the latter case, all the aristocrats had to stick together; no one was allowed to deviate from their community; common interests had to trump an individual's wishes or desires. So there could be no quarrel among the elite under any circumstances. From this point of view, the quarrel between Achilles and Agamemnon was a bad and terrifying example, a warning how not to act or react. And yet: if the cause of this quarrel were those very norms fundamental to society, was it not unavoidable? Should such a quarrel then not be permissible or even be encouraged in certain situations because, after all, social cohesion can only be based on clearly understood and commonly held norms? And was not such a quarrel necessary to provide leaders with ways to deal with newly arising circumstances? If so, could Achilles not demonstrate how much better a strong protest against Agamemnon's absolute authority would turn out to be than the conformity and appeasement, as we might call it, of an Odysseus?

These are the fundamental questions the *Iliad* raises, of topical concern to eighth-century Greeks and not at all unfamiliar to us today since we live in an age of a technological revolution that is comparable in its global reach to the impact which the first phonetic script ever introduced in human history had on the Mediterranean world. Should or can we continue today on the well-trodden paths of our political institutions? Or should we instead begin to think about the feasibility of entirely new forms of government? Homer makes such questions his main subject since no other medium of communication existed at the time to function as the aristocrats' mouthpiece. For centuries epic poetry alone had been the aristocracy's means to state and rethink its social position and the demands made on it by changing times. Homer's epic about Achilles represents an attempt at dealing with the urgent contemporary problem, as yet unsolved, of how the aristocracy should define itself and its rights and responsibilities. So Homer presents his audience with several characters – Achilles, Agamemnon, Nestor, Odysseus, Ajax, and Diomedes among others – who discuss or exemplify various ways of reacting to new situations or problems. All this occurs in a plot which pushes its conflicts, once arisen, to such an extreme, an extreme imaginable only in great literature, that the kind of compromise that must have been a common way out in reality should here become impossible.

Once we read the *Iliad* from this perspective, that of Homer's original audiences, we begin to realize that everything in the epic that is of primary interest to us – the matter of Troy and the Trojan War – was of only secondary importance to its poet and audiences. They were far less concerned with that war than with their own problems, for which Troy and the whole Trojan War provided only the backdrop. What then does this leave us with? The story of Troy as a whole is a narrative web comprising a period of about forty years, a web far too complex in its episodes, characters, connections, and ramifications to be the invention of one poet. Homer composed the story of Achilles and his wrath in an epic which later generations came to call the *Iliad*. He embedded his own narrative, which comprises only fifty-one days but which points to important contemporary issues, within the already existing, widely familiar, and much larger narrative of Troy. In this way he freed himself from having to provide a framework for his story. He selected a specific segment from the wider narrative, a part he then examined in close-up, as it were. In this way he directed his original audiences' and our attention to a circumscribed number of characters and to a particular problem and its impact.

Such a narrative technique can be found in the history of world literature again and again. Various segments from the same mega-narrative of Troy recurred, for example, in Greek tragedy of the fifth century B.C. and in Roman myth-based epic poetry like Virgil's *Aeneid*. The pattern continues in modern works like Derek Walcott's *Omeros* or Christa Wolf's *Cassandra*, to mention only two highly sophisticated representative examples. The figure of Achilles, too, has undergone significant changes in the ways authors have presented him.[3] Such literature reprises ancient myths and is indebted to Homer's example. French literary scholar Gérard Genette calls such literature a palimpsest, using the Greek term for a piece of papyrus whose original text has been erased (*palimpseston* = "scratched off") and whose surface has been covered

---

3   Cf. on this topic my *Achilleus: Wandlungen eines europäischen Heldenbildes* (Stuttgart: Teubner, 1995).

with a new text. Genette has developed a sophisticated theory that is applicable to practically all literature. Small wonder that Homer is his starting point.[4] (For comparison's sake, consider the Bible and its influence.) As a result, today we possess an enormously complex web of interrelated texts and visual narratives that deal with the matter of Troy. But all of them have certain features in common. They all fit or can be embedded into a system of narratives that has become canonical. It allows of numerous variations and deviations from one version to another, but it demands that its basic structure remain fundamentally unchanged. In turn, this system guarantees that readers and viewers can recognize the pattern. Themes and variations are familiar, useful, and pleasant each time we encounter the story or parts of it. Within the overall frame, of course, much can be newly invented or made to serve new purposes, such as contemporary concerns. All this ensures the survival even across millennia of the original frame story within which the new versions are placed.

Evidently it is this technique that the author of our *Iliad* adopted when he took over the familiar story of Troy as the frame within which to present his own narrative, voicing his own concerns. Consequently the story of Troy and the Trojan War must have been available to him when he began the *Iliad* and must have afforded him a vast array of events and characters; otherwise we could not account for the large number of references or allusions that the *Iliad* contains to parts of the whole that are far removed in time from its own plot. Nor could we explain the presence in the *Iliad* of certain motifs that it does not fully develop but seems only to play with. This means that the matter of Troy must have been quite ancient at the time the *Iliad* was composed and must have reached a level of great complexity. The very size of the Troy story as we know it makes the conclusion unavoidable that long before Homer many *aoidoi* had embedded their own versions into the old frame of the matter of Troy, also expressing their own contemporary concerns and in turn contributing to the story's expansion. They are certain to have used plot material already embedded by their predecessors, just as later generations of oral poets and eventually the literate poets from antiquity until today were to do. The tradition of epic poetry composed and transmitted orally that has survived into the twenty-first century, for example in Serbo-Croatia, provides us with a modern analogy. For professional reasons alone each of these modern *aoidoi* was and is keenly

4   Gérard Genette, *Palimpsests: Literature in the Second Degree*, tr. Channa Newman and Claude Dubinsky (Lincoln: University of Nebraska Press, 1997).

interested in becoming familiar with as many versions of the stories in his colleagues' repertory as possible. The same must have been the case with Homer himself. When he took it up again in the eighth century to address current concerns, Homer could count on his listeners' knowledge of its frame. He could have found no more effective a subject than this old story with its long-familiar characters, making it, or rather a part of it, fresh and newly meaningful. In this way he did not have to start by inventing his own plot and characters; instead, he could immediately concentrate on what was of prime importance to him.

It is highly regrettable that all of the pre-Homeric uses of the frame story about Troy have been lost, since they had been performed only orally. Before the art of writing came to Greece in the eighth century, they could not have been preserved beyond a poet's death, except as part of the continuing, if anonymous, palimpsest tradition. Only after writing became common could the Greeks begin to preserve a version of the old tale that they considered to reveal exceptional value or beauty. This version was Homer's. It was later called *Iliad*, but this name is quite erroneous, as we know by now. For all of Western culture Homer's poetry came to be the prototype of literature, and the *Iliad* became the ancestor of all written narratives until today. We can already see what this means for Petersen's *Troy*, the most recent kind of palimpsest to address the matter of Troy, although one that primarily uses images rather than words.

2. *Petersen's* Troy

The title of the film, as mentioned, directs us not so much to Homer's *Iliad* as to the story that people from antiquity to today have associated with the name of that famous city. As we have seen, this is a subject far larger than what the *Iliad* deals with. It was, and still is, the story of the destruction of a mighty and rich city brought about in a war against a Mediterranean superpower, the allied kingdoms in areas that roughly correspond to modern Greece. The Greeks – Homer's Achaeans – apparently wanted to eliminate Troy for some reason. If the story is based on fact – and more and more discoveries indicate that it is – a possible reason is that the city was an obstacle to the Greeks' access to the Black Sea and to its rich coastal regions. To make such a story immediately accessible and visually impressive to modern audiences who do not know the entire wide-ranging background that is involved, Petersen and David Benioff, his screenwriter, had to do two things. First, they had to condense the extensive ramifications of the Troy narrative of which ancient sources, and not only the *Iliad*, tell us and to concentrate on a limited number of crucial plot points. Secondly – and this is crucial for any appreciation of the film – they had to do the very thing that Homer had done in order to present audiences with something more meaningful than an empty if grandiose historical spectacle. To draw them into the narrative in such a way that viewers today, just like Homer's original listeners almost 2750 years earlier, could emotionally and intellectually respond to a tale they were experiencing before their eyes or in their imagination, the filmmakers had to introduce contemporary references or parallels readily recognizable to most viewers, and they had to focus less on the gigantic extent of the matter of Troy and the Trojan War than on the personal experiences of those embroiled in it either as combatants or as bystanders, showing their deeds and sufferings, their achievements and losses. In order to reach their goals within a limit circumscribed by cost, time, and other aspects of film production, Petersen and Benioff had to accept a number of compromises. One of these is Petersen's recourse to formulaic presentations of battle scenes that viewers have come to expect from the long tradition of sword-and-sandal films, although I believe that Petersen's direction of these scenes subtly subverts audience expectations, at least as far as he could do so without arousing suspicions on the part of studio bosses or members of his team. Clearly, historical accuracy concerning the thirteenth century B.C. – something that not even archaeologists, Bronze-Age historians, or Homeric scholars have fully achieved, given the current if constantly increasing state of our knowledge of that time – did not have to be Petersen's chief concern. Nor could it have been. Nor had it been Homer's chief concern. This is the main reason why criticism of the film on the part of scholars who miss accurate reproductions of ancient buildings, ships, weapons, tools, clothes, social institutions, etc. are beside the point, are indeed inappropriate. Modern Homeric scholarship knows only too well that Homer himself was severely limited in his factual knowledge of Troy, having never laid eyes on the city he was telling about. Scholars also know that neither Homer nor his listeners, who had never seen the Troy of the story and so could not check the extent of Homer's knowledge of it, greatly cared about what we call historical accuracy. Homer's concerns, as we saw, lay altogether elsewhere. He cared about presenting conflicts, feelings and passions, intrigues, fear and suffering, honor and treason, and many other related aspects of the human condition that a great war brings out in people and that go beyond their everyday lives. Petersen took direct recourse to this perspective. Notwithstanding some weaknesses in dialogue or plot construction, Petersen's film will be a surprising achievement for anybody who knows the *Iliad*.

Petersen and Benioff should not be criticized that, in order to achieve such effects, they sometimes changed the sequence of events, had characters die earlier than they do in Homer or in other ancient sources, omitted whole plot strands, or invented connections between and among characters and events about which our texts say nothing at all. The filmmakers are actually in excellent company. For example, Aeschylus, Sophocles, and Euripides, besides many other playwrights in fifth-century Athens, had done just that. They surprised their audiences with variants of the venerable matter of Troy, which was a recurring subject of their tragedies. These variants of their own invention forced the Athenians to think anew about something they thought they already knew intimately. All this was far more than merely theatrical entertainment; it was the very goal of the annual festivals held in honor of the god Dionysus. We may conclude that Petersen, who as a student at the Johanneum, an elite *Gymnasium* (high school) in Hamburg, had read Homer in the original, seems to have understood much more about the nature and spirit of classical mythology and literature than most of his critics, even academic ones. Petersen was even aware of modern research concerning Troy. His Nestor says to Agamemnon after the death of Menelaus: "If we leave now, we lose all credibility. If the Trojans can beat us so easily, how long before the Hittites invade?" The Hittites were unknown to Homer; only modern scholarship has known of them after their language was deciphered in 1915.

The true substance of the *Iliad* and of *Troy* alike is to be found in the scenes between individuals who are faced with critical issues. Such private and intimate scenes, for example those between Hector and Andromache, convey an emotionally touching immediacy. Or consider the Trojan brothers Hector and Paris. They have achieved a peace treaty between Troy and Sparta and are now sailing back home. Paris shows Hector a stowaway: Helen, the wife of the Spartan king Menelaus. Paris and Helen have fallen in love. Hector knows that Helen's secret eloping with Paris constitutes a cause for war, annihilating years of diplomacy and setting aside the peace treaty. So Hector immediately wants to return Helen to Menelaus, but Paris threatens to go back with her. His death would be unavoidable, and so Hector relents. Brotherly love wins out over reasons of state. But tragedy ensues.

In another scene, Achilles and Briseis, here a priestess of Apollo and Achilles' captive, are discussing the gods. A bitter Briseis, who has considered Achilles to be no more than a killing machine, "a dumb brute," comments on his apparent lack of reverence for the gods ("All the gods are to be feared and respected"). In return, Achilles observes that the gods admire humans for the mortality that gives meaning to their existence: "The gods envy *us*. They envy us because we're mortal, because any moment might be our last. Everything is more beautiful because we're doomed." Briseis now begins to understand Achilles better. The scene reveals that one of the main charges critics have leveled against Petersen – that he omitted the gods from his narrative – is wrong. The gods *are* present in *Troy*. They are *inside the humans*. As a result, Petersen's conception of Achilles is appropriate. Yes, Achilles is a ruthless killer, as he had been in the *Iliad*. But he takes no pleasure in his killings, as his facial expressions reveal. (The same, by the way, is true for Hector, Achilles' greatest antagonist.) Achilles is a solitary character, a lonely hero. Like Homer's, Petersen's protagonist shows that greatness of spirit that allows him eventually to rise above the inhumanity of war. He returns the body of Hector, whom he has killed in a duel, to Hector's father. The depth of Priam's love for his dead son conquers Achilles. When he himself is dying, he sends Briseis, whom he loves, away. Achilles is fated to die, but Briseis he wants to live. The film intends to show us that peace is far better than war. So it had been for Homer.

Petersen has understood Homer. Following the examples of Homer and other ancient poets, he did the only right thing: he emphasized several, if not all, of the themes that had already been important to Homer and his audiences. *Troy* is not an empty spectacle but an estimable attempt at presenting great literature in the popular medium of film. For this Petersen deserves our gratitude.

Translated by Martin M. Winkler

CHAPTER THREE

The *Iliad* and the Cinema

Martin M. Winkler

Probably the most famous verdict ever passed on a translation of Homer was that of Richard Bentley, the great classical scholar of eighteenth-century England. Bentley told Alexander Pope about his translation of the *Iliad*: "it is a pretty poem, Mr. Pope; but you must not call it *Homer*."[1] Comparable negative views that classicists have held about translations and adaptations of ancient literature have echoed Bentley ever since. Usually these scholars have been disappointed that the new work is insufficiently faithful to the original. Classicists tend to reserve their greatest scorn, however, for adaptations of ancient masterpieces to modern mass media. Cinema and television, they believe, only turn sacred texts into fodder for the undiscriminating millions. Vulgarity is inevitably the result, for how can a profit-driven industry like Hollywood avoid catering to the lowest common denominator? Rare exceptions apparently only prove the rule.[2]

---

1 Quoted from *Lives of the English Poets by Samuel Johnson, LL. D.*, ed. George Birkbeck Hill, vol. 3: *Swift–Lyttleton* (Oxford: Clarendon Press, 1905), 213 note 2, with references; cf. also 275–276 (Appendix N) for other contemporary views of Pope's *Iliad*. See further Maynard Mack, *Alexander Pope: A Life* (New York: Norton/New Haven: Yale University Press, 1985), 348, 642, and 877 (note on 348). Bentley's words are sometimes quoted slightly differently.

2 A representative recent example of a scholar's contempt for a film deriving from a canonical text is the review of *Troy* by Daniel Mendelsohn, "A Little Iliad," *The New York*

Creative or artistic engagement with a text, however, is not scholarship, and adaptations of classical literature do not have to conform to the strictures of philology. Nor are scholars meant to be the primary audience of such works. Rather, there is room for both scholarly exposition and creative adaptation of classical and all other literature. So the dismissive attitude toward modern visual adaptations of ancient texts is short-sighted. On the one hand, it ignores the strong presence of the past in modern popular culture, usually much wider than can be found in the high culture of theater, painting, or opera. Traditionalists would have a much better reason to complain about contemporary popular culture if antiquity were *not* such a conspicuous force in it. On the other hand, even if modern adaptations are well below the artistic level of their originals, scholars' dismissals ignore the long tradition of adaptation that goes back to antiquity. This is most evident in regard to myth, the chief subject matter of ancient narratives. Greek and Roman authors and visual artists were fully aware that myth is by nature variable.[3] As a result, there was no unequivocally correct and no unequivocally false retelling of a myth in antiquity, even if some poets and philosophers claimed to know the truth behind certain tales and proceeded to correct them accordingly.[4] Nor can there be any today. To state this is not to

Review of Books (June 24, 2004), 46–49. Examples of exceptions to this attitude on the part of classicists, calling for their involvement in philological approaches to film, are my "Introduction" to *Classical Myth and Culture in the Cinema*, ed. Martin M. Winkler (New York: Oxford University Press, 2001), 3–18, at 5–6; my "Introduction" to *Classics and Cinema*, ed. Martin M. Winkler (London and Toronto: Associated University Presses, 1991), 9–13; the latter book's review article by Maria Wyke, "Classics and Contempt: Redeeming Cinema for the Classical Tradition," *Arion*, 3rd ser., 6.1 (1998), 124–136, and my "Altertumswissenschaftler im Kino; oder: *Quo vadis, philologia?*" *International Journal of the Classical Tradition*, 11 (2004), 95–110, at 95–102.

3   Two books by Susan Woodford deal with ancient retellings of myth in the visual arts: *The Trojan War in Ancient Art* (Ithaca: Cornell University Press, 1993) and *Images of Myths in Classical Antiquity* (Cambridge: Cambridge University Press, 2002; rpt. 2003). Cf. further Jocelyn Penny Small, *The Parallel Worlds of Classical Art and Text* (Cambridge: Cambridge University Press, 2003). Margaret R. Scherer, *The Legends of Troy in Art and Literature*, 2nd edn (New York: Phaidon, 1964), is a survey from antiquity to the twentieth century.

4   The *Palinodes* ("Recantations") of Stesichorus, turned against Homer and Hesiod, are among the best-known ancient literary examples. On corrections of myth see now the instances examined in *Mythenkorrekturen: Zu einer paradoxalen Form der Mythenrezeption*, ed. Martin Völler, Bernd Seidensticker, and Wolfgang Emmerich (Berlin: de Gruyter, 2004). In their introduction ("Zum Begriff der Mythenkorrektur," 1–18, especially 2–8), the editors distinguish among variation, correction, and criticism of myth and briefly discuss several instances from Greek literature.

ignore that many specific versions of certain myths came to overshadow others and became canonical. But being canonical is not the same as being correct. The early Greek poet Hesiod addresses the flexibility of myth when he has none other than the Muses, the divine inspirers of poets, state outright:

> We know to tell many lies resembling the truth,
> but we also know, when we want, to pronounce truths.[5]

We may compare what two modern voices have observed on this subject in connection with Homer. First, that of a famous scholar and representative of high culture. In his introduction to *Homer in English*, an anthology of translations and adaptations, George Steiner speaks of a "perennial ubiquity of translations from Homer, of Homeric variants, re-creations, pastiches and travesties." Steiner further observes: "I believe our *Iliad* to be the product of an editorial recension of genius, of a wonderfully formative act of combination, selection and editing of the voluminous oral material."[6] Second, the voice of a representative of mass culture. What film director Wolfgang Petersen has said about *Troy* is a close echo of Steiner's perspective: "If there is something like a tree of storytelling, on which each book, each film, is a tiny leaf, then Homer is its trunk."[7] Steiner's and Petersen's views are apt to do greater justice to the endless web of storytelling, in whatever language or medium, than do haughty dismissals of adaptations of a revered author's works. Petersen's understanding of storytelling exemplifies the concept of the narrative palimpsest that French literary scholar Gérard Genette has developed in connection with Homer's *Odyssey*.[8] Petersen's mention of a tree and its leaves, an immediately comprehensible image to emphasize his point, may even remind readers of Homer of a famous simile in the *Iliad*.[9]

---

5   Hesiod, *Works and Days* 27–28; my translation.

6   *Homer in English*, ed. George Steiner (London: Penguin, 1996), xvii and xxviii.

7   Quoted from an interview with Petersen by Tobias Kniebe, "Homer ist, wenn man trotzdem lacht: 'Troja'-Regisseur Wolfgang Petersen über die mythischen Wurzeln des Erzählens und den Achilles in uns allen," *Süddeutsche Zeitung* (May 11, 2004), at http://www.sueddeutsche.de/kultur/artikel/607/31576/print.html; my translation.

8   Gérard Genette, *Palimpsests: Literature in the Second Degree*, tr. Channa Newman and Claude Dubinsky (Lincoln: University of Nebraska Press, 1997).

9   *Iliad* 6.146–149: the generations of man as compared to the regeneration of the leaves on a tree.

1. Can the *Iliad* Be Filmed?

The end of Petersen's *Troy* carries a written acknowledgment that the film was inspired by the *Iliad*. As such, it is a conspicuous leaf on the tall and wide tree of Homeric storytelling. Still, neither *Troy* nor any other film ever made about the themes or the plot of the *Iliad* is a close adaptation – a visual translation – of Homer's text. Instead, all these films deal in different ways with the Trojan War, usually beginning with the abduction of Helen and ending with the fall of Troy. Strictly speaking, the *Iliad*, unlike the *Odyssey*, has never been filmed. The likeliest reason for this is the epic scale of the original. A film of the *Iliad* would be far too long for most viewers' taste, running to at least six or seven hours. It would also be enormously expensive. In addition, the scenes of extreme violence in battle, in which the *Iliad* abounds so much that Simone Weil could characterize it in a famous essay as "the poem of force," would have to be handled very carefully, even today when viewers have been inundated with graphic acts of on-screen bloodshed.[10] A film of the *Iliad* would throw its viewers into the midst of carnage, death, and all the horrors of war for most of its running time. The effect might be numbing or sickening more than anything else, and the depth of Homer's characterization of the Greek and Trojan heroes, their families, their societies, and their gods would suffer accordingly. As a result, the *Iliad* has attracted filmmakers mainly as the basis for free retellings.

Nevertheless, one filmmaker stands out from all others. For many years, Italian writer-director Franco Rossi hoped to make an epic film faithful to the *Iliad*. Rossi had earlier directed and co-written *L'Odissea* (1969), the most accomplished *Odyssey* ever put on the screen. His was and still is the only version to communicate to viewers the beauty and profundity of its model. The film, a good six hours long, was an international production financed by Italian, German, and French public television. Almost every scene reveals that the film had been a labor of love, probably not only for Rossi. Three years later Rossi followed his *Odissea* with a distinguished companion piece, also for international television. His six-hour *Eneide* is the only film version of the *Aeneid* worthy of Virgil. It is likely that Rossi would have filmed the *Iliad* in a comparable manner. But he could never get the necessary financing, although a screenplay, co-written by him, had been completed. Had Rossi succeeded with this project, he would have achieved the unique distinction of making

---

10   Simone Weil, *The Iliad or The Poem of Force: A Critical Edition*, ed. James P. Holoka (New York: Lang, 2003), is the most scholarly reissue of this 1939 essay.

memorable screen adaptations of all three of antiquity's greatest and most influential heroic epics. After his death in 2000, a film of the *Iliad* on the high level of his style and sensibility is unlikely ever to be made.[11] So there still is no film of the *Iliad*. The question then arises: can the *Iliad* be filmed at all?[12]

The difficulties inherent in the subject matter, length, and overall complexity of the *Iliad* mentioned above, all formidable obstacles to any serious adaptation, may incline us to answer this question with "No." Moreover, to modern sensibilities the *Iliad* is wordy and repetitive, especially in its epithets and formulaic language, integral to its style as these are. An even greater problem for today's audiences is a lack of realism on both the divine and the human levels. Gods and goddesses play important parts in the *Iliad*; they take sides in the Trojan War, and some of them fight in it. Warriors deliver lengthy speeches right on the battlefield. The *Iliad* may be too alien in its historical, cultural, religious, and social aspects to be put on screen in a manner that is appropriate to its greatness and at the same time capable of reaching a large audience. That modern viewers are far less familiar with its plot and cast of characters than ancient audiences had been is an additional, and by no means negligible, factor. As a film today, the *Iliad* would need extensive verbal and visual annotation to prevent audiences from being puzzled by what they see or hear. Explanation would be necessary for major aspects and small details alike. As a result, a film would have to be expanded significantly and would inevitably distort the original. Annotation of the kind mentioned is the filmic equivalent of a scholarly commentary accompanying modern editions of ancient texts, so classical scholars might welcome the application of its principles to a film. But

11 Brief comments by Rossi on his films set in antiquity appear in the interview in Francesco Bolzoni and Mario Foglietti, *Le stagioni del cinema: Trenta registi si raccontano* (Soveria Mannelli: Rubettino, 2000), 253–258. Bolzoni and Foglietti appropriately give this section of their book the heading "Franco Rossi: *L'ultimo Ulisse*."

12 *Singe den Zorn* (2004), a German film whose title renders the opening of the *Iliad*, was made with the avowed goal of remaining faithful to the poetic nature of Homer's epic. It is not a film of the *Iliad* but of a staged declamation. Matthias Merkle and Antje Borchardt developed their project for the Dramatisches Theater in Berlin in 2003 and put on a revised version at and around the archaeological site of Troy in 2004. This performance is the basis of their film, which runs to 96 minutes and comprises about 2,500 lines. The *Iliad* has more than 15,000 lines. – At the beginning of their careers, Stanley Kubrick and his friend Alexander Singer contemplated a film of the *Iliad* based on Singer's screenplay; it never materialized; cf. Joseph Gelmis, *The Film Director as Superstar* (Garden City; Doubleday, 1970), 312. Kubrick later directed the science-fiction and historical epics *Spartacus* (1960), *2001: A Space Odyssey* (1968), and *Barry Lyndon* (1975).

there is a decisive difference. A philological or historical commentary can be kept separate from the text while explanations in a film, either verbal or visual, cannot; they are an integral part of the film itself. And where should a screenwriter or director draw the line concerning expository or explanatory additions? Besides many other aspects of life and death in Bronze-Age antiquity, there would have to be explanations of the major ancient customs, for example during funerals; of concepts like duty, honor, and ethical behavior; of religious practices and the importance and functions of numerous gods. All this would be cumbersome and bring any narrative drive to a standstill, doubtless alienating large segments of the audience. Screenwriters and directors would equally defeat their purpose if they provided too much or too little information.

Nor is the *Iliad* a narrative complete in itself. Its storyline is part of a much larger plot with which ancient audiences were familiar. Homer could refer to it briefly but could otherwise keep it out of his narrative. Such familiarity is no longer the case today. So an expansion of the "backstory" of the *Iliad* would become necessary for a coherent film plot. Homer himself on several occasions refers to his story's background and its aftermath. The full story, of which he tells only a segment, begins with the Judgment of Paris and his elopement with Helen, if not even earlier; it continues well beyond the funeral of Hector during the Greeks' siege of Troy, the last scene in the *Iliad*. The death of Achilles, the fall of Troy, and the return home of the surviving Greeks are all part of the matter of Troy. And this does not even include the continuation of the Trojan myth in the historical mythology of the Romans, whose ancestor was the Trojan prince Aeneas, one of the few survivors of the destruction of the city.

Petersen's *Troy* and its cinematic predecessors since Giovanni Pastrone's *La caduta di Troia* (*The Fall of Troy*, 1910) all adhere to the pattern of plot expansion here summarized. If not even someone as experienced and uniquely qualified as Rossi could make a film of the *Iliad*, we might indeed have to conclude that Homer's epic is unfilmable. This conclusion, however, will strike any lover of both Homer and the cinema as highly regrettable, as we will see next.

2. The Cinematic Nature of the *Iliad*

The additions outlined above that a film of the *Iliad* would need are themselves highly cinematic. The beginnings of the illicit affair between the most beautiful woman on earth and her handsome prince, the big spectacle of the Trojan War, Odysseus' trick with the wooden horse (itself a suspenseful and irresistible part of the story, as the histories of painting and film both attest), the tragic deaths of Hector, his father, and his son, the destruction of his people, city, and culture, and the remarkable deaths of Achilles and Agamemnon and the no less remarkable survival of Odysseus – all this is the stuff of cinema. Again and again the Trojan War has attracted filmmakers for its timeless plot – heroism, war, forbidden love, the most famous *femme fatale* ever – and for its visual appeal. More importantly, the *Iliad* itself is inherently visual, even cinematic, on the levels of plot and style. So we can adduce a number of substantial points to argue against the conclusion reached above.

The plot of the *Iliad* is full of action, the lifeblood of cinema: a great war hero's anger at the mistreatment he receives from his commander-in-chief and the effects of his withdrawal from fighting on himself and others on both sides in the war. The *Iliad* also has enough beautiful women (Aphrodite, Helen, Briseis) and happy marital love (Hector and Andromache) to satisfy any viewer's expectations. It also takes its readers to an exotic past. Its setting, or an imaginative version of it, can be re-created on film, most attractively in a widescreen format and with color cinematography. Computer-generated images can show us the impossible or barely imaginable and seamlessly integrate its amazing sights into live-action footage. *Troy* is an example: "Even I don't know where the CG starts and our extras end," Petersen has said.[13] So what more could a filmmaker want? Even considered by itself, the plot of the *Iliad* is a natural for large-scale visual retellings. American writer-director Samuel Fuller, playing himself in Jean-Luc Godard's *Pierrot le Fou* (1965), famously defined the cinema in terms directly applicable to the *Iliad* because everything he points to is central to Homer's epic: "The film is like a battleground: love, hate, action, violence, death. In one word: emotions."[14] Humans show emotions primarily through action. Action implies motion, and the cinema, whose very name means "motion," may well be the best artistic medium for the representation of emotions and all they entail. Petersen has echoed Fuller by summarizing his view of the *Iliad* as follows, if in rather colloquial terms: "The *Iliad* is an anticipation of eternal human drama. Men bash each other's

13   M. E. Russell, "Helmer of Troy," *In Focus*, 4 no. 5 (May, 2004); quoted from the complete interview at http://www.infocusmag.com/04may/petersenuncut.htm.
14   Fuller's words, spoken in English in the film, are often quoted in slightly different wording or punctuation; cf., e.g., *Pierrot le Fou: A Film by Jean-Luc Godard*, tr. Peter Whitehead (New York: Simon and Schuster, 1969), 28 and 33 ("Emotion").

heads in, love each other, torture each other. Homer understood this overwhelmingly: the Beautiful, but also violence and the desire to exterminate each other."[15] So a filmic treatment of the *Iliad* independent of its surrounding mythical narratives is long overdue. Presumably, Rossi would have made such a film.

The second level on which the *Iliad* works cinematically, that of style, could greatly have aided a director like Rossi in his undertaking. To an astonishing degree, the *Iliad*, the very first work of Western literature, reveals features of the art of cinematic storytelling long before modern technology made this art a reality. That is to say, the *Iliad* provides a director with numerous clues for translating its story to the screen. The text, as it were, contains its own screenplay, with staging directions, hints at camera angles, and points about editing. In a 1977 interview, film director George Cukor made the case for literary adaptations in general: "The text tells you where the camera should be. I don't think that's a question of your judgment . . . If the story is good, the director is halfway there."[16] Evidently, these words apply to the *Iliad*.

Great narrative literature is highly visual and prompts readers or listeners to see in their mind's eye the story in which they are engaged. This is especially true for a large number of Greek and Roman works.[17]

15   Wolfgang Röhl, "'Menschen hauen sich die Köpfe ein'," *Stern* (April 19, 2004); quoted from http://www.stern.de/unterhaltung/film/index.html?id=522904&q=petersen%20menschen.
16   Quoted from Paul F. Boller and Ronald L. Davis, *Hollywood Anecdotes* (New York: Morrow, 1987), 93. Cukor directed several films adapted from works of literature and had extensive experience as a stage director.
17   On this see especially Sergei Eisenstein, "Dickens, Griffith, and the Film Today," in Sergei Eisenstein, *Film Form: Essays in Film Theory*, ed. and tr. Jay Leyda (1949; rpt. San Diego: Harcourt Brace Jovanovich, 1977), 195–255, and "Word and Image," in Sergei Eisenstein, *The Film Sense*, ed. and tr. Leyda (1942; rpt. New York: Harcourt Brace Jovanovich, 1975), 1–65. Cf. William C. Wees, "Dickens, Griffith and Eisenstein," *The Humanities Association Review/La Révue de l'Association des Humanités*, 24 (1973), 266–276, and Ana L. Zambrano, "Charles Dickens and Sergei Eisenstein: The Emergence of Cinema," *Style*, 9 (1975), 469–487. J. K. Newman, "Ancient Poetics and Eisenstein's Films," and Fred Mench, "Film Sense in the *Aeneid*," both in my *Classical Myth and Culture in the Cinema*, 193–218 and 219–232, apply Eisenstein's principles to classical literature. Italian poet Gabriele D'Annunzio had expressed his awareness of the connections between ancient Roman literature and the cinema in February, 1914, in an interview published in *Il Corriere della Sera*; the text is reprinted in *Interviste a D'Annunzio (1895–1938)*, ed. Gianni Oliva (Lanciano: Rocco Carabba, 2002), 278–285. D'Annunzio was greatly taken with Ovid's *Metamorphoses* in this regard – "There you have a true cinematic subject" (*Ecco un vero soggetto cinematografico*) – and particularly with the story of Daphne (282). The cinematic equivalent of Ovidian metamorphosis is the dissolve, one of the earliest and most common "special effects" since the days of film pioneer Georges Méliès.

Ancient poets' and audiences' creative imagination supplied what lack of technology denied them. In an essay first published in 1946, André Bazin, the influential French critic and theoretician of film, made this point explicit: "The cinema is an idealistic phenomenon. The concept men had of it existed, so to speak, fully armed in their minds, as if in some Platonic heaven, and what strikes us most of all is the obstinate resistance of matter to ideas rather than of any help offered by techniques to the imagination of the researchers." Bazin adduces an apposite analogy from Greek myth: "the myth of [Daedalus and] Icarus had to wait for the internal combustion engine before descending from the Platonic heavens. But it had dwelt in the soul of every man since he first thought about birds."[18]

The *Iliad* demonstrates the accuracy of Bazin's observation. In Book 8, Zeus comes down from Olympus to the highest peak of Mt. Ida, on which he has a grove and an altar. Here he sits down and, "looking out over the city of Troy and the ships of the Achaians," watches the battle between Trojans and Greeks.[19] Zeus resembles the viewer of an epic film.[20] He delights in watching the heroic exploits on the battlefield purely for the sake of spectacle. His elevated position affords him a panoramic overview of the Trojan War, one that corresponds to today's filmgoer looking at an extreme long shot as composed for the kind of wide screen onto which historical epics have been projected for over fifty years. A number of high-angle battle shots in Petersen's *Troy* come close to showing us what Zeus may have seen from his vantage point.

---

18   André Bazin, "The Myth of Total Cinema," in *What Is Cinema?*, tr. Hugh Gray, vol. 1 (Berkeley: University of California Press, 1967; rpt. 1974), 17–22; quotations at 17 and 22 (slightly altered and corrected). I discuss Bazin in related context in my "Introduction" to *Classical Myth and Culture in the Cinema*, 3–22, at 14. Fredric Jameson, *Signatures of the Visible* (New York: Routledge, 1990), 5, has repeated Bazin's point (if without reference to him): "was some cinematographic dimension of human reality always there somewhere in prehistoric life, waiting to find its actualization in a certain high-technical civilization?" The answer is evident.

19   *Iliad* 8.41–52; the last line of this passage is quoted in the translation by Richmond Lattimore, *The Iliad of Homer* (Chicago: University of Chicago Press, 1951; several rpts.), 183.

20   A recent film epic specifically makes this point. In *Alexander* (2004), writer-director Oliver Stone includes bird's-eye views of the battle of Gaugamela that are intended to represent Zeus, Alexander the Great's putative father (an ancient legend that the film takes care to include), witnessing his son's victory: "The eagle that dominates the film's imagery represents by tradition Zeus . . . I use the eagle in that scene to represent Zeus's point of view." Quoted from Gary Crowdus, "Dramatizing Issues That Historians Don't Address: An Interview With Oliver Stone," *Cinéaste*, 30 no. 2 (2005), 12–23, at 20.

Throughout the *Iliad*, Zeus and the other gods watch from on high the epic scenes that take place on earth. The poem reminds us time and again that its story is a spectacle in the word's literal sense. But there is much more. The chief cinematic clues contained in the *Iliad* may be found in its similes and ecphrases. Both are famous aspects of Homeric style.[21]

2.1. Similes

Epic similes are an integral part of Homeric narrative. A revealing instance of their function occurs in a complementary pair of similes in Book 22, when Hector is about to face Achilles for their decisive duel. As the very first lines of the *Iliad* have made evident, the hero whose anger is most devastating in the entire Trojan War is Achilles. But now his greatest foe, Hector, is full of heroic fury, too. He refuses to heed his parents' pleas not to fight Achilles but to save himself. Homer expresses Hector's state of mind in a long soliloquy, the ancient equivalent of an interior monologue. (Films usually render this as voice-overs.) In the passage that describes Hector waiting and Achilles approaching, Homer sets the scene by cutting, as it were, from Priam and Hecuba to Hector. (The cut is implied in the second "but" in the lines quoted below.) I quote the passage without Hector's soliloquy:

> So these two in tears and with much supplication called out
> to their dear son, but could not move the spirit in Hector,
> but he awaited Achilles as he came on, gigantic.
> But as a snake waits for a man by his hole, in the mountains,
> glutted with evil poisons, and the fell venom has got inside him,
> and coiled about the hole he stares malignant, so Hector
> would not give ground but kept unquenched the fury within him
> and sloped his shining shield against the jut of the bastion.
> Deeply troubled he spoke to his own great-hearted spirit . . .
> So he pondered, waiting, but Achilles was closing upon him
> in the likeness of the lord of battles, the helm-shining warrior,
> and shaking from above his shoulder the dangerous Pelian
> ash spear, while the bronze that closed about him was shining
> like the flare of blazing fire or the sun in its rising.

21   On Homer's descriptive techniques and on his similes see especially Mark W. Edwards, *The Iliad: A Commentary*, vol. 5: *Books 17–20* (Cambridge: Cambridge University Press, 1985), 24–41, and *Homer: Poet of the* Iliad (Baltimore: Johns Hopkins University Press, 1987; rpt. 1990), 82–87 and 102–110, with additional references.

And the shivers took hold of Hector when he saw him, and he
　could no longer
stand his ground there, but left the gates behind, and fled, frightened,
and Peleus' son went after him in the confidence of his quick feet.
As when a hawk in the mountains who moves lightest of things flying
makes his effortless swoop for a trembling dove, but she slips away
from beneath and flies and he shrill screaming close after her
plunges for her again and again, heart furious to take her;
so Achilles went straight for him in fury, but Hector
fled away under the Trojan wall and moved his knees rapidly.[22]

The paired similes of the snake coiled on the ground and of the hawk
pursuing a dove high in the air contain clear hints at the way we are to
visualize Hector and Achilles. Homer takes care to guide us, for the first
adjective describing Achilles anticipates both the similes and the result
of the duel. Achilles arrives "gigantic," that is to say, towering above
Hector. The filmic equivalent of this adjective is a low-angle shot, from
Hector's point of view, of Achilles rushing straight toward the camera.
Then a cut to the next shot, which is expressed in the snake simile: a
high-angle long or medium shot of Hector ready for battle. By contrast
to the preceding shot of Achilles, Hector appears dwarfed. The fact that
the animal to which Hector is likened is found on the ground reveals
how a viewer should imagine the moment: by looking down. The detailed description of the coiled snake's venomous fury expresses how an
actor is to portray Hector at this moment: tense and crouching down
but ready to spring up into action. Homer reinforces the high viewing
angle and Hector's low position by a double reference to the serpent's
hole and by the observation that Hector's shield is "sloped." The snake
simile describes Hector's posture as it appears simultaneously to obser-
vers outside the immediate action, such as his parents (who see him) and
the poem's listeners or readers (who imagine seeing him), and to a par-
ticipant in the action, an Achilles swooping down on him. When Homer
likens Achilles, now closer, to the god of war himself, he again does so in
visual terms, emphasizing the flashing metal of Achilles' divine armor, a
sight both beautiful and terrifying. No alert reader can fail to visualize
Achilles and Hector at this moment.

　The second simile, which uses different animals to make the scene it
describes more vivid, expresses Achilles' superiority to Hector by pitting

---

22　*Iliad* 22.90–98 and 131–144; quoted from Lattimore, *The Iliad of Homer*, 437 and
438–439. For the sake of consistency I substitute "Achilles" and "Hector" for Lattimore's
"Achilleus" and "Hektor."

a bird of prey against a helpless victim. This simile is more accomplished and even more cinematic than the preceding one in that it contains high- and low-angle shots on the movements of both birds. Words denoting height, as when Achilles moves upon Hector as if from above ("swoop," "plunges"), find their counterpart in the dove slipping away "from beneath" the hawk. The phrase "again and again" expresses continuous back-and-forth movements that in a film call for rapid back-and-forth cutting from high-angle and low-angle shots of the two enemies in close-ups and medium shots. Such intercutting is one of the oldest filmic techniques to create in viewers a sense of suspense, even of mounting doom, concerning the fate of the people they are watching. Heightening readers' suspense is Homer's purpose in the simile, too. The fast cutting in a film corresponds to his numerous words for swift movement on the part of both birds ("quick feet," "moves lightest," "effortless swoop," "plunges").

Two scenes in Petersen's film visually express Homer's similes. In the opening sequence of *Troy*, Achilles comes down on his victim by rising in the air and stabbing him from above. This moment prepares us for two others in the scene of the duel between Achilles and Hector. In less than a second, Achilles whirls up and around Hector and, while still in the air, lunges downward at him with his sword. Shortly after, he brings Hector to his knees when he stabs him, again from above, in the shoulder. Then he kills him by thrusting his sword downward through Hector's chest.

If these two Homeric similes describe individual heroes, others give us panoramic overviews of the Greek and Trojan armies in battle. One of them finds a direct equivalent in *Troy*. This passage occurs in Book 4. It contains two similes as frames; their purpose is to make the action narrative in between immediate and easy to envision. The Greek army is advancing on the Trojans, who are holding their ground; then both sides clash in furious battle. The first simile is of waves breaking on the shore. The description implies an observer stationed on an elevation, such as a mountain top, and looking down along the beach. In the second simile two rushing rivers commingle. The poet also provides the "soundtrack" that accompanies the action: the Greeks' menacing silence and, in yet another simile, the Trojans' cries. These lines I omit. Here is the decisive part of the passage:

> As when along the thundering beach the surf of the sea strikes
> beat upon beat as the west wind drives it onward; far out
> cresting first on the open water, it drives thereafter

to smash roaring along the dry land, and against the rock jut bending
breaks itself into crests spewing back the salt wash;
so thronged beat upon beat the Danaans' close battalions
steadily into battle, with each of the lords commanding
his own men . . .
  Now as these advancing came to one place and encountered,
they dashed their shields together and their spears, and the strength
of armoured men in bronze, and the shields massive in the middle
clashed against each other, and the sound grew huge of the fighting.
There the screaming and the shouts of triumph rose up together
of men killing and men killed, and the ground ran blood.
As when rivers in winter spate running down from the mountains
throw together at the meeting of streams the weight of their water
out of the great springs behind in the hollow stream-bed,
and far away in the mountains the shepherd hears their thunder;
such, from the coming together of men, was the shock and the
    shouting.[23]

Description of the repeated waves of the Greek attack on a stationary
Trojan line yields to that of close combat between the two armies by
means of the second simile involving water; it is prompted by the observation within the action narrative that the ground already "ran blood."
A filmic retelling of these lines has to be realistic. No actual waves could
appear on screen. They would only divert viewers' attention from the
battle instead of involving them in it more closely, as the similes do. If
staged effectively, an on-screen battle needs no extraneous enhancement
anyway. Still, Petersen shows us how a real-looking attack can express
Homer's imagery. Modern computer technology makes it possible. In
my description I include the time at which the important shots in this
scene occur according to the film's DVD edition.[24]

After the non-Homeric death of Menelaus at Hector's hands,
Agamemnon orders an attack on the Trojans by the entire Greek army,
Achilles and his men excepted. (Achilles is watching the attack from
an elevated position.) The Trojans are arrayed in battle line, with the
walls of Troy at their back. The camera shows us the attack of the Greeks
first from an eye-level position on the side of their battle line, as if from a
combatant's point of view. Then, in a fluid motion and without a cut,

---

23 *Iliad* 4.422–429 and 446–456; quoted from Lattimore, *The Iliad of Homer*, 124 and
125.
24 Readers who wish to view the scene I am about to describe can find it at 1:17:19–
1:23:31 in chapters 22–23 of the DVD edition of *Troy*. I identify individual shots according to this edition's timer.

the camera soars up and above the men (1:17:23–30). An extreme long shot beginning at 1:17:31 is also from a high angle, but this time the camera watches from behind the advancing Greeks. At 1:18:12 Petersen gives us a corresponding shot from the opposite position: above and behind the Trojans we see, as they do, the Greeks storming near. Shortly after this comes the shot that is closest to Homer's simile of the crashing waves (1:18:15–26). The camera is now positioned high above the battlefield, looking down over both armies from the side so that the Trojans appear screen left, still standing firm, while the Greeks are attacking them from screen right. The camera begins to move along and above the entire battle line, in the process swooping down closer but still remaining above all the soldiers. The shot continues while the Greeks break into the Trojan line. The Homeric nature of the moment in which both armies make contact is made evident when the shields of the Greek warriors rise wavelike above the Trojans and tumble down over their heads. Only then does Petersen cut to close-up images of hand-to-hand combat. The wavelike nature of this fight continues in three very brief shots in which we see a few Greek soldiers who have jumped up into the air descending on the Trojans (1:18:26–30). In this battle sequence the attack of the Greeks is indeed cresting, smashing, driving, and breaking on the Trojans while shields massive in the middle clash against each other. Still images can capture neither the fluidity of these shots, graceful even in the context of the carnage that is about to ensue, nor the movements contained within them. As viewers realize soon after, the ground runs blood, too, because numerous Greeks die under the missiles of the Trojan archers (whom Homer does not mention here). The individual fights and deaths which Homer describes after the passage quoted find their equivalent in *Troy* in several brief duels; they culminate in the ferocious combat between Hector and Ajax, which is followed by another wavelike Greek attack (1:21:03–09) filmed from different angles but not as long or visually expressive as the preceding one. Even the Trojans' counterattack has a wavelike quality, although it is seen only momentarily.

Like Homer's shepherd who overhears the roar of the rushing streams, we watch and hear the shock and the shouting of Greek and Trojan warriors in the film's battle sequence. Homer closes Book 4 with the comment: "on that day many men of the Achaians and Trojans / lay sprawled in the dust face downward beside one another."[25] Petersen includes shots that exactly correspond to these lines. When they see a

---

25   *Iliad* 4. 543–544; quoted from Lattimore, *The Iliad of Homer*, 127.

chariot being driven over dead bodies lying on the ground (1:22:17–22), viewers familiar with the *Iliad* may even think of a specific moment later in the epic. Achilles, too, drives his chariot over dead bodies. His horses "trampled alike dead men and shields, and the axle under / the chariot was all splashed with blood."[26]

The Homeric similes of storms, fires, streams rushing down mountains, or waves breaking bring home to us the irresistible power of the elements, with which man must deal in his daily life. But they also express the devastating force of man-made conflicts like war and battle. So it is very much to the point that Petersen gives us a visual equivalent of the simile of the waves to intensify our sense of the Greek army's furious onslaught on the Trojans. (We still use the phrase "wave of attack" today.) The equivalent of Homer's simile in *Troy* has a precursor in *The Perfect Storm* (2000), the film Petersen directed immediately before. This drama deals with the impossible odds faced by the intrepid crew of a small fishing boat against a gigantic gale on the Atlantic Ocean. Images of their boat dwarfed by waves of overwhelming proportion express the insignificance of man before nature's implacability. The most monstrous wave imaginable eventually destroys the boat and kills its crew. The immediacy of this unusual storm derives from Petersen's use of state-of-the-art computer technology, for filming in an actual storm would have been impossible. *The Perfect Storm* was perhaps Petersen's perfect preparation for the epic battle scenes in *Troy*. *Das Boot* (1981), Petersen's submarine epic about heroism and death in a World War II setting, a film that made him internationally famous and paved his way to a successful career in Hollywood, is also likely to have influenced his approach to the material of *Troy*.

2.2. Ecphrases

Similes heighten listeners' or readers' sense of immediacy and help them imagine themselves present at the scenes described. Homeric ecphrases equally appeal to their visual imagination. An ecphrasis gives a detailed description of an object, frequently a work of art. The most famous ecphrasis in the *Iliad* occurs in Book 18, when the god Hephaestus forges a shield for Achilles that is decorated with numerous scenes.[27] This

---

26 *Iliad* 20. 499–500; quoted from Lattimore, *The Iliad of Homer*, 417.
27 On the shield see Klaus Fittschen, *Der Schild des Achilleus* (Archaeologia Homerica II.N.1; Göttingen: Vandenhoeck and Ruprecht, 1973), and Edwards, *The Iliad: A Commentary*, 200–232, especially 206–208 on scene arrangement, the difficulties of actually

detailed ecphrasis symbolizes the process of the poem's composition.[28] The most remarkable quality of the scenes that Hephaestus puts on the shield is that they tell stories. The images represent complete narratives rather than individual – that is, static – moments in a story. As such, they show a cinematic (rather than a photographic) imagination. The two representative scenes I examine below can deepen modern readers' appreciation of the nature of Homeric epic. My first scene is comparatively simple and may serve as a suitable starting point. The second is more important for the themes of the *Iliad* and considerably more complex.

One of the scenes Hephaestus fashions concerns two lions attacking a herd of cattle. In my quotation of the text I italicize those words that indicate motion or movement. In themselves such terms are not conclusive evidence for the cinematic nature of these lines, for most of them describe a particular moment in a manner comparable to a modern photograph or a freeze-frame in a film. Nevertheless, they show us that the image is to be understood as the narrative of an action in constant progression:

> He made upon it a herd of horn-straight oxen. The cattle
> were wrought of gold and tin, and *thronged in speed* and with lowing
> *out of* the dung of the farmyard *to* a pasturing place by a sounding
> river, and beside the *moving* field of a reed bed.
> The herdsmen were of gold who *went along* with the cattle,
> four of them, and nine dogs *shifting their feet followed* them.
> But among the foremost of the cattle two formidable lions
> had caught hold of a bellowing bull, and he with loud lowings
> *was dragged away*, as the dogs and the young men *went in pursuit* of him.
> But the two lions, breaking open the hide of the great ox,
> gulped the black blood and the inward guts, as *meanwhile* the herdsmen
> *were in the act* of setting and urging the *quick* dogs on them.
> But they, *before* they could get their teeth in, turned back from the lions,
> but *would come* and take their stand very close, and bayed, and kept
>   clear.[29]

The first six lines move herdsmen, cattle, and dogs from the farm to a pasture and are simple in their expressions of motion. But this simplicity

fashioning a shield from the information given in the text, and "the normal Homeric technique for physical objects to be described by means of action and movement" (207). See also Edwards, *Homer: Poet of the* Iliad, 278–286.

28   Cf. Keith Stanley, *The Shield of Homer: Narrative Structure in the* Iliad (Princeton: Princeton University Press, 1993).

29   *Iliad* 18. 573–586; quoted from Lattimore, *The Iliad of Homer*, 390–391.

ends as soon as we find out about the lions. Now we observe a short action story that is broken down into different stages. Most noteworthy for the linear progression in which the story unfolds is its first element, the past-perfect tense of the verb that expresses the beginning of the lions' attack. They "had caught" their prey already – the tense indicates that the actual moment of their capturing the ox does not appear on the shield. But since it is the logical beginning of their hunt, the narrator provides us with this information, just as a film would have started at that point. Next comes the action in progress: the bull was being "dragged away" while herdsmen and dogs "went in pursuit." Again the verb tenses are important for us to visualize the scene in that they denote a continuing action. (Cf. "in the act" a few lines later.) Then comes stage two of the lions' story on the shield: they are now feasting on their prey. This tells us that a necessary but unmentioned prior stage has occurred, in which the lions stopped dragging the ox away and killed it. By now we have followed the ox on its journey all the way from farmyard to pasture and to its death. The last scene is stationary on the part of the lions feeding but at the same time highly agitated on the part of the actions of the dogs. They run up, then turn tail, then come close again. The verb form "would come" indicates their repeated and ongoing movements.

If we take the narrative in these lines strictly literally, we must assume that Hephaestus presented a series of at least three unmoving images in sequence: 1) animals and people leaving the farm, with the pasture perhaps visible in the distance or on one side; 2) the lions dragging the bull and being pursued by herdsmen and dogs; 3) the lions gorging themselves while being harried by the dogs. The individual moments could be broken down even further; the first, for example, could be shown in two separate images (departure from farm, arrival at pasture). The third in particular almost demands to be shown in more than one still image to reveal the dogs' frantic back-and-forth motions. In principle, the sequential arrangement of still images on the shield resembles the sequence of individual exposures on a film strip: an action in progress is broken down into its constituent static elements. With film, the rapid change of twenty-four frame exposures per second deceives the eye into perceiving not static images but motion, an illusion of movement that really does not exist. This impression is caused by the retina's "persistence of vision," which blurs individual images into a continuous flow. With ecphrasis, our imagination supplies the connections that are not actually present in the images on the shield but that the words prompt us to "see." Our imagination makes us visualize – "imagination" derives from "image" – a progressing story that can only be shown and is shown in still pictures.

These images, like all others on the shield, are in color ("gold and tin," "black blood") and have, as it were, a soundtrack ("lowing," "sounding," "bellowing," "loud lowings," "bayed").[30]

Such cinematic analysis can be applied to all the individual scenes on Achilles' shield. For the episode that takes the greatest amount of verbal description, Hephaestus fashions a contrasting pair of complex images.[31] The first depicts a peaceful city with its marriages and festivals. Expressions of motion – people "were leading the brides," "young men followed" the dance – and accompanying sounds of bridal songs and musical instruments (492–496) express the fluid nature of the scene and prepare us for the much more dramatic one that follows, a court trial (497–508). As again the verb tenses make evident, Hephaestus tells a complete and self-contained story. Below, I italicize words and phrases that reveal its temporal aspects. Hephaestus provides first a prehistory ("a quarrel / *had* arisen," 497–498) and its impact ("two men *were* disputing over the blood price / for a man who *had been* killed," 498–499; note the different past tenses and their non-chronological sequence). The background information continues in such a way as to signify the progress of time: "One man promised full restitution" but "the other refused" (499–500). We can easily visualize this two-part phase. The next stage follows: "Both *then* made for an arbitrator" (501). Now comes the climax, the actual trial. Its agitated nature, expressed on a screen in rapidly intercut shots of the different participants from various angles, is conveyed in the text through verbs and conjunctions (502–505): "people *were* speaking up on either side . . . *But* [a word corresponding to a cut in a film] the heralds *kept* the people in hand, as *meanwhile* [a transitional panning shot in a film to a different view of the court] the elders *were* in session . . . The two men *rushed* before these, and *took turns* speaking . . ." The scene of the trial, whose resolution Hephaestus does not render since it can be deduced from the preceding description of the peaceful city with its well-functioning laws, ends with another cinematic equivalent. The mention of gold lying on the ground between the antagonists, a reward for the most just among the elders (507–508), indicates a more distant view of the court than before. On film, it would appear in a long shot of the entire court, perhaps with the camera further receding from the scene.[32] Such a long shot or traveling

---

30   Edwards, *The Iliad: A Commentary*, 208: "Even sound effects are included" in individual scenes on the shield. Note his use of a term familiar from film.

31   *Iliad* 18.490–540; Lattimore, *The Iliad of Homer*, 388–389.

32   The opposite camera movement, a zoom, is mentioned by Edwards, *Homer: Poet of the Iliad*, 86, in connection with Homeric descriptions.

shot might in turn be followed by a fade-out or by a dissolve to the next description.[33]

The second city is at war, besieged by two armies (509–540). This part of the story is even more intricate in its details and thus more cinematic than the one just described. Again, verbs of both motion and inaction, adverbs like "quickly," "meanwhile," or "presently," and conjunctions like an adversative "but" and a temporal "as" impart both scope and complexity to a kind of small-scale epic of war, a miniature *Iliad*. Attentive readers cannot fail to visualize this passage, to translate it into a sequence of mental images. Their imagination, prompted by the clues in the text, turns them into their own directors, cinematographers, and editors.

The scenes on the shield of Achilles are short films expressed in words. All represent action narratives that progress through different stages. Our understanding of them as a kind of proto-cinematic approach to narrative does justice to their intricate and highly visual nature, but it also leads us to an important question. Could Hephaestus really have put images of all the individual parts of the several different stories mentioned in the text onto the surface of a single shield? Such a feat would be impossible even for a divine craftsman. A shield of a size that accommodates all the scenes described in such loving detail would be so large as to be useless for any practical purposes. Evidently, we are not meant to understand the ecphrases on the shield in purely realistic terms.

What then is the purpose of such detailed descriptions? If they are not intended to be factual, they must be intended to appeal to our imagination. That is to say, they have a double function. On the one hand, the ecphrases refer to actual scenes which most likely consist of only one image each. In the case of the cattle and lions, it may well have

33 Joachim Latacz, *Kampfparänese, Kampfdarstellung und Kampfwirklichkeit in der Ilias, bei Kallinos und Tyrtaios* (Munich: Beck, 1977), 78, adduces the analogy of a still camera with a lens of a focal length (cf. modern zoom lenses) suitable to describe the epic poet's view of the battlefield. His book contains several diagrams to illustrate the synchronic and diachronic battle actions in the *Iliad*. On Zeus' and other gods' bird's-eye view of human actions and on this perspective's analogy to the omniscient narrator's position cf. Latacz, 97. His work has influenced, among others, the study by Irene J. F. de Jong, *Narrators and Focalizers: The Presentation of the Story in the* Iliad, 2nd edn (Bristol: Bristol Classical Press, 2004). Cf. further Irene J. F. de Jong and René Nünlist, "From Bird's Eye View to Close-Up: The Standpoint of the Narrator in the Homeric Epics," in *Antike Literatur in neuer Deutung*, ed. Anton Bierl, Arbogast Schmitt, and Andreas Willi (Munich: Saur, 2004), 63–83. (This book is a *Festschrift* for Latacz.) Such work indicates that classical scholarship has become aware of the cinematic aspects of ancient texts. A systematic study, however, does not yet exist.

been the moment numbered third in my summary above. On the other hand, the ecphrases also surround the actual images with a context; they provide narrations of the actions that precede and follow each image. These are the moments in the narrative that a real image can only imply but that the text prompts our innate sense of the visual to supply subconsciously. Such a technique of description works well because we are dealing not with static images – as in a still life, for instance – but with images of actions in progress. As classical art historian Susan Woodford has recently put it:

> A photographic snapshot records a single moment in time. The Greeks and Romans did not have cameras and probably did not have a very rigid concept of what could be seen at any one moment. It is unlikely, therefore, that they found it particularly odd if a single image suggested a number of different things, all of which could not be happening at the same time.

She also observes: "Words can sometimes conjure up images that defy visual representation."[34] So the individual ecphrases on the shield of Achilles take on a life of their own. They become independent of their material setting, as the very language of the text reveals. Verb tenses expressing a developing action are crucial for this independence, for they let the ecphrases soar above the level of mere realism and engage us mentally and emotionally as recipients of a gripping story. This is to say that Homer expresses verbally what he has already imagined visually and what he expects his readers or listeners to translate back into sequential images. With his ecphrases Homer has made a complex, even an epic, kind of film, mirroring the epic of the *Iliad* as a whole. It is fitting that the very impulse for the recent film *Singe den Zorn* should have come to one of its directors when he realized that the description of Achilles' shield is inherently dramatic.[35]

So the very first work of Western literature already demonstrates an understanding of cinematic storytelling *avant la lettre* and *avant la technologie*. Bazin's statement about film as an idealistic phenomenon turns out to be correct, for it is fully applicable to ancient epic. Greek and

34   Woodford, *Images of Myths in Classical Antiquity*, 39 (at beginning of a chapter section entitled "A Synoptic View") and 165 (opening sentence of a chapter entitled "Showing What Cannot Be Seen").

35   See Antje Borchardt, "Singe den Zorn: Homers Ilias in Troia," *Pegasus-Onlinezeitschrift*, 4, no. 3 (2004), 65; at http://www.pegasus-onlinezeitschrift.de/agora_3_2004_borchardt.html.

Roman poets after Homer continued the tradition of complex ecphrases by means of what we may legitimately call "motion pictures" in the literal sense of the phrase and also in its cinematic sense. The ecphrasis of the shield that Vulcan, the same god as Hephaestus, forges for Aeneas in Book 8 of Virgil's *Aeneid* is the most famous instance.

3. Iliadic Themes in the Cinema

We should therefore modify our initial conclusion that the *Iliad* cannot be filmed. A film that does justice to Homer's complex epic is difficult but not impossible to make after all. It requires a committed producer or studio with very deep pockets, a first-rate writer and director, a sensitive cast, and a creative technical crew. All involved should have a measure of knowledge of the *Iliad* and the plot, characters, time, and society it portrays. Ideally, in return they deserve sophisticated audiences, at home in classical literature and in the history and aesthetics of narrative cinema. This is, of course, a task on a gigantic scale. But we can imagine what a film of the *Iliad* could be like if we keep Homeric epic and its cinematic qualities firmly in mind when we ask how a true film of Homer might look. Rossi's *Odissea* and *Eneide* already exist to provide us with useful models.

In addition, the history of epic cinema can reinforce our mental construction of a film of the *Iliad*. Even films that are not set in antiquity provide us with clues. The cinema has produced numerous historical epics or other films that present archetypal themes and timeless issues comparable to those raised in the *Iliad*. Many of such films belong to well-established action genres (e.g., the war film) and may be related to the underlying themes and the poetic qualities of the *Iliad* even if Homer was not in their makers' minds. The best of them show at least a measure of Homer's humanity and depth, portraying human nature in all its greatness and debasement. Their number is too large, the level of their artistry too varied, and their range across genres too wide for me to list them here.[36] But two great films exemplify best what epic cinema can

---

36　I direct interested readers to some of my previous work, which contains further references: "Homeric *kleos* and the Western Film," *Syllecta Classica,* 7 (1996), 43–54; "*Dulce et decorum est pro patria mori?* Classical Literature in the War Film," *International Journal of the Classical Tradition,* 7 (2000), 177–214; and "Homer's *Iliad* and John Ford's *The Searchers,*" in *The Searchers: Essays and Reflections on John Ford's Classic Western,* ed. Arthur M. Eckstein and Peter Lehman (Detroit: Wayne State University Press, 2004), 145–170.

tell us about a film of the *Iliad*. Both describe war, heroism, suffering, and the toll these take in ways comparable to the *Iliad*, although they are radically different from each other in content and style. Since their stories are long and complex, they consist of several installments produced over a number of years. They are the Japanese *Ningen no joken* (*The Human Condition*, 1959–1961), written and directed by Masaki Kobayashi, and the Russian *Voyna i Mir* (*War and Peace*, 1965–1968), an adaptation of Lev Tolstoy's novel by writer-director Sergei Bondarchuk. The first of these films is in six parts that together last for more than nine and a half hours. The second is in four parts and lasts for over seven hours. Kobayashi's work, filmed in black and white, is one of the most harrowing depictions of World War II. It shows the bleakness and doom of all wars, as did the *Iliad*. The film's title is exactly appropriate for its content. By contrast, Bondarchuk's film is in color, ranging from the brightness of aristocratic elegance – as in the sequence of Natasha's dance, as ravishing a set piece in the film as it was in the novel – to the dark inferno of Moscow burning. Bondarchuk uses his color palette for thematic purposes. Both he and Kobayashi filmed in widescreen formats to show the epic scale of their subjects. Their films are intense labors of love on an immense scale, deeply moral in their portrayal of the past and of its importance for the present and the future. Their titles, taken together, aptly express the fundamental sides of human life and society, reminding us of the two cities on Achilles' shield. (War and peace *are*, we might say, the human condition.) Kobayashi's and Bondarchuk's films show us the stylistic and thematic reaches that epic cinema is capable of achieving; taken together, they could serve as models from which to shape a film of the *Iliad*.

A related aspect is an awareness of Homer on the part of epic filmmakers who are telling a modern story. Explicit recourse to the *Iliad* reveals the thematic affinity of epic cinema with Homer. An example is a film whose subject is the most notorious aspect of World War II. *Holocaust* (1978), a seven-hour American television film directed by Marvin J. Chomsky, cites one of the most famous scenes of the *Iliad*. The film tells the story of a fictional Jewish-German family. Their destruction exemplifies the fate of German and European Jews. *Holocaust* was a popular success in the United States; when shown on West German public television, it generated a nationwide renewal of the debate over German war crimes, anti-Semitism, and the Final Solution. In the film, a meek and baby-faced young German bourgeois will become the main architect of the Holocaust. He is originally an apolitical and non-violent law-school graduate, a husband and the father of two little children. He is also unemployed and unable to provide for his family. On the urging of his stronger-willed wife, he enters the SS and swiftly rises to positions of power. On the day he is wearing his black uniform for the first time, his wife and children are watching him put on its cap in front of a mirror. The mother has been holding her son in her arms. When she puts him down, the boy runs off in fear and hides behind a door. The dialogue now refers to the *Iliad*, but the entire scene puts a sinister twist on its Homeric model:

> *Husband*: Peter, how do you like your father? . . . Uniform's too much for him.
> *Wife*: Erik, you look heroic. [*The boy is peering out from behind the door.*] . . . Peter, it's only Daddy's uniform.
> *Husband* [*diffidently*]: I'm afraid my first day as a policeman is a dead loss. Like a scene from the *Iliad* – Hector goes to put on his shining helmet with the plume, and his little son moves away in terror, screaming, frightened at the aspect of his own father. Can't recall the rest; something about Hector asking Zeus to make the boy braver than he was.
> *Wife*: I'll make you both brave.

In the *Iliad*, Hector's farewell from his wife Andromache and from his terrified child shows the anguish of all warriors going off to battle, their uncertainty of survival and return, and their hope for a good outcome – often against all hope, as will be the case for Hector.[37] The farewell scene in the *Iliad* is one of the most humane moments in literature. Every sensitive reader or listener feels for Hector and Andromache. Our knowledge that despite Hector's heroism Troy is doomed to utter destruction in a kind of ancient holocaust even increases our involvement. The brief scene in *Holocaust* turns the humanity in Homer's scene into its opposite. Erik (better: Erich) is not going out to defend his country, which will soon willfully and without provocation precipitate a worldwide war, and neither he nor his wife and children will be remembered the way Hector, Andromache, and their child will be. The man whom we see leaving his family is anything but heroic; rather, he is about to turn himself into a soulless bureaucrat who rationally and without any pangs of conscience administers mass murder on an unprecedented scale. Erik organizes the country-wide violence against

---

37 *Iliad* 6.390–502. The specific lines to which *Holocaust* refers are 399–400 (Hector's son in the arms of his nurse), 466–470 (the boy's terror at seeing Hector in his helmet with its moving horse-hair crest), and 476–481 (Hector's prayer on behalf of his son).

Jews which signals the onset of the Holocaust and leads to the death camps. His descent into barbarism begins during the infamous *Kristallnacht*, the "night of smashed glass," of November 9–10, 1938, and ends after the war when he kills himself with a poison capsule to avoid trial for crimes against humanity. There is only one brief moment in the entire film in which Erik exhibits something resembling an awareness of his crimes and his guilt. The fact that he has studied law and should know something about justice and morality is a revealing irony, echoing the situation in Sophocles' *Antigone* that political or ideological "right" may temporarily supersede genuine right and law. The scene in *Holocaust* described above is a chilling comment on the dehumanizing side of modern war, which is the more devastating because of its virtually unlimited killing potential. Most of the film's viewers will probably not have recognized the Homeric scene to which Erik refers, but some may have recognized Homer's name and deduced that Erik is well educated. Presumably, he read parts of the *Iliad* as a student in high school. This inference is important because it tells viewers that not even a classical education can prevent a man's descent into the abyss. The scene is the more effective through its understated quality. The ominous comment by Erik's wife which closes it reveals to us that she is as different from a loving wife like Andromache as can be imagined.

4. Vestiges of Ancient Epic

The tradition of extensively reworking Homeric epic and related stories for large-scale visual adaptations began on the Athenian stage in the fifth century B.C.[38] This tradition has never ended. Since the early twentieth century it has expanded to include the furthest-reaching medium for artistic and not-so-artistic expression that modern technology has made possible. Today, films are the most influential way in which we tell stories, our most powerful means to preserve the memory of ancient legends and myths. Sometimes films themselves hint at the truth of this observation.

Giorgio Ferroni's *La guerra di Troia* (1962) is a loose adaptation of parts of the *Iliad* and the *Aeneid*.[39] During the night of Troy's fall, the

---

38   Horst-Dieter Blume, "Homer auf der tragischen Bühne," in *Homer, Hellas und Europa*, ed. Pantaleon Giakoumis (Aachen: Verlag Mainz, 2004), 57–69, provides a recent introduction and references to ancient drama based on Homer.
39   The film's English titles are *The Wooden Horse of Troy*, *The Trojan Horse*, and *The Trojan War*.

Trojan princess Cassandra tells Aeneas, the film's hero, that despite its destruction the city will survive forever in the imagination of future generations. I quote her words from the English-language version:

> Troy is living her last night. For millenniums to come, men will search in her ashes to find the vestiges of her noble walls . . . The horrors we have seen in these years [of war] will always live in legend.

Cassandra is correct in her prophecy, and the film in which she makes it is itself an example of the legend she has in mind. But there is another level. *La leggenda di Enea*, directed by Giorgio Rivalta, was released the same year as a sequel to Ferroni's film.[40] Rivalta includes a number of shots from the earlier film when his Aeneas remembers the fall of Troy. Here a cinematic retelling of the Trojan War, that of *La guerra di Troia*, becomes elevated to a quasi-mythical level when it is reprised in *La leggenda di Enea*. Not only do ancient myths and epics survive in a new popular medium, but this medium is also highly suited to mythmaking itself. Ferroni's and Rivalta's films are leaves on one and the same branch of the tree of Homeric storytelling.

It is not difficult to imagine what Richard Bentley or any of today's traditionalists might think of all this. So we are better advised to remember the words of another British classicist. Not too long ago, J. B. Hainsworth, co-author of major scholarly commentaries on the *Iliad* and the *Odyssey*, observed in a book entitled *The Idea of Epic*: "At the beginning of literature, when heroic poetry reached society as a whole . . . society *listened*; in the twentieth century society *views*." Hainsworth concluded: "the modern heroic medium is film, and not necessarily the productions that are held in highest critical regard."[41] A number of films on Homeric themes made throughout the twentieth century bear out Hainsworth's view. Petersen's *Troy* shows that his words continue to apply in the twenty-first century.

---

40   The film's English titles are *The Avenger*, *The Last Glory of Troy*, and *War of the Trojans*. Aeneas is played by the same actor as in Ferroni's film.

41   J. B. Hainsworth, *The Idea of Epic* (Berkeley: University of California Press, 1991), 148. Hainsworth wrote the commentary on Books 5–8 of the *Odyssey* in Alfred Heubeck, Stephanie West, and J. B. Hainsworth, *A Commentary on Homer's Odyssey*, vol. 1: *Introduction and Books I–VIII* (Oxford: Clarendon Press, 1988; rpt. 1990). He is the author of *The Iliad: A Commentary*, vol. 3: *Books 9–12* (Cambridge: Cambridge University Press, 1993), among other publications on Homer.

CHAPTER FOUR

The Story of Troy Through the Centuries

Georg Danek

When we meet Achilles for the first time in Wolfgang Petersen's *Troy*, a little boy asks him: "Are the stories about you true? They say your mother is an immortal goddess. They say you can't be killed." His words remind us of the story we know:[1] Achilles' mother Thetis is a goddess living beneath the sea, and Achilles is invulnerable except in his famous heel.[2] But in the film Achilles replies to the boy: "I wouldn't be bothering with the shield then, would I?" So we learn that Achilles is not invulnerable. Later on, when he meets his mother, she is not diving up from the depths of the sea but walking in the flat water of the shore and collecting shells. When she tells her son about his future (as she does in the *Iliad*), she ends with the words: "If you go to Troy . . . I shall never see you again." So we understand that she is not a goddess who can visit her son wherever he is (as in the *Iliad*) but resembles a mortal woman endowed with an unusually high amount of prophetic power.

To modern audiences, all this sounds like a playful rationalization of a Greek myth, especially when we compare the text of the *Iliad*, in which

1 On Achilles through the centuries see Katherine Callen King, *Achilles: Paradigms of the War Hero from Homer to the Middle Ages* (Berkeley: University of California Press, 1987).
2 Servius on Virgil's *Aeneid* 6.57: "Achilles, dipped by his mother in the water of the Styx, was invulnerable on his whole body, except the part by which she held him." Apollodorus, *Epitome* 5.3: "at the Scaean gate he was shot with an arrow in the ankle by Alexander [Paris] and Apollo." Translations are my own.

the intimate relationship between Achilles and his divine mother is crucial for our understanding of his more-than-mortal ambitions.[3] In the film, the gods are simply left out of the plot. So, what has our cinematic storyteller done with the ancient myth? To understand the relationship between this modern and the ancient versions, we should take into account several different levels: the allusion to the original version (Achilles' heel), the realistic correction of the original version (the hero as vulnerable mortal), and, maybe, a parody of this correction (the tone in which Achilles mentions his shield). Stories about invulnerable heroes fighting in full armor are illogical and verge on the ridiculous.

But there is even more, for in the penultimate sequence of the film we receive an explanation of the meaning of the old myth: Paris hits Achilles with an arrow in his ankle. Achilles does not die from this wound, and Paris continues to shoot arrows at him, striking him in the chest. Now the great hero finally sinks to his knees. Even then he pulls all the arrows out of his chest, and when the Greeks find him lying dead on the ground, they see only one arrow sticking in Achilles' heel. So, we could say, the film tries to explain rationally how the myth came into being: Achilles was not killed by the arrow in his heel, for how on earth can anyone be killed by such an arrow? Nevertheless, this was the arrow that doomed him.

Very modern? Well, not quite as modern as it may seem. As early as 1855 Thomas Bulfinch wrote in *The Age of Fable*, his handbook of Greek mythology:

> While in the temple of Apollo, . . . Paris discharged at him [Achilles] a poisoned arrow, which . . . wounded Achilles in the heel, the only vulnerable part about him. For Thetis his mother had dipped him when an infant in the river Styx, which made every part of him invulnerable except the heel by which she held him.

In a footnote Bulfinch comments:

> The story of the invulnerability of Achilles is not found in Homer, and is inconsistent with his account. For how could Achilles require the aid of celestial armour if he were invulnerable?[4]

---

3   Cf. Laura M. Slatkin, *The Power of Thetis: Allusion and Interpretation in the* Iliad (Berkeley: University of California Press, 1991).

4   Thomas Bulfinch, *The Age of Fable* (now accessible on numerous websites), ch. 28. David Benioff mentions Bulfinch as one of his sources for his script of *Troy*; see "David Benioff's Epic Adaptation, TROY: Interview by Daniel R. Epstein," at www.ScreenwritersUtopia.com.

Bulfinch, too, explains ("poisoned arrow") and corrects ("inconsistent") the myth. But he did not invent this approach to ancient myth that is found in most modern handbooks of Greek mythology. In what follows I will show how the Greeks themselves, from Homer until the end of antiquity, worked on the myth of Troy by using the same methods we have already noticed in the film: citation, allusion, explanation, correction, and parody. And as does *Troy*, they worked with and against their one great model: Homer's *Iliad*. An excursion through the history of the myth of Troy in antiquity will give us a better background for asking what *Troy* is doing with the *Iliad*.

If we search for the roots of the method of arguing for and against the traditional myth, we may start with the *Iliad* itself, our first written text. We can still use the motif of Achilles' heel as our example. In the *Iliad*, Achilles is *not* invulnerable. But during his heroic fight he has become as good as invulnerable, because he wears invulnerable armor made by the god Hephaestus.[5] When, for once, Achilles' survival is at stake, it is because he fights against the river god Scamander, who threatens to drown him (*Iliad* 21.1–384).

It may even be that we find in the *Iliad* a hidden polemic against the traditional version of Achilles' death as caused by Paris' arrow to the heel. In Book 11, the hero Diomedes is fighting against the Trojans. Diomedes has by now been established as the most important surrogate for Achilles, who is not fighting. Paris, hiding behind the pillar of a tomb in the plain, shoots an arrow at Diomedes and hits him in the right foot. Diomedes reacts coolly: he curses Paris as a coward, pulls the arrow out of his foot, and retreats on his chariot to the Greek camp to have his wound treated.[6]

These scenes are a clear statement by the poet of the *Iliad* about his approach to traditional myth. He prefers a rationalist manner, he does not believe in all of the old myth's supernatural features, and he prefers to tell his story on a human – and humane – level, cleansed from monsters and daemons. With this humanistic approach he sets himself apart from the oral pre-Homeric tradition.[7]

---

5   *Iliad* 20.259–272. Cf. the description of armor and shield at 18.477–613.

6   *Iliad* 11.369–400. For a full discussion see Wolfgang Kullmann, "Oral Poetry Theory and Neoanalysis in Homeric Research," *Greek, Roman and Byzantine Studies*, 25 (1984), 307–323, at 313–315.

7   Cf. Jasper Griffin, "The Epic Cycle and the Uniqueness of Homer," *Journal of Hellenic Studies*, 97 (1977), 39–53.

So, as early as with the *Iliad*, myth fights against myth, poet against poet, just as Hesiod will describe it a little later.[8] In epic, rationalizing explanations or corrections of competing versions of myth concern only small aspects, mostly the plausibility of minor details. On a larger scale, epic narrative usually sticks to the heroic view of the world, depicting its heroes as human beings who lived a long time ago. They were separated from our world and acted on a higher level and in close contact with the gods. Many of them were themselves sons or grandsons of gods, able to carry out heroic deeds that men of our own generations could never match.

Problems about mythological thinking arose only in the sixth century B.C. with the first philosophical critics of Homer's theology and world view. Two kinds of responses developed in defense of Homer. First there was an allegorical reinterpretation of myth that tried to discover philosophical meanings lying beneath the surface of the Homeric texts. This method was much used by philosophers. In its popularized Stoic form, it intruded back into mythological poems.[9] Second, and more to the present point here, were the earliest historians, who traced the past back over several generations. They were confronted with the fact that no written records existed but only oral stories, transmitted from generation to generation and often as family records.[10] Within this oral memory there was no difference between mythical and historical tales, for most noble families traced their origins back to the one or the other hero of mythology. So there was a continuum from the Age of Heroes to the Age of Men. For the first historians, the only possible way of referring to the generations of heroes consisted in reinventing and rewriting mythical stories in the style of men's history. With this, the rationalizing interpretation of myth was born.[11] The heroes became human beings

8 Hesiod, *Works and Days* 24–26. I have dealt at length with similar narrative techniques in the *Odyssey* in *Epos und Zitat: Studien zu den Quellen der Odyssee* (Vienna: Verlag der Österreichischen Akademie der Wissenschaften, 1998).

9 For a comprehensive survey see Ilaria Ramelli and Giulio Lucchetta, *Allegoria*, vol. 1: *L'età classica* (Milan: Vita e pensiero, 2004); for poetical reuse cf. Philip R. Hardie, *Virgil's Aeneid: Cosmos and Imperium* (Oxford: Clarendon Press, 1986).

10 Cf. Rosalind Thomas, *Oral Tradition and Written Record in Classical Athens* (Cambridge: Cambridge University Press, 1989).

11 Cf. Wilhelm Nestle, *Vom Mythos zum Logos: Die Selbstentfaltung des griechischen Denkens von Homer bis auf die Sophistik und Sokrates*, 2nd edn (Stuttgart: Kröner, 1941; rpt. 1975), 126–152. For recent approaches see *From Myth to Reason? Studies in the Development of Greek Thought*, ed. Richard Buxton (Oxford: Oxford University Press, 1999), especially the editor's "Introduction" at 1–21.

like everyone else and so had to follow the same rules of behavior. Most importantly, the gods had to be eliminated from these heroes' stories. The historians' chief criteria were credibility and plausibility, principles first expressed about 500 B.C. by Hecataeus, who opened his historical work with the following words:

> Hecataeus of Miletus speaks like this: I write this the way it seems to be true to me, because the accounts of the Greeks are manifold and laughable as they present themselves to me.[12]

Hecataeus belongs to the first generation of mythographers. He began a long tradition that would eventually lead to mythographical handbooks like that attributed to Apollodorus in the first or second century A.D. Apollodorus took a good deal of his material from Pherecydes of Athens (fifth century B.C.). The first genuine ancient historian, Herodotus, who wrote about 430 B.C., started his *Histories* by stating that you cannot get any reliable information about the "beginnings," which lie in the dark realm of conflicting mythological stories. Even so, Herodotus makes ample use of old stories, but controlled by his rationalist approach. After telling the story, told by Egyptian priests, of how Helen came to Egypt and stayed there during the whole Trojan War, Herodotus comments:

> This is what the priests of the Egyptians said. As for me, I agree with the account given about Helen, adding this: if Helen had been in Ilium, they would have given her back to the Greeks whether Alexander [Paris] agreed or not. For Priam was not really so foolhardy, nor his other relatives, that they wanted to endanger their own bodies, children, and city so that Alexander could sleep with Helen. If even in the early times [of the war] they had decided on that [keeping Helen], when many of the other Trojans, joining battle with the Greeks, were killed and for Priam himself it came out that two or three or even more of his sons died in battle – if we must make some use of the epic poets in our argument – when all that had come out like this, I suppose that, even if Priam himself was sleeping with Helen, he would have given her back to the Achaeans in order to be set free from the evils at hand . . . But in fact they could not give back Helen nor . . . did the Greeks trust them . . . And the preceding has been stated as it appears to me.[13]

---

12   Hecataeus, *Histories*, fragment 1.
13   Herodotus, *Histories* 2.120. Cf. Robert L. Fowler, "Herodotos and His Contemporaries," *Journal of Hellenic Studies*, 116 (1996), 62–87.

Herodotus argues against Homer – by taking his proofs from the text of the *Iliad*. The same is true for Thucydides, who polemicizes against historical accounts that are too near to what he calls *to muthôdes* ("myth-like manner"). Nevertheless, Thucydides takes his proofs for a rationalizing explanation of the mythical past from the *Iliad* by correcting and retelling it, as when he argues about the conditions of war in the heroic past:

> I think Agamemnon was able to raise the army because he was superior in strength and not because Helen's suitors were bound by the oaths to [her father] Tyndareus . . . [and] because he also had a navy far stronger than all the others. I think he assembled the army not so much because he was well liked but because he was feared. For it appears that he arrived with the largest contingent of ships and furnished that of the Arcadians as well; this at least is what Homer says, if his testimony may be sufficient for anybody.[14]

Like Herodotus, Thucydides explains and corrects the *Iliad* by allusively citing passages and constructing from them a new, coherent meaning that corroborates his view of the heroic past.[15] The picture remains the same through the following centuries. The Trojan War is used as a historical argument in the same way as the Persian Wars were used by Athenian politicians, mostly in burial speeches,[16] or by philosophers.[17] They purge the story of Troy from any divine involvement in human actions and assimilate the events to everyday war-time reports.

Euhemerus of Messene (about 300 B.C.) is the first to construct a theoretical background for this rationalizing method by writing a story of a (fictional) journey that carried him to an island in the Indian Ocean. There he detected an inscription from which he learned that the gods of Olympus had once been mighty kings among humans and had come to be worshipped as benefactors and gods after their deaths. Later authors use this perspective to retell all kinds of myth and include fantastic elements. In the first century B.C. Diodorus of Sicily starts his *World History* with a detailed account of Greek and other mythologies, refashioning the traditional stories in the historians' rationalizing style. It is a pity that his sixth book, which contained the Trojan myth, has been lost.

---

14 Thucydides, *The Peloponnesian War* 1.9.
15 For both historians' approach to the mythical past see Virginia Hunter, *Past and Process in Herodotus and Thucydides* (Princeton: Princeton University Press, 1980), 93–115.
16 Isocrates, *Panathenaicus* (12), 71; Demosthenes, *Epitaphius*, 10.
17 Plato, *Hippias Minor*, passim; *Symposium* 221c2–d1.

People still believed in the Trojan myth as historical fact down to the second century A.D., when Artemidorus of Daldis gives the following advice to professional interpreters of dreams:

> Remember that you should take into account only those stories [or: histories] which are thoroughly trusted to be true from many important proofs, as for example the Persian War and, in earlier times, the Trojan War, and things like that. Because it is from these wars that people show localities, battlefields, sites of army camps, foundations of cities, constructions of altars, and whatever else comes with these things.[18]

Artemidorus represents the mainstream of popular belief in the value of myth. But by his time there also existed a more sophisticated approach to myth. The second to third centuries A.D. are the heyday of the Second Sophistic, a time of prospering schools of rhetoric with a newly heightened interest in older themes. Interest in the myth of Troy abounds once again, but now a more distanced, critical, and ironic approach prevails. In a rhetorical exercise called *Trojan Speech*, subtitled "Ilion was not conquered," Dio Chrysostom (about 100 A.D.) argued with and against the *Iliad* that Paris had not abducted Helen but had legally married her and that the Greeks besieged Troy for ten years without success. Dio, like Herodotus, quotes (11.37–43) an Egyptian priest as telling him "the true story" that originated in an eye-witness account of Menelaus and was transmitted in Egyptian writings through the centuries.

In the third century A.D. the sophist Philostratus has the ghost of the hero Protesilaus talk about the course of the Trojan War in his dialogue *Heroicus*, sometimes agreeing with, sometimes correcting, Homer.[19] By that time, the eye-witness motif has become a literary game that indicates fictionality. The best proof of this development is the satirist Lucian of Samosata, who lived in the second century A.D. In paragraph 17 of his dialogue *The Dream, or The Cock*, Lucian has a cock claim to be the reincarnated Trojan hero Euphorbus. This eye-witness, of course, knows much more than Homer, who had lived many centuries later and at the time of the Trojan War had been "a camel in Bactria." But when the cock comes to his report, he confines himself to correcting Homeric minutiae, like this:

> I tell you only so much, that nothing was extraordinary then, and Ajax was not as tall, and Helen herself not as beautiful, as people think.

18   Artemidorus of Daldis, *The Interpretations of Dreams*, 4.47.
19   Cf. Peter Grossardt, "Ein Echo in allen Tonlagen: Der *Heroikos* von Flavius Philostrat als Bilanz der antiken Troia-Dichtung," *Studia Troica*, 14 (2004), 231–238.

Because I saw her with a rather white skin and a long neck, as if to think
that she was the daughter of a swan; on the other hand, she was rather
old, about the same age as Hecuba, because Theseus raped her for the
first time and kept her at Aphidnae in the time of Heracles, and Heracles
took Troy earlier, about the time of our fathers.

Lucian, too, laughs at the myth – Zeus begot Helen, as we know, disguised as a swan – but his parody of mythical thinking includes a parody
of the rationalizing method of correcting myths. So we may conclude
that, by the time of the Second Sophistic, an intertextual method of retelling the story of Troy has been established which uses, reuses, misuses,
changes, and corrects the traditional story, concentrating mostly on the
plot of the *Iliad*. At the same time and from the same literary background the first and only presentations of the whole story of the Trojan
War in narrative form that survive from antiquity were produced, except
for mythographic handbooks. They are in two historical narratives, the
Diary of the Trojan War by Dictys the Cretan and the *Report of the Trojan
War* by Dares the Phrygian.[20] Both versions survive only in Latin translations of the fourth to fifth centuries. A few pages of the Greek original
of Dictys have come to light on papyrus. We have no firm proof for the
existence of a Greek Dares, but the Latin text shows that the original
must have been directed at sophisticated readers who enjoyed the contrast between the dense web of refined allusions to minor details in the
Iliad and the rude, laconic, diary-like presentation of "pure facts."

Both authors claim to be eye-witnesses. Dictys tells us that he wrote
the annals of the war on the order of his king Idomeneus; he had the
book buried with him in a tin box until an earthquake during the rule of
Emperor Nero uncovered the tomb. Dares claims to be a Trojan who
fought from the beginning to the end of the war. (A minor character
by this name appears once in the *Iliad*.) His Latin translator only tells
us that he found the Greek account during his studies in Athens. The
same kind of fictional discovery of an eye-witness account occurs in *The
Wonders Beyond Thule*, a fantastic travel novel by Antonius Diogenes
written in the second century A.D. Petersen's *Troy* uses this motif in its
frame when a narrator, Odysseus, talks about his heroic experience and
personal involvement in voice-over.

20   English translations: *The Trojan War: The Chronicles of Dictys of Crete and Dares
the Phrygian*, tr. Richard M. Frazer, Jr. (Bloomington: Indiana University Press, 1966).
Stefan Merkle, "The Truth and Nothing But the Truth: Dictys and Dares," in *The Novel in
the Ancient World*, ed. Gareth Schmeling (Leiden: Brill, 1996), 563–580, provides a good
survey.

In the Middle Ages, Dictys and Dares were widely read (in Latin), imitated, and reworked, mainly because they give the impression that they are telling the real story about Troy, an impression corroborated by their dry prose style and matter-of-course narrative. Keeping to the rationalizing manner, they eliminate the gods from the war on earth. They change Homer's course of events, add new elements, and follow a strictly chronological order. On the one hand, Dictys and Dares turn Homer's epic into history oriented on the historians' sub-genre of the *commentaries*; on the other, they turn it into romance. In this way they "correct" the *Iliad*.

Dictys and Dares developed precise methods to deal with the *Iliad*, their subtext. I will concentrate on a sample of their narrative devices that show how these "fringe novels," as we may call them, construct an alternative account of the Trojan War. Some of these techniques appear in *Troy* as well.

1. Verbal Citations of the *Iliad*

The early historians argued against Homer by quoting him. They were followed by authors like Lucian, Dio Chrysostom, and Philostratus. Dictys and Dares, on the other hand, do not argue with the *Iliad* but tell the whole story of Troy anew. With them, every citation signals to the audience that the new version sticks closely to the subtext and that the new account as a whole is trustworthy. But, since they translate the content of the *Iliad* into prose, they do not use verbatim quotations, and close correspondences can be checked only from the content. There are differences as well: Dictys every now and then stays close to the text of the *Iliad* while Dares does his best always to turn events into the exact opposite of Homer.

Troy, on the other hand, operates with a dense web of verbal citations of the *Iliad* that are taken from Robert Fagles's translation, although with minor variations.[21] As a result, the film's dialogue is frequently elevated to a highly poetic level. In this way audiences can recognize citations as such even if they are not familiar with the *Iliad*. Connoisseurs may enjoy the differences from the *Iliad*. I give a few examples of this technique:

Agamemnon says about Achilles before the Trojan War has even started: "Of all the warlords loved by the gods, I hate him the most." In

---

21   Homer, *The Iliad*, tr. Robert Fagles (New York: Viking, 1990; several rpts).

the *Iliad* it sounds like this: "You – I hate you most of all the warlords / loved by the gods" (Fagles, 1.208–209 = *Iliad* 1.176).

A priest recalls his conversation with some farmers: "They saw an eagle flying with a serpent clutched in its talons." This derives from "That eagle flying high on the left across our front, / clutching this bloody serpent in both its talons." Both times, Hector replies by exclaiming: "Bird-signs" (Fagles 12.253–254 [= *Iliad* 12.219–220] and 280 [no exact equivalent in the Greek]). But the roles have changed: in the *Iliad*, the priest warns against an attack, and Hector wants to fight; in the film, it is the other way round.

Priam on the walls of Troy: "Helen! . . . Sit with me!" This recalls "Sit in front of me" (Fagles 3.196 = *Iliad* 3.162). Contrary to the *Iliad*, in which Helen tells Priam about individual Greek heroes down on the plain, Priam and Helen do not talk about the Greek army in *Troy*.

Achilles before his duel with Hector: "There are no pacts between lions and men." This keeps close to "There are no binding oaths between men and lions" (Fagles 22.310 = *Iliad* 22.262).

When Priam arrives in Achilles' tent, he kisses Achilles' hands. His first words are: "I have endured what no one on earth has endured before. I kissed the hands of the man who killed my son." This is a variation of "I have endured what no one on earth has ever done before – / I put to my lips the hands of the man who killed my son" (Fagles 24.590–591 = *Iliad* 24.506–507). Priam answers Achilles' question "Who are you?" with a quotation from the *Iliad*.

The same high poetic diction sounds through in places where the script does not stick to the wording of the *Iliad*, as with Thetis' prophecy about Achilles' future: "If you go to Troy, glory will be yours . . . But if you go to Troy, you'll never come home. For your glory walks hand in hand with your doom." In this we find only some catchwords from the *Iliad*: Thetis says: "All I bore was doom" (Fagles 1.493 = *Iliad* 1.414), and Achilles says: "If I hold out here and I lay siege to Troy, / my journey home is gone, but my glory never dies" (Fagles 9.500–501 = *Iliad* 9.412–413). Here the film sounds even more poetic than Fagles's translation. The heightened language functions as a signal for the audience that the original is being referred to.

2. Hidden Allusions

These are attested since the very beginnings of Greek literature. Authors allude to the *Iliad* in such a way that readers without an intimate knowledge of Homer cannot catch the whole meaning of a text. These intertextual signals give the works of Dictys and Dares an extra meaning while the narrative itself remains understandable even without knowledge of Homer. In *Troy*, there are two problematic cases.

Advancing toward the Trojan leaders for negotiations before the first full battle, Agamemnon raises his sword while turning back to the Greek army. Not all spectators know what this gesture means. Only when we turn to Book 3 of the *Iliad* do we catch its full significance. When Hector starts to arrange a duel between Paris and Menelaus, he steps forward and keeps the Trojans back from advancing by holding his spear in the middle. The Trojans understand his sign and sit down on the ground; the Greeks do not understand and shoot at him with arrows and stones. Agamemnon intervenes and explains Hector's purpose to the Greek army (*Iliad* 3.76–85). The scene in the film is an abbreviated and condensed variation on this, incomprehensible to anyone who does not remember the *Iliad* in detail. Is this negligence on the filmmakers' part?

Aeneas appears in one of the last scenes of *Troy* only to disappear immediately. He is introduced to the external audience, the viewers, by a silly question from Paris ("What's your name?") that is pointless in regard to the internal audience, the Trojans in this scene, and to the action. But there is no necessity to reveal Aeneas' name concerning the function he has to fulfill – to save and keep the Sword of Troy – to all those spectators who know that he will found a New Troy that is to become Rome. Those viewers who already knew Aeneas are likely to find the allusion to Virgil's *Aeneid* flat; whoever did not know Aeneas is unlikely to remember him afterwards.

3. Variations of a Scene: The Duel between Paris and Menelaus

Variation, combination, and reversal are the underlying principles of most of the plot changes in Dictys and Dares and in *Troy* as well. A list of people in Dictys, Dares, and *Troy* who kill, die, or survive contrary to the *Iliad* or to traditional myth, or who appear in the "wrong" place, would be long indeed. Some of the most surprising effects in the film are due to such violent changes from tradition, as when Menelaus is killed by Hector and Agamemnon by Briseis. I here describe in detail three variations of a single Homeric scene, the duel between Paris and Menelaus.

In the *Iliad* there is a formal duel, spun out in a long series of individual scenes and delayed by several interruptions. Menelaus hits Paris first with his spear, then with his sword, then drags him behind himself by the helmet. Aphrodite causes Paris' helmet to come off. Menelaus is left holding the helmet, while Aphrodite carries Paris into his bedroom in Troy and unites him with Helen. Menelaus is still searching for Paris on the battlefield when Athena entices the Trojan warrior Pandarus to shoot an arrow at him. Pandarus shoots and wounds Menelaus (*Iliad* 3.15–4.219).

Dictys (2.39–40) has Paris challenge Menelaus to a duel. They fight, Menelaus stabs Paris with his spear in the thigh, and Paris falls to the ground. Menelaus pulls his sword and rushes at Paris to kill him. At this moment Pandarus' arrow hits him, and, while the Greeks are shocked, the Trojans save Paris behind the lines. This change of action is caused primarily by the elimination of the gods, which reduces the action to the human level, and by a process of rationalization, for how could Paris escape if he was not saved by a god? Dictys' condensation of the sequence of events leads to a logically more consistent plot.

As for Dares, I give the full text of paragraph 21 to show his extremely terse style:

> Menelaus starts chasing Alexander. Alexander looks back at him and hits Menelaus' thigh with an arrow. This man is struck by the pain, but together with Ajax the Locrian proceeds to chase him. When Hector realizes that they do not stop chasing his brother, he comes to his aid together with Aeneas. Aeneas protects him with his shield and leads him out of the battle to the city.

Dares here aims at a reversal of Dictys, because in the *Iliad* nobody is hit in the thigh. The course of action becomes progressively more banal, the formal duel of heroes is reduced to a trivial battlefield incident, and Paris is saved in quite a normal way by his comrades.

Troy preserves the formal duel of the *Iliad*. Menelaus gives Paris a thrashing and hits him with his sword in the thigh. Paris falls to the ground, and Menelaus throws his sword to kill him. Paris crawls back to Hector, whose knees he clasps. Menelaus comes after Paris, has a short discussion with Hector, who is protecting Paris, and raises himself up to kill Paris with his sword. Hector stabs him in the belly. The result is a total surprise as it goes against all traditional versions. Menelaus' death makes the war senseless since now the Greeks will no longer fight for the return of Helen. But the audience is satisfied because Menelaus has been a "bad guy" who did not deserve to get Helen back. So we are left with greedy Agamemnon, for whom Helen was only a pretext for war on Troy.

4. Achilles as Lover and Hero

One of the most fascinating developments of the Achilles myth through the centuries is that of the love motif. There is none yet in the *Iliad*: Achilles' wrath caused by the abduction of Briseis does not mean that he is in love with her, and his pain caused by the loss of Patroclus concerns friendship, not a sexual relationship. It is only in the post-Homeric tradition that we can observe an additional love element, one that involves Achilles with Priam's daughter Polyxena. We do not know who was the first to tell the story of Achilles' desperate love for Polyxena, but traces of this motif occur in the earliest post-Homeric epics, which may go back to the pre-Homeric oral tradition, and in a large number of vase paintings from the seventh century on. Achilles tries to ambush and capture Polyxena together with her brother Troilus near the temple of Apollo outside the city.[22] In all our sources Polyxena is killed or buried next to Achilles' tomb.[23] Not surprisingly, Dictys and Dares took over this story and turned it into an elaborate bourgeois tragedy of love.

Dares (27–34) leaves out Briseis, and Patroclus' death has no consequences for Achilles' behavior. Achilles falls in love with Polyxena when she visits Hector's tomb together with her family. He starts wedding negotiations, keeps away from the battlefield, and is trapped into an ambush and killed by Paris in the temple of Apollo. Dictys keeps Briseis separate by moving her forward to the beginning of the war. Polyxena's story occupies a large portion of the whole plot and is worked into a complicated web of actions involving Achilles, Patroclus, Priam, Hecuba, Hector, and Troilus. Dictys, too, has Achilles fall in love while meeting Polyxena in the temple of Apollo and start wedding negotiations. She offers herself as a slave to him when she comes with Priam to obtain Hector's body, but Achilles, despite his burning desire for her, sets her free. His marriage negotiations almost lead to his betraying the Greeks, but then he is caught in an ambush laid by Paris in Apollo's sacred district.

In *Troy*, this love motif is transferred to the person of Briseis, who is taken over from the *Iliad*. But this Briseis incorporates five other women

---

22   There exists no comprehensive work on the archaic myth of Polyxena. For the pictorial documents see the articles in the *Lexicon Iconographicum Mythologiae Classicae*, s.vv. "Achilles" (vol. 1.1 [1981], 37–200, here 72–95) and "Polyxene" (vol. 7.1 [1994], 431–435).

23   For various aspects of the Polyxena tradition see King, *Achilles*, 184–201.

of the *Iliad* and the myth. Briseis' first appearance reminds us of Cassandra: both are virgin priestesses of Apollo and close relatives of Priam's. When, at the end, Agamemnon tries to drag Briseis away from the statue of Apollo, we are reminded of Ajax the Locrian, who dragged Cassandra out of Athena's temple. Agamemnon threatens to sleep with Briseis as he does with Chryseis in the *Iliad*.[24] When Briseis stops Achilles from killing Agamemnon, she behaves like the goddess Athena in the *Iliad* (*Iliad* 1.188–218). When she kills Agamemnon, she takes over Clytemnestra's part. And, most importantly, Briseis is more and more assimilated to Polyxena. This development starts when Achilles saves Briseis from the Greek army mob. Achilles falls in love with her and sets her free when Priam comes to get Hector's body back. Achilles is shot by Paris in the area of Apollo's temple in Priam's palace while trying to save her from being killed during the conquest of Troy.

All of this fuses several traits of the traditional myth that make Briseis a much more complex character than any single model of her had ever been. Achilles has become the kind of love hero he was in the post-Homeric tradition. But contrary to the tradition represented by Dictys and Dares, he also remains a war hero, fighting for Briseis until the end. And he remains the Achilles of the *Iliad* when he reflects on the value of heroic fighting, decides not to fight for Agamemnon, reflects on going home, but then does fight for Briseis even at the cost of his life.

5. The Duration of the War

In the *Iliad* the Trojan War lasts ten years, but the story occupies only fifty-one days of action, with no more than seven or eight days of fully narrated action and four days of battle. Even so the *Iliad* represents the whole war. Its first third refers us to the beginning of the war, its last third to the end, and its middle third to the long time of fighting. When we ask what happened in the first nine years of war, we learn that it was almost not worthwhile: the Trojans avoided fighting Achilles in open battle, and there were not too many victims. Only the fighting told in the *Iliad* led to the decisive events of the war. The plan of Zeus mentioned at the beginning of the *Iliad* consists not only of his decision to

---

24   Agamemnon's words ("Tonight I'll have her give me a bath. And then – who knows?") allude to *Iliad* 1.29–31: "slaving back and forth / at the loom, forced to share my bed!" (Fagles 1.34–35).

favor Achilles by helping the Trojans in battle but also in his strategy of bringing the war to its long-desired end in just this way.[25]

Dictys and Dares explain the long duration of the war in a rationalizing manner. Dictys long delays the beginning of the war because its preparations and its unsuccessful first campaigns take eight and a half years. The war itself lasts for only a year and a half. In Dares (19–20 and 22), the war is full of long truces and negotiations. The two armies fight for two days, during which Hector kills Patroclus, and then arrange a truce. During the funeral games for Patroclus the Greeks start quarreling about leadership, and the fighting starts up again only after an interval of two years. Soon afterwards, a new truce lasts three years.

Troy condenses the war to a sort of Blitzkrieg. There are only three days of regular fighting, then a truce of twelve days for Hector's funeral, and then we witness Odysseus' ruse of the Wooden Horse. The film blends the method of the *Iliad* of condensing the narrated action to just a few days and focusing on the stories of Achilles and Hector while still representing the "war that will never be forgotten" with the rationalizing explanation that the ten years of war did not mean ten years of continuous battle action.

I close with two observations. Pausanias briefly states his opinion about the true meaning of the Wooden Horse:

> Every one who does not suppose that the Phrygians [Trojans] were the veriest ninnies, is aware that what Epeus [the horse's builder] made was an engine for breaking down the wall.[26]

Dictys and Dares avoid the danger of having the climax of their tale turn on an improbability. In their versions, the Greeks do not take Troy with the Wooden Horse but by treason. The film gives us a lot of rationalizing explanations of mythical thought but still serves up the Wooden Horse, without any meaningful explanation for the Trojans' stupid behavior except for a vague hint at superstition. So we must conclude that these Trojans *are* "the veriest ninnies."

Secondly, in the course of their conversations in Achilles' tent, Briseis says to him: "I thought you were a dumb brute . . . I could have

---

25   On this see my "Achilles and the *Iliad*," in *Eranos: Proceedings of the Ninth International Symposium on the Odyssey*, ed. Machi Païsi-Apostolopoulou (Ithaca: Centre for Odyssean Studies, 2001), 165–179.

26   Pausanias 1.23.8, quoted from J. G. Frazer, *Pausanias's Description of Greece*, 2nd. edn (London: Macmillan, 1913), vol. 1: *Translation*, 34.

forgiven a dumb brute."[27] But why do we get the feeling that Achilles *is* a dumb brute despite all attempts to cleanse his character? In the *Iliad*, we need the gods to understand Achilles. As soon as the filmmakers drop the divine apparatus to explain otherwise inexplicable human behavior, their audiences can no longer fully grasp what forces drive Achilles to behave like a madman – unless he really is nothing but a dumb brute. So there is a choice. Either find a new motivation for Achilles' behavior, the way Dictys and Dares painted him as being sick of the political corruption in the Greek army and sick in his love for Polyxena, or simply state that the Achilles of the *Iliad* is a dumb brute because you do not believe in Homer's gods. *Troy* tells us that Achilles is not a dumb brute only because he feels intense emotions even in the face of death. Most people today will not excuse his behavior on these grounds. So there remains, in the film, a gap between the rationalizing tradition and the epic and tragic mood that we find in the *Iliad*.

The original Greek "true stories" of Dictys and Dares were intended for well-informed readers who enjoyed the intellectual game of detecting similarities with and differences from the *Iliad*. The best terms to describe this literary genre are "parody" or "travesty." This holds true even if most readers of the Latin versions, from late antiquity until the eighteenth century, did not catch this hidden meaning and believed in the "historical truth" of these eye-witness accounts. In the Greek originals and in the Latin translations, part of the parody consisted in their trivializing style, which is in stark contrast to the sublime poetic language of the *Iliad*. Another, and more important, aspect of this parody is the authors' method of sticking closely to the sacred tradition on the whole but every now and then employing a surprising or paradoxical twist that turns the story upside down and gives it a wholly different color.

Screenwriter David Benioff was as ambitious about improving on the plot of the *Iliad* as his colleagues Dictys and Dares had been almost 2000 years ago. He succeeded in constructing a coherent plot with dramatic unity by condensing the myth to a few storylines and concentrating on the characters of Achilles and Hector and, to a lesser degree, Paris and Helen. Benioff's approach closely resembles the intertextual methods of Dictys and Dares, even if Benioff may have taken over some of their

---

27   German writer Christa Wolf also has him referred to as "Achilles the brute," but this is probably not what the filmmakers were thinking of. See Christa Wolf, *Cassandra*, tr. Jan van Heurck (New York: Farrar, Strauss and Giroux, 1984), 57. The German has "Achilles, das Vieh" (i.e., "Achilles, the beast").

scenes from modern mythological handbooks like Robert Graves's *The Greek Myths*.[28] Contrary to the times of the Second Sophistic, nowadays only few people know the *Iliad* well enough to enjoy most of Benioff's allusions. The allusive method may work best with people who have both the DVD of *Troy* and Fagles's translation of the *Iliad* at hand and so can trace the film back to its sources. But most people will confine themselves to doing what readers of Dictys and Dares have done through the centuries: enjoy the old story in its "true version" that tells us "what really happened" with a seasoning of "modern" rationalism.

28   Robert Graves, *The Greek Myths* (1955; rpt. New York: Penguin, 1993). Benioff mentions Graves as one of his sources ("David Benioff's Epic Adaptation, TROY").

CHAPTER FIVE

Viewing *Troy*: Authenticity, Criticism, Interpretation

Jon Solomon

When classicists view a film set in antiquity for the first time, their reaction to the film is never the same as that of the non-classically trained audience. The viewing process bypasses the usual modes of passive reception and sensual spectatorship that apply to the viewing of most contemporary Hollywood films and becomes by default an intellectual endeavor.[1] Because of the critical and pedagogical nature of their discipline, classicists approach the cinema with essentially the same mindset they apply to evaluating a colleague's article or even a student's term paper. Classicists are on the lookout for a variety of irregularities, scanning a broad spectrum of signals that do not belong to the vision of the classical world they have honed during decades of study, research, and teaching. Did the Greeks reside in huts or tents outside Troy? Could Achilles have been blond? Is that an accurate portrayal of a sexual encounter between Achilles and Briseis? And wasn't Agamemnon killed in his bath at home by his wife Clytemnestra and not in Troy by Briseis?

Academic concerns tend to dominate scholars' viewing experiences. For two or three hours we are responsible for knowing more about the

---

1 Contemporary theorists recognize that artistic illusion is not unique to film viewing. See Richard Allen, "Representation, Illusion, and the Cinema," *Cinema Journal*, 32 (1993), 21–48, and Murray Smith, "Film Spectatorship and the Institution of Fiction," *The Journal of Aesthetics and Art Criticism*, 53 (1995), 113–127.

ancient world than we could possibly know. Many of the questions we ask ourselves are easily answered from our areas of general knowledge or fields of specialization, but some lie on the outer fringes of, or even completely outside, our familiarity. What actually happened during the Greek landing at Troy? How long did the historical Trojan War last? Our expertise is potentially challenged at every new line of dialogue or camera angle: art historians and archaeologists search their philological memory banks, and philologists search their visual memories.

When the viewing is finished, the classicist may expect a barrage of questions from students, colleagues, family, and even the press and ultimately may be asked for a "thumbs up" or "thumbs down" judgment about the film's merit. With all its mistakes and oddities, can such a film be shown in class?

This is no way to watch a movie.

Viewing circumstances can be even less suitable. Films like *Troy*, Oliver Stone's *Alexander* (2004), or Ridley Scott's *Gladiator* (2000) have such high-profile releases that a number of classicists attended premieres or early showings, sitting bundled together in small groups. Some may be pondering what this or that colleague knows or is thinking that they themselves do not. Professional prestige and even competition come into play, and if a junior faculty member attends a showing with a senior, the former's career is a consideration. A similar mindset will also interfere with the teacher who views one of these films with students who will expect from the scholar to know everything about the film's historicity and authenticity.[2]

This is no way to watch a movie.

The phrase "watch a movie" is itself loaded with cultural bias. In a professional sense, one views a film as a narrative or submits to the group experience of spectatorship. Experiencing cinema is an academic and intellectual exercise. In the popular sense, one "watches a movie" for the purpose of emotional stimulation, be it laughter, fear, tears, or Aristotelian catharsis. The "thumbs up" or "thumbs down" decision inevitably follows the latter experience; the former does not require it. In 2005 practically no one watches Orson Welles's *Citizen Kane* (1941) or the expressionist silents of Weimar Germany in the popular sense; film scholars have long since determined them to be classics. Although students are entitled to make an aesthetic judgment about films produced two to four generations ago, such films have become monuments

---

2   On film, history, and students see Ron Briley, "Reel History: U.S. History, 1932–1972, as Viewed through the Lens of Hollywood," *The History Teacher*, 23 (1990), 215–236.

and cannot be as easily dismissed as audiences can dismiss, say, Charles Herman-Wurmfeld's *Legally Blonde II: Red, White & Blonde* (2003) as disappointing, inferior, derivative, or plain dumb. Milestone films boast the patina of time, have survived the initial period of judgment, and no longer need to be tested in the popular sense, although even some "classics" can fall out of favor with film scholars. A classic like *Citizen Kane* can even reverse such a process. While not very successful in a popular sense for long after its initial release, the special attention awarded it in graduate film departments in the past few decades resulted in a surge in its popularity in the 1990s to the extent that in 1998 the American Film Institute voted *Citizen Kane* the greatest movie of all time.[3]

Classicists will recognize in this contemporary cinematic reception process patterns well established in the reception of classical literature during the past 2,700 years. Was Homer more popular than Hesiod? We know that they had their own popular face-off. Although the historicity of the *Contest Between Hesiod and Homer*, a poem dating to the reign of the Emperor Hadrian, is very questionable, the kernel of that poetic debate dates back at least to the sophist Alcidamas in the late fifth century B.C. The process described in the later poem was an equally unscientific survey, in which Homer defeated Hesiod in the popularity contest. Still, the Euboean Paneides, sponsor of the contest, determined Hesiod the victor on the basis of what we might describe today as "values."[4] Of course, the context of popular culture was much more confined and much less commercial in the late eighth to early seventh century B.C., the period of the poem's setting, and in the late fifth century, but popular culture is by nature unscientific in its preferences. And we should also consider that, while the actual reasons for the preservation of the poem may be serendipitous, it did survive the collapse of Greco-Roman civilization whereas, for instance, the majority of the Epic Cycle on the Trojan War did not.

Popularity also often seems to be unwarranted or inexplicable to those with whom what is popular is, well, not popular. It was not the scholarly poetry of Callimachus that thrilled Roman nobles but Aratus' *Phenomena*. Ovid's popularity was hardly dimmed, if not actually advanced, by the imperial dislike Augustus seems to have had for him.

3 For the unscientific method of the AFI voting procedure see, for instance, the CNN news release at http://www.cnn.com/SHOWBIZ/Movies/9806/17/afi.top.100.final.
4 For a recent rhetorical and historical analysis of this poem see Neil O' Sullivan, *Alcidamas, Aristophanes, and the Beginnings of Greek Stylistic Theory* (Stuttgart: Steiner, 1992), 63–105, and cf. note 246. The setting's historicity is briefly discussed in *Hesiod: Theogony*, ed. M. L. West (Oxford: Clarendon Press, 1966), 43.

The consensus of scholarly opinion still finds the texts of Seneca's tragedies incapable of being performed, but Elizabethan dramatists mined them for both their lurid narratives and their richness of expression and rendered them into stage dramas that were popular for decades.[5] So let us imagine, which is all we can do, how Homer would have reacted to learning that the silly but delightful short mock-epic *Battle of the Frogs and Mice*, the *Batrachomyomachia*, was printed in 1486, two years before Demetrius Chalcondyles published the *editio princeps* of the *Iliad*.

Popularity is also fleeting, although it can sometimes take an extended period to fleet. While the quasi-historical ramblings in Justin's *Epitome* of Pompeius Trogus and Valerius Maximus were considered so intriguing in the early eighteenth century that the Habsburg court librettist Metastasio could boast of employing them as reliable historical sources for his *Ciro riconosciuto*, an opera about the ancient Persian King Cyrus, nearly three hundred years later these authors have been widely discredited and entirely lost their popularity and their influence on popular culture.

The tragedian Euripides provides a well-known paradigm for the vagaries of popularity. Euripides' reason for accepting, in 408 B.C., King Archelaus' invitation to Macedonia, where he died after two years, was later attributed to his dislike for Athens, either for political or professional reasons.[6] Perhaps one of the reasons for the latter speculation was the relative paucity of victories he had won at the annual tragic contest during the Festival of Dionysus in contrast to Aeschylus and Sophocles. Biting literary criticism and personal attacks in the comedies of Aristophanes furthered Euripides' reputation of lacking popularity in fifth-century Athens. At some point the legend developed that he found quiet refuge by hiding away in a cave on the nearby island of Salamis. Nonetheless, by the Hellenistic period his reputation had been reclaimed along with the popularity of his works, and nearly five centuries after his death Seneca admired him to the extent that he modeled four of his nine dramas after Euripidean originals. But then came about fifteen centuries in the Latin-speaking West when Euripides was utterly neglected. Not until the resurgence of Greek tragedy in the form of opera under the royal patronage of Frederick the Great, Catherine the Great, and the Habsburg Joseph II in the mid-eighteenth century did the dramas

---

5   In general cf. Robert S. Miola, *Shakespeare and Classical Tragedy: The Influence of Seneca* (Oxford: Clarendon Press, 1992).

6   Cf. Mary R. Lefkowitz, *The Lives of the Greek Poets* (Baltimore: Johns Hopkins University Press, 1981), 90–91.

of Euripides, albeit mostly his later, more romantic, plays, again achieve popularity on stage.

Essential for any comparison of the reception history of classical texts with contemporary reception of cinema is not the factual basis of ancient biographical detail about authors like Hesiod, Homer, or Euripides but the popularity of the fictional or legendary material associated with them. In Homer's case, only his popularity counts – unsurprisingly, given the absence of virtual any reliable information about himself and the immense influence of the *Iliad* and *Odyssey*. Dante and Chaucer, for instance, both treat Homer with reverence although neither had read a word of his poetry.[7]

Whether in ancient Chalcis or today on the Internet, all judgments on artists and their output, be they by royal preference, a panel of peers and critics, or a vote of the general public, are subjective, unscientific, and, in the minds of most of the unsuccessful participants, unfair, but that is just the point. Popularity is often inexplicable and offensive, even despicable, to any number of artists, intellectuals, and academics and so is dismissed as the result of a vulgar preference, as the unlearned opinions of the masses.[8] The historian Thucydides provided an early example of this when he articulated his observation that the Athenian tyrant Pisistratus was succeeded by "Hippias, and not Hipparchus, as is vulgarly believed."[9] That Thucydides then recounts at length – by his own admission and with an almost Herodotean self-satisfaction of having scooped the correct story – the homoerotic motivation of the two tyrannicides suggests that it was important to him to demonstrate the inaccuracy and innate unworthiness of popular opinion.

Both popular opinion and the popularity of an artistic product almost necessarily lack the historical accuracy and scholarly rigor that intellectual evaluation and critical standards require. We have only an imprecise understanding of the composition of the ancient Athenian audiences who attended the original performances of fifth-century tra-gedy, but it is reasonable to assume that these audiences were primarily composed of adult male citizens. This suggests a limited demographic of educated – relative to the rest of the population – and mature men, far different from the all-inclusive, multi-demographic audiences who watch contemporary cinema. But the spectrum still ranges from the highly

---

7   Dante, *Inferno* 4.88–90; Chaucer, *Troilus and Criseyde* 1.141–147.
8   Cf. William Warner, "The Resistance to Popular Culture," *American Literary History*, 2 (1990), 726–742.
9   Thucydides, *The Peloponnesian War* 6.54.1–4.

educated, sharply critical, and thoroughly experienced to the uneducated, gullible, and youthful: sophisticated cinephiles are different from uneducated or casual movie-goers.

Probing several points along the classical tradition in this way should help us broaden our perspective of spectatorship insofar as a film like Wolfgang Petersen's *Troy* is concerned. The primary purpose of producing a commercial artistic project costing almost $200,000,000 is not to please either academics (least of all classicists) or film critics who like to think that their reading of the *Iliad* in college qualifies them as Homeric scholars. The primary purpose is to create a successful product, that is, a work popular enough to earn back the investment and many millions in profit. To accomplish that, the product has to inspire considerable initial interest; epics do not qualify for the status of "sleepers" whose reputation slowly spreads via word of mouth. The pre-release advertising campaign of a blockbuster like *Troy* is itself a multi-million dollar project. The release itself involves another large investment when a film opens on as many as several thousand screens simultaneously. All who have large stakes in the outcome hope that television and newsprint critics will complement the enthusiasm generated among initial audiences viewing the film in theaters. In many instances there are also simultaneous and subsequent merchandising campaigns, all aimed at generating additional millions of dollars. Simultaneous sales usually include posters, books, toys, and other retail products; for the highest-profile releases there are tie-ins with fast-food franchises. After-market sales include DVDs, soundtrack CDs, and, in rare instances, theatrical re-releases.[10] Each of these is a multi-million dollar enterprise.

This summary is not intended to be an amateur business primer for anyone interested in developing a Hollywood property based on an ancient text or narrative. It is intended to highlight how unimportant the classicist is in any part of the business of popular filmmaking. As a result, while it is inevitable that classicists will analyze, criticize, and make professional judgments about a film like *Troy* in the process of viewing the film, especially for the first time, it is important for us to put such analyses, criticisms, and judgments in perspective. Everyone is entitled to their opinion, and *de gustibus non est disputandum*. But errors in authenticity, anachronisms, improprieties, and other faults, or the judgment that the filmmakers have failed to generate the same depiction of the

10   *Gladiator* was re-released in Argentina, Peru, Brazil, Germany, the Netherlands, and Taiwan in March, 2001. More than 500,000 copies of the DVD were sold in the United Kingdom in 2000, surpassing the sales of any other film.

Trojan War that scholars have developed after years of research and thought, do not mean that the film is neither good nor successful. At the very least, such a conclusion is an unfair criticism of a commercial product that has not been designed to meet scholarly standards; in the extreme, it also reveals ignorance of the progress that scholarship in popular culture has made in the past three or four decades.

If classicists could transform themselves briefly into journalists, policemen, lawyers, or soldiers while viewing such well-received films as *Citizen Kane*, Sidney Lumet's *Serpico* (1973), Billy Wilder's *Witness for the Prosecution* (1957), or Lewis Milestone's *All Quiet on the Western Front* (1930), they would soon realize that no professional could watch a popular film without identifying numerous errors, inconsistencies, improprieties, and downright impossibilities in the depiction of what falls under the purview of their professional knowledge and experience. On the other hand, a filmmaker who pays painstaking attention to technical detail, as Tyrone Guthrie did with his *Oedipus Rex* (1957), does not necessarily create a great or successful film. By far the most influential sequence of Stanley Kubrick's *Spartacus*, hailed as "the thinking man's epic," was its most unhistorical moment, the rousing shouts of "I'm Spartacus!"[11]

Even if the approval of the academic guardians of classical antiquity were required for a film about the Trojan War, there would still remain a very wide range of what constitutes historical accuracy or authenticity. Homer's *Iliad* describes both Bronze-Age and Late-Geometric artifacts and presents its story through a poetic vision, while the mound presently being excavated by teams from the universities of Tübingen and Cincinnati at Hisarlık has been claimed recently to represent Homer's Troy vividly or not at all.[12] If a film could have been made in the 1870s, it would have been regarded as authentic if it reflected Heinrich Schliemann's Troy, but by only a few decades later it would have become inauthentic. The cinema was not yet invented, but there was an "authentic" opera of 1770, *Paride ed Elena* (*Paris and Helen*). Its

---

11 Despite the fact that *Spartacus* was produced well over forty years ago, the "I'm Spartacus" scene still reverberates, most recently in a Pepsi Cola commercial first aired during the 2005 Academy Awards. Other examples are David Seltzer's *Punchline* (1988), Tom Hanks's *That Thing You Do* (1996), Frank Oz's *In and Out* (1997), Martin Campbell's *The Mask of Zorro* (1998), and perhaps Spike Lee's *Malcolm X* (1992). The scene was spoofed in Terry Jones's *Monty Python's Life of Brian* (1979).

12 See Joachim Latacz, *Troy and Homer: Towards a Solution of an Old Mystery*, tr. Kevin Windle and Rosh Ireland (Oxford: Oxford University Press, 2004), and Dieter Hertel, *Troia: Archäologie, Geschichte, Mythos* (Munich: Beck, 2001).

composer and librettist, Christoph Willibald Gluck and Ranieri de' Calzabigi, portrayed Paris as a historically accurate Phrygian and Helen as a historically accurate Spartan, even to the point of changing their artistic style to conform to what they considered historical truth. Gluck explained his decision to do so in this way:

> I was obliged to find some variety of color, seeking it in the different characters of the two nations of Phyrgia and Sparta, by contrasting the roughness and savagery of one with the delicacy and tenderness of the other. I believed that since singing in opera is nothing but a substitute for declamation, I must make Helen's music imitate the native ruggedness of that nation, and I thought that it would not be reprehensible if in order to capture this characteristic in the music, I descended now and then to create a coarse effect. I believed that I must vary my style in the pursuit of truth.[13]

If we go almost exactly one century further back, we come to John Dryden's rendition of *Troilus and Cressida* of 1679. In 1699 Dryden would publish his translation of Book 1 of the *Iliad*, but here he was retelling the tale told toward the end of antiquity by Dares and Dictys, both of whom claimed to be eyewitnesses to the Trojan War. Dictys claimed to be a companion of the Cretan Idomeneus, while Dares has the same name as the Phrygian priest of Hephaestus mentioned at *Iliad* 5.9–10. Throughout the medieval period in Europe, Dares and Dictys were considered to be more accurate in describing the Trojan War than Homer. Despite the reintroduction of Homer's text into Europe by Petrarch and Boccaccio in the middle of the fourteenth century, Dares and Dictys had already influenced Benoît de Sainte-More, who then invented the romance of Troilus and Bressida, soon to be renamed Cressida in the wake of Boccaccio's *Filostrato*.

The influence of the Troy tale as told by Dares and Dictys was pervasive and long. Their versions were rendered into a variety of vernacular languages and lasting from the end of antiquity to Shakespeare and Dryden (and trickling on beyond them), so long in fact that it cannot be attributed merely to the medieval mindset. Even before the medieval period, the Second Sophistic produced several powerful anti-Homeric exercises in rhetoric. The *Heroicus*, for instance, attributed to Flavius Philostratus, derives its superior accuracy in relating actual events of the Trojan War from the ghost of Protesilaus, who was the first Greek

---

13   Quoted from Patricia Howard, *Gluck: An Eighteenth-Century Portrait in Letters and Documents* (Oxford: Clarendon Press, 1995), 98.

killed during the landing at Troy. In view of Petersen's film, it is particularly telling that the *Heroicus* features Protesilaus as an important and authentic source, for the landing at Troy was an event not represented in the *Iliad*; it is a major and ambitious sequence in *Troy*. Similarly, Dio Chrysostom in his eleventh ("Trojan") oration (11.95–96 and 123–24) anticipates Petersen's narrative transgressions by having Hector kill not Menelaus or Ajax, as does Petersen's, but Achilles and claiming also that the Greeks never did conquer Troy.

Clearly, authenticity is an ephemeral aspect of knowledge, subject to change from one generation or chronological period to the next. For that reason alone authenticity is a poor criterion by which to judge either the validity or the quality of a film like *Troy*. And this does not even take into consideration the reports we have from people who have served as historical advisors to films set in antiquity, which inform us that film directors will follow an advisor's manual only insofar as it does not interfere with their artistic vision or their budgetary constraints.[14]

All this leaves classicists who view a film like *Troy* with several possibilities of judgment which are less dependent on their expertise but which demand a measure of familiarity with film, its history, and its place in modern culture. But, once divorced from their classical training and methodology, many flounder. At professional colloquia and conferences and in private conversations one hears the tell-all clichés of the modern movie-goer even from the mouths of the educated elite: "It was boring." – "It was too long." – "So-and-So can't act." – "It's not like the book." None of these criticisms is any more useful than to say: "It was not authentic." They reveal more about the spectator than about the spectacle. Boredom is a passive experience of inactivity that comes from disengagement. Finding a film boring usually suggests that the viewer has failed to find the film's approach, voice, intent, rationale, or style. But it is always our task as scholars to understand an artist's intent. An additional misstep is to assume that the director of such a large-scale film is not an artist worthy of serious consideration or, worse, that a director, even one who has a body of work of highly regarded and artistically innovative or challenging films, has now made one that is utterly devoid of any artistic merit. Complaints about the length of a film are often a by-product of boredom. Conversely, the extremely successful *Lord*

14   Cf. my discussion in *The Ancient World in the Cinema*, 2nd edn (New Haven and London: Yale University Press, 2001), 29–32, and Kathleen M. Coleman, "The Pedant Goes to Hollywood: The Role of the Academic Consultant," in *Gladiator: Film and History*, ed. Martin M. Winkler (Oxford: Blackwell, 2004), 45–52.

of the Rings trilogy not only lasted for nearly nine hours but was also expanded on its DVD releases by several additional hours. William Wyler's *Ben-Hur* (1959) ran for nearly four hours but won a record number of Academy Awards and earned back several times its production costs.

As for acting, spectators have unrealistic expectations if they want an actor to portray the Achilles or Hector they have envisioned for themselves when they read the *Iliad*. For some viewers of *Troy*, Brad Pitt and Eric Bana did just that; for others they did not. For the latter group of viewers, Pitt or Bana "can't act." But there is no rational basis for that judgment. The task of the actor attempting to portray a legendary literary character is different from that of the actor who portrays a contemporary or more recent historical person, as when Anthony Hopkins portrays the title character of Oliver Stone's *Nixon* (1995) or Will Smith plays Muhammad Ali in Michael Mann's *Ali* (2001). Both actors were nominated for Academy Awards in the "Best Actor in a Leading Role" category. At the very least, the spectator should attempt to understand the characterization the actor was attempting to create and should also assume that the actor's performance was satisfying to the director. Of course there are film productions so flawed by personality clashes or fundamental artistic misconceptions that the innate problems of the project spill over into its screenplay and performances, but high-profile releases are rarely so.

In most instances the sole narrative requirement of a major Hollywood release based on a work of literature is that the film tell a compelling story, not necessarily the original story and not a story fully appropriate to the text in every detail. A film is not even required to have the same theme as the original, nor should it be. Why not? Film is not only a different medium, it is also a different art form. It has different structural components and methods of organization, there are different economic and time-related production pressures, the end product is usually much sooner viewed than the original is read, and it is received by a very different type of audience and perceived in an emotional rather than an intellectual context. A producer, director, and screenwriter are artists who have worked in film, studied film, thought about film, and then read the original text and reacted to it as commercial artists responsible for an important project; they may also have seen previous film adaptations of their text.[15] They respond to all of this by developing

15   For example, visual motifs from the prelude to the chariot race of Fred Niblo's version of *Ben-Hur* (1925) served as models for the same sequence in Wyler's version. Wyler had been one of Niblo's assistant directors at the chariot race.

their own cinematic version of the text, making their own artistic decisions.

So a far more appropriate response to a film set in antiquity is to examine it with some of the same analytical tools with which one approaches a work of ancient literature. Textual analysis is unnecessary in most instances, at least until the DVD appears with additional footage; at that point there are indeed textual matters to consider. But Joseph L. Mankiewicz's *Cleopatra* (1963) that we view today offers only about half of the footage originally shot for what its director had hoped would be two four-hour epics. Various drafts of a script also require textual analysis, but they, too, are only rarely available.[16]

I conclude with an examination of a single sequence in *Troy*. My goal is to attempt to offer an example of how we may appreciate a sequence which classicists would by nature and training automatically dismiss as un-Homeric. Instead, I consider Petersen's unique adaptation of the first book of Homer's *Iliad* as a positive, even avant-garde contribution to the tradition of the Trojan War rather than as an ill-conceived, poorly acted, poorly written, overly long, inauthentic rendition of one of the integral passages of the *Iliad*. The first book of the *Iliad* is such an integral part of the story that filmmakers would be hard pressed to explain its omission.

Preceding *Troy* there were several films about the Trojan War. I here examine three of them: Robert Wise's *Helen of Troy* (1955), Marino Girolami's *L'ira di Achille* (*Fury of Achilles*, 1962), and John Kent Harrison's *Helen of Troy* (2003) for television. Wise's *Helen of Troy*, the first project of the twentieth century about the *Iliad* to be introduced into the popular culture after World War II, abbreviates Book 1 significantly.[17] The narrator establishes the length of the siege of Troy: "As time went on they looted and raped the surrounding villages." (Petersen chose not to use a narrative voice-over, a cumbersome technique in a visual medium that inserts an additional layer between the story and the audience.) Then the Greek generals carouse in a tent, Agamemnon and Achilles quarrel over a nameless concubine, Achilles delivers an ultimatum, Agamemnon laughs at him, and Achilles calls Agamemnon

16   I analyze the drafts of *Gladiator* in "*Gladiator* from Screenplay to Screen," in *Gladiator: Film and History*, 1–15.

17   Earlier films like Giovanni Pastrone's *La caduta di Troia* (1911), Georges Hatot's *Le jugement de Paris* (1922), Manfred Noa's *Helena* (1924) and *La regina de Sparta* (1931) were all non-Iliadic. John Erskine's novel *The Private Life of Helen of Troy* (1925), which Alexander Korda filmed two years later, takes place after the Trojan War has ended. Jean Giraudoux's drama *La Guerre de Troie n'aura pas lieu* (*The Trojan War Will Not Take Place*, 1935) converts Hector into a pacifist, as, to a certain extent, does Petersen's film.

and his followers "Dogs! Jackals!" and swears never to fight for Greece again. This all takes up one minute and eleven seconds. It is a scene charming in its conciseness, silly in its lack of Homeric profundity, but effective in conveying the most transparent reason for the quarrel between Achilles and Agamemnon and Achilles' refusal to fight any longer for the Greek cause.

In the Italy of the 1950s and 1960s, scores of films set in antiquity, often called "sword-and-sandal" films or *pepla*, were produced and distributed by small consortia. One of them brought together a trio of B-film figures: director Girolami, writer Gino De Santis, and American bodybuilder-actor Gordon Mitchell. *L'ira di Achille* begins just as the *Iliad* does – literally, by paraphrasing Homer's opening line ("Oh heavenly goddess, tell me of the many woes brought on the Greeks by the wrath of Achilles"), and then chronologically, by putting on screen the attack on Lyrnessus to capture, among others, Chryseis and Briseis. The film ends, as the *Iliad* almost does, with the conversation between Priam and Achilles and the ransom of Hector's corpse. Thirty-four minutes into the film, Briseis raises a dagger and jabs it into an unwary Achilles' shoulder. But the stab fizzles away, and Achilles explains that "the vagrant gods protect all of me, except one spot . . . I do not know where the fatal spot is." This adds some mystery to the part of the myth, although not Homer's, that Achilles is invulnerable except in one place. The music softens, Achilles and Briseis fall in love, and a few minutes later Chryses enters the Greek camp and demands the return of his daughter Chryseis. We are now forty-three minutes into the film. Chryses offers a wagon of treasure, a kind of redistribution of Agamemnon's ransom for Briseis in Book 9 of the *Iliad*, but Agamemnon responds by reminding Chryses that he, too, had lost a daughter when he had to sacrifice Iphigenia. He threatens Chryses and banishes him from the camp. Halfway through the film comes the quarrel of Achilles and Agamemnon from Book 1. Achilles protects Calchas, Calchas explains the problem (to the viewers as much as to the Greeks), Agamemnon returns Chryseis but demands recompense, ultimately Achilles' Briseis. Achilles goes for his sword, Athena (in double exposure) stops him, and Achilles withdraws from the war.

Here we have a reasonably authentic realization of the *Iliad* that consumes as much as one-fifth of the film, nearly 25 minutes of 118. But the dialogue is stiff and badly dubbed, and whereas fidelity to Homer is unsurpassed, the cinematic quality is low. This is a subjective opinion, but it will hardly be contradicted by any sober critic or scholar. Girolami provides a wonderfully instructive example of how a film that offers a

sincere attempt at rendering an ancient text into film can fail cinematically and so demonstrates better than many other films that authenticity
does not guarantee artistic or commercial success.

Harrison's *Helen of Troy* was part of the spate of films that followed the
success of Ridley Scott's *Gladiator*. Here the dominant and plot-driving
romantic triangle of Paris, Helen, and Menelaus is preceded by Theseus
abducting Helen and followed by Agamemnon raping her. It also precludes any romance between Achilles and Briseis, who does not appear
at all.

Petersen's *Troy*, on the other hand, uses the psychological tensions
of the first book of the *Iliad* to eliminate the importance of the gods from
his retelling of the story and to concentrate on the romantic relationship between Achilles and Briseis and the dislike between Achilles and
Agamemnon. Like the vast majority of the different versions of the
Trojan War myths, Petersen's broadens the scope of the tale well beyond
the *Iliad*. He shows the Greeks landing on the shore of Troy and Achilles
storming the temple of the sun god Apollo. Achilles' faithful Myrmidons
present him with Briseis, a priestess of the god and a member of the
royal Trojan household. In their initial encounter in Achilles' hut, Briseis
accuses him of impiety and warns him of Apollo's vengeance, but Achilles only scoffs. Immediately after, Achilles is summoned to Agamemnon's
tent, where the other Greek kings are paying homage to Agamemnon.
When Achilles enters, Agamemnon dismisses everyone else. The two
disagree about who deserves the glory of the initial victory, Agamemnon
claiming it for himself, Achilles pointing out that it was the soldiers
who won the battle for him. Achilles then generously offers him the
gold from the temple he sacked ("take what you wish"). Agamemnon
responds: "I already have" and summons two men to bring in Briseis.
Achilles draws his sword, but Briseis herself interferes ("Stop!") and pleads
for an end to violence. Achilles does indeed stand down, although he
points his sword at Agamemnon and threatens him, if without the
Homeric animal curses.

Petersen is not ignorant of the narrative of the *Iliad*. He knows as
well as anyone that in Homer it is Athena who appears to stay Achilles'
sword. But he chose to emphasize the role of Briseis in order to de-
emphasize the importance of the gods. Briseis not only takes command
over Achilles but also announces to the spectators of the film who are
familiar with the *Iliad* that she is replacing Athena. In this way Petersen
makes it clear that his version of the Trojan War is a battle between
humans and that the tensions and emotions among the leading characters are human. Twenty minutes later, the duel between Paris and

Menelaus breaks off when a defeated Paris crawls away from Menelaus and in desperation and exhaustion grasps the legs of his mightier brother, Hector. In Homer's version, in Book 3 of the *Iliad*, Aphrodite miraculously picks up the defeated Paris and deposits him with Helen in Troy while Menelaus is amazed to find his opponent missing. Again Petersen specifically removes the gods from his narrative and emphasizes the human element, in this instance the close relationship between Hector and his younger brother.

In addition, Petersen uses his version of Book 1 of the *Iliad* to establish the fondness that Achilles is beginning to feel for Briseis. At first, Achilles merely assured Briseis that she had nothing to fear from him, but now the arrogant and hated Agamemnon has taken her from him. This loss of face forces Achilles to defend her and value his possession more. It also establishes Briseis' hatred for Agamemnon, whom she will kill near the end of the film.

Petersen is innocent of the charge that he trivializes the *Iliad* by establishing romantic relationships. One of the film's closing credit screens claims that *Troy* was only "inspired by Homer's 'The Iliad'." More importantly, romance has been part of the Trojan tale for several thousand years. Among the Cyclic Epics, the *Cypria* incorporated the romantic relationship between Paris and Helen; the late ancient versions by Dares and Dictys include a romance between Achilles and Polyxena; the late medieval adaptations by Benoît de Sainte-More and Boccaccio feature the romances between Achilles and Bressida, then Cressida. Earlier films equally featured the romantic elements of the tale. Popularity has always demanded, and still demands, the romance that the *Iliad* lacks.

The significance and quality of Petersen's version of the Trojan War is open to discussion. My purpose with the preceding pages is not to limit debate but quite the opposite, to open up such a discussion by directing our attention away from the accusation of inauthenticity, an easy default mode of criticism, to a more appropriate and sophisticated kind of judgment.

CHAPTER SIX

Troy and the Role of the Historical Advisor

J. Lesley Fitton

Troy had no official historical advisor. No such person appears in the credits, and the process by which historical or archaeological research supported the design and the action of the film was diverse, depending largely on its director, writer, producers, and designers – in fact, on the whole team responsible for the film. Their sources were manifold, and the result is visually very rich. The various elements of the environment in which the action takes place, from the largest buildings to the smallest details of costumes and props, show influences from many different ancient cultures from a wide chronological and geographical span.

The reaction of professional archaeologists and historians seems to have been equally varied. Some seem to have enjoyed what one might describe as a game of "spot the source": identifying the original context of various visual elements. Others pointed with indignation to anomalies in the material culture shown in the film. Similarly, general audiences will have included people who, for example, had visited Knossos and who realized that the Troy of the film bore obvious resemblances to the capital of Minoan Crete.

The question becomes, then, whether the film should have had a historical advisor, what such a person would have been able to achieve, and whether the overall effect would have been an improvement. In fact, the creative art of filmmaking took precedence over the creative art of archaeological reconstruction. And rightly so. After all, the filmmakers' aim was not to create an academic or didactic document but a dramatically satisfying film for large audiences worldwide. The two things are quite different.

Nevertheless, the question of the film's historical accuracy was widely raised. It seems that audiences do care about accuracy or are at least interested to know where facts end and imaginative reconstruction begins. For many epic films, particularly those set in the Roman Empire, an answer to such a question can be offered.[1] Hence perhaps the expectation that the same could be done for *Troy*. But the story of *Troy* occupies the most difficult territory between fact and fiction. If we briefly review the situation, its complexity emerges.

1. A Complex Question

Although they had no historical record of the events described, the ancient Greeks believed in their historical validity. The story of the Trojan War came to them through the tradition of oral recitation. Such oral traditions can preserve memories of historical events but can also distort them, not least in the interests of a good story being told. So even in antiquity the art of storytelling took precedence over the craft of the historian. A shadowy but much-revered poet named Homer was preeminent among the many bards who used elements of this story that had been handed down from an indefinable time in the past. His epic poems, the *Odyssey* and the *Iliad*, represent the earliest Greek literature. They were probably written down in the second half of the eighth century B.C.

The works of Homer became a staple of Greek education and a cornerstone of Greek thought. Themes taken from the story of Troy proliferated not only in literature but also in the visual arts. Sculptors, vase painters, and other artists usually showed the events and protagonists in contemporary trappings.[2] They were doing exactly what the makers of *Troy* were doing in their attempts to portray various elements of the Troy story. On the whole, however, their approach was radically

---

1 Cf., e.g., the comments by P. M. Pasinetti, "*Julius Caesar*: The Role of the Technical Adviser," *Film Quarterly*, 8 (1953), 131–138, in connection with Joseph L. Mankiewicz's *Julius Caesar* (1953), and by Kathleen M. Coleman, "The Pedant Goes to Hollywood: The Role of the Academic Consultant," in *Gladiator: Film and History*, ed. Martin M. Winkler (Oxford: Blackwell, 2004), 45–52, in connection with Ridley Scott's *Gladiator* (2000).

2 On this see Susan Woodford, *Images of Myths in Classical Antiquity* (Cambridge: Cambridge University Press, 2002; rpt. 2003), ch. 12 ("Life and Myth in Art").

different. The Greeks did not aim for conscious archaism, still less for historical reconstruction, although they had their own artistic means to separate the heroic world of the poems from their contemporary reality. An example is the ancient convention of heroic nudity: heroes are shown naked in circumstances such as battlefields in which any real warriors would have been clothed. In general, artworks that depict clothes, armor, physical settings, and other accoutrements are usually based on contemporary classical reality and do not strive toward the re-creation of times past.

The classical Greeks did not have information about their past from archaeology as, by contrast, the modern world does. Excavations at Troy, Mycenae, and elsewhere have provided us with detailed information about the material world of the earliest periods of Aegean history. If the equation of the Late-Bronze-Age world with the world of Homer's heroes is accepted, then visualizations of the Trojan War can at least attempt accurate reconstructions, if within the limitations of archaeological evidence.[3]

These limitations themselves pose a great problem, for much remains unknown. Creators of archaeological reconstructions for didactic purposes have a choice. They need only attempt to reconstruct on the basis of actual evidence; where gaps remain, they can simply leave a blank. A filmmaker has no such latitude. Sets must be built, actors clothed, action must be continuous. A cogent whole must be created and presented to the audience. This is problematic for any historical setting, even one from a well-documented era. It is particularly difficult for Greek prehistory, where by definition no written sources can help and where excavations reveal remains more than three thousand years old. The world of Mycenaean Greece or Late-Bronze-Age Troy does not spring from the ground as if new-minted. Archaeologists are fully aware that details remain obscure and that there are many gaps even in the broader picture. Moreover, is this really the world in which any events that lie behind the tradition of the Trojan War should be set? It is a plausible but not a provable setting. Archaeology shows that Mycenae and Troy were rich and important places in the Late Bronze Age and that they were in contact. We know, too, that the fortification walls of Late-Bronze-Age Troy are battered and may have been attacked many times. The current excavators date a particularly devastating destruction around 1180 B.C. and interpret the archaeological record as showing that Troy lost a major

---

3   For a general discussion of the archaeological pursuit of the world of Homer's heroes see my *The Discovery of the Greek Bronze Age* (London: British Museum Press, 1995; rpt. 2001).

battle.[4] This certainly could be archaeological evidence for the event handed down in the literary and artistic tradition as the Trojan War, although archaeology does not make clear who the attackers were. And no Agamemnon or Achilles, Priam or Hector, Helen or Menelaus could possibly appear in archaeological findings.

The *Iliad* is of little help for pinning down the material culture and the date of the events described. Much scholarly effort has been spent addressing this question, with interesting results. Certainly some well-known specifics demonstrably describe Bronze-Age reality – Odysseus' boar's-tusk helmet is often quoted in this connection – and we can see many general correspondences between the Bronze-Age world and the world of Homer.[5] But the main difficulty resides in the fact, fully recognized from classical antiquity onwards, that Homer is a poet, not a historian. The world he creates may be half-remembered, but it is equally certainly half-imagined. It is an age of heroes and has to be bigger and better than anything in the audience's experience or the poet's own time. The description of Priam's palace in Troy, for example, demonstrates this. Its endless rooms and courtyards and its living quarters for the king's fifty sons and their families make it bigger and more complex than any real building ever was or could have been.

So imagination and exaggeration must be taken into account. The same is true for the possibility of accretions, losses, and changes that occurred during the centuries of the story's oral transmission from the end of the Bronze Age around 1200 B.C. to the time when the poems were written, perhaps around 700 B.C. This leaves the possibility of a very broad approach to material culture in a film such as *Troy*. If we keep all this in mind, it becomes evident that the inclusion of elements from the whole period of the story's creation and transmission in a film is entirely defensible. Indeed it is defensible to include almost anything if modern imagination is allowed to mirror that of the poet himself.

2. The Filmmakers' Approach

It must be said, though, that the makers of *Troy* did not adopt this rationale. Rather, they thought that they were aiming for a Late-Bronze-Age

---

4   Cf. the contribution by Manfred O. Korfmann in this volume and the references cited there.
5   *Iliad* 10.261–265. On this helmet see, e.g., Hilda Lockhart Lorimer, *Homer and the Monuments* (London: Macmillan, 1950), 212–214, and Frank H. Stubbings, "Arms and Armour," in *A Companion to Homer*, ed. Alan J. B. Wace and Frank H. Stubbings (1962; rpt. New York: Macmillan, 1974), 504–522, at 513–517.

setting somewhere around 1200 B.C. At the same time, they consciously included some elements that fitted in with the modern world's expectations of ancient Greek behavior, particularly as transmitted by Hollywood and popular culture. So the placement of coins on the eyes of the deceased for burial purposes was anachronistic even within the loose rationale outlined above. Coinage was not introduced until later than any of the possible "ages of Homer," probably not much earlier than about 600 B.C. Nonetheless the gesture appeared in the film both as a poignant farewell to the dead and as part of the repertoire of things that people "know" the Greeks used to do. We might question whether the inclusion of coins was a wise decision. It invites accusations of anachronism without adding substantially to the plot. But in other instances the very nature of the story and its sources force the filmmaker's hand. This is the case when it comes to the statues of the gods.

As is well known, the gods in Homer appear as a big supernatural family, gossiping, banqueting, quarreling, and not only taking sides in the Trojan War but personally interceding on behalf of their favorites. The decision to omit them from the action of the film was perhaps necessary; certainly it strains the modern imagination to contemplate how they could have been incorporated successfully. But while the gods took no part in the film's action, they had to be present, as it were, as the deities whom the protagonists worshipped. They were therefore represented in the form of statues.

The walls of Troy built for the film were based on reconstruction drawings of what archaeologists call Troy VI (about 1700–1200 B.C.). These walls could not possibly have protected the statues of the gods seen in Priam's throne room or council chamber, which were loosely modeled after the *kouros* ("young man") and *kore* ("young woman") types of the Archaic period, which emerged fairly late in the seventh century B.C. The adaptations used in the film were elaborate enough to include the attributes associated with the Olympian deities. For example, Apollo carried a bow and Poseidon a trident. But such sculptures do not fit the rationale of "anything from the period of origin or the period of transmission" of the story. They are too late.

Their inclusion, far from being simply a blunder, is a response by the filmmakers to an impossible situation. The problem is that Homer describes the Olympian deities with characteristics and spheres of influence that could be recognized in classical Greece. Clearly this way of looking at the gods had evolved by the late eighth century B.C. But it is much less clear whether these deities were viewed in a similar way in 1200 B.C. We know from the Linear B tablets of the Mycenaean world that some of the deities who would later be numbered among the Olympian gods and goddesses were already being worshipped. The names of Zeus, Hera, Athena, and Poseidon occur along with some others. But too little is known of Mycenaean religion for it to be clear whether these deities were already being worshipped in the same way as they were in classical times.

Even more problematic is the visual representation of deities in the Mycenaean world. One of the striking things about Late-Bronze-Age Greek art is that most of it is relatively small-scale.[6] There are no big sculptures of either gods or rulers of the sort that are found in contemporary Egypt and Mesopotamia. And it is often difficult to recognize deities with any certainty. A number of terracotta figurines and some figures on frescoes or seal rings are generally thought to represent deities. Yet cult statues remain elusive and the gods remain small. The filmmakers therefore faced a serious difficulty concerning representations of the gods, a difficulty that arises from the very nature of the Homeric account, which cannot easily be linked with the material record of the Bronze Age. Even in the poet's own time large-scale statuary was not yet common. A purist's attempt at Late-Bronze-Age authenticity would have the film's protagonists worshipping very small terracotta figures, no doubt puzzling audiences and running the risk of looking rather odd. The argument that larger-scale statues of wood may have existed in the Bronze Age and later is of limited help in this dilemma since we have little idea what such statues would have looked like. Again, any attempt at reconstruction would have been confusing.

The film's designers were keen not to use classical prototypes. From the beginning of the design process they avowedly wanted to avoid classical styles in both architecture and sculpture, especially the fluted columns and draped figures that have already become visual clichés of ancient Greece in popular culture. They wanted at the very least to retain a sense of earliness and of the pre-classical throughout the film. This goal was not always achieved – Helen's dress and wreath look very Hellenistic, to name only one example. Nonetheless, the compromise of adopting and adapting archaic statue types to represent the gods in *Troy* was perhaps the best option.

---

6   For small-scale representations of Mycenaean deities see the chapter entitled "Religion and Cult Centres" in Lord William Taylour, *The Mycenaeans*, 2nd edn (New York: Thames and Hudson, 1983; rpt. 1990), 43–64.

3. *Troy* and the British Museum

The above reflections arose during the time that I spent on the sets of *Troy*, at Shepperton Studios for the interiors and in Malta for exteriors, and when I lectured to audiences at a small exhibition that we mounted at the British Museum to coincide with the film's release. This display took as its theme *Troy Retold* and incorporated some of the costumes from the film.

I have said that the film had no historical advisor, and this is strictly true. My own contact with *Troy* began after sets and costumes had been designed. Much was already fixed, and my discussions with director and producers were concerned mainly with various details, such things as movements, ritual gestures, and others. My impact on the final product was minimal, but it is a pleasure to record my association with it here.

I believed that the film was worthy of support by historians and archaeologists because it aimed to bring the story of Troy to new audiences around the world. Moreover, it rapidly became clear that Wolfgang Petersen and his team were taking an extremely thoughtful view of the subject matter. Particularly striking was the way in which the equality of the Greeks and the Trojans emerged. Both had their virtues and their flaws in a way that exactly echoed the *Iliad*. And the inclusion of such a great Homeric set-piece as Priam ransoming the body of Hector seemed to show that the spirit of the original would indeed be at the heart of this new version for the twenty-first century.

Certainly reservations can be expressed about the liberties taken with the story toward the end of the film, when the fates of certain characters were radically different from what the ancient tradition tells us. Of course one could argue that the ancient world knew variants of traditional stories, but these were not motivated by what seemed in the film to be a very Hollywood need for the evil to be punished and the good to prosper. The ambivalent position of Helen in particular has been the subject of much fascination and poetic and scholarly debate down the ages, replete with speculations about what her life could possibly have been like when she returned to Sparta with Menelaus, with Troy a smoldering ruin. The ending of *Troy* undercuts such speculation, and the story becomes far less interesting.

Audiences who saw some of the costumes displayed at the British Museum almost invariably asked whether they were accurate. The truth was that the costumes, though magnificent creations in their own right, bore no close relationship to any ancient period or culture. Instead, like the film as a whole, they reflected mixed influences. The question of accuracy was easy to ask but hard to answer, and any reply had to try to summarize the complexity of the issues outlined above. Our intention was not to use the costumes as any sort of archaeological resource. Instead, we attempted to put them and the film itself into the context of a long series of retellings of the Troy story from antiquity to the present day. We wanted to explore not the archaeology of Greece or Troy, which can be pursued in our permanent galleries, but the phenomenon of the story itself, its reception throughout later ages, and its continuing power.

4. Conclusion

We return, then, to the original question whether *Troy* should have had a historical advisor and whether the film would have been improved by full incorporation of historical and archaeological advice from the outset. In spite of the difficulties outlined above, it would no doubt have been possible to create a more consistent Late-Bronze-Age environment of considerable grandeur, given the extensive resources available. Many of the elements were already there, particularly in the large sets. And the film's Wooden Horse could scarcely have been improved.

Yet my personal view is that the story is not history, that Homer was not a historian, and that something of Homer would certainly have been lost in a purist archaeological approach. Ultimately, dramatic success matters more than the archaeological accuracy of Helen's hairpins. It matters more for modern audiences to feel for Achilles in his progress from war machine to man, to sympathize with Hector in his efforts to defend all that was dear to him, and in the end to mourn for Priam and for Troy. In this regard the film takes an honorable place as the latest, if not the last, instance in the long series of retellings of the tale of Troy.[7] Perhaps what matters most of all is that audiences still gather to see and hear this story as they have done for three thousand years. We share a common humanity with the heroes and with the early audiences – in spite of the differences between a Mycenaean megaron and a cinema multiplex.

7   The meticulously researched *Age of Bronze* comics by Eric Shanower deserve honorable mention here. They show that it is possible, at least in graphic form, to retell the story of Troy in an exclusively Mycenaean setting. At the same time they illustrate the difficulties inherent in showing worship of small-scale gods. The first nineteen issues of this ongoing series have been collected in two books: *A Thousand Ships* (2001) and *Sacrifice* (2004). For details about the production of these comics see *Age of Bronze: Behind the Scenes* (2002). All books mentioned are published by Image Comics of Orange, California.

CHAPTER SEVEN

From Greek Myth to Hollywood Story: Explanatory Narrative in *Troy*

Kim Shahabudin

Before the release of *Troy* scriptwriter David Benioff was asked how he felt about adapting the *Iliad*, the foundation of Western literature. He replied that this was not his intention and that his script had borrowed ideas from several different sources. He called it "an adaptation of the Trojan War myth in its entirety, not The Iliad alone."[1] Despite Benioff's declaration and subsequent similar statements from others involved in the film, the close association with Homer's epic refused to go away. When *Troy* was released critics were quick to seize on the rather vague statement in the credits that the film had been inspired by Homer's *Iliad*. Consequently, much of its critical reception has been concerned with how well or badly the film adapts the poem.

In view of Benioff's statement, this seems rather unfair. But if *Troy* is not a literary adaptation, it is also not simply a film version of the Trojan War myth. Any scriptwriter working from existing sources must select and discard from the material he or she collects. Although many of the major names and places connected with the myth are present in *Troy*, a whole layer is missing. The decision to exclude the gods as a motivating force makes man (and woman) the measure of all things and transforms the mythological story of the Trojan War from a web of interactions

---

1 "David Benioff . . . Web Access" at www.bbc.co.uk/print/films/webaccess/david_benioff_1.shtml.

between mortals and immortals to a chronicle of strictly human cause and effect. Structure, content, and style of the film provide rational explanations for events explained in antiquity by the irrational.

However, the reception of a film depends not only on its narrative content but also on how its audience understands it as a story. Long ago F. R. Leavis objected to popular cinema because he believed that it encouraged passivity in the audience: viewers simply absorb the visual and aural features presented on the screen.[2] Today it is generally recognized that audiences play a much more dynamic role, not simply accepting but actively interpreting what they view and hear. Along with this concept of the active viewer comes the awareness that such interpretations may differ according to the preconceptions that individual viewers bring to a film. The teenage boys who are the primary target audience of action adventure films will view *Troy* differently from classical scholars who may look primarily for its sources, from film scholars who are most interested in, for instance, its cinematography, or from fans of a particular actor. This is the theory; in reality these and other possible ways of viewing overlap. To claim under these circumstances that any one mode is the right one seems rather arrogant.

Yet if it is wrong to assume that there is a single correct way, it is also wrong to assume that all are equal or equally valid. A variety of off-screen factors are important, such as the persona of a star, previous films which may bear a resemblance, genre conventions that prompt us to expect certain elements from certain kinds of films, and the promotional rhetoric that accompanies a film's release. So to understand how *Troy* uses its version of antiquity to present myth we must think about both text and context: how cinematic narrative lets features of myth appear natural and how extra-cinematic factors encourage viewers to accept such a construction.

1. Myth and History

Viewers rarely watch a film without some prior knowledge of what it will be about. In the past such knowledge may have come from posters and trailers and from reviews in newspapers and magazines. The Internet now provides new ways to find out about films before their release. Official websites operate as electronic pressbooks with stills and on-location photographs, actors' biographies, and production information. Online

---

2   F. R. Leavis, *Mass Civilisation and Minority Culture* (Cambridge: Minority Press, 1930).

message boards host fan discussions and spread rumors. If they give viewers greater access to information about a film, such sources also give filmmakers instant feedback on how their product is being received by its audience. Commercial pressures often mean that the paying customer's opinion is more important than that of the filmmakers. As a result, commercial cinema has become largely audience-driven and perhaps more conservative.

Online promotion of *Troy* revealed the producers' perspectives early on. First versions of the official website included a "Production Journal" by the film's publicist with information on the film's background: Benioff's original pitch to Warner Bros., director Wolfgang Petersen joining the project, problems with the choice of location. However, the journal's opening paragraph concerned Heinrich Schliemann's excavations at Hisarlık in 1871. His discovery of what he reported to be the historical location of Homeric Troy transformed the view of the *Iliad* as a recounting of myth to one that might have been based on historical fact. This opening gambit in the film's publicity directed viewers to the idea of Troy as historical reality. In addition, a large part of the journal was devoted to "An Historical Primer" that set the *Iliad* in the context of the fall of Mycenaean civilization and observed that in antiquity Homer's "historical accuracy" did not seem to have been disputed. Added to this ancient validation was a modern one from archaeologist J. Lesley Fitton, who had been employed as a kind of historical consultant for the film and whose credentials were given as "the British Museum's expert on the Bronze Age." By involving a scholar whose primary objects of study are the physical remains of the past, *Troy* declares that its story will be founded on empirical evidence. The message is clear: Schliemann's excavations explained Troy as historical reality; Homer wrote about events that took place there in the *Iliad*; and *Troy* will adapt Homer's history.

Another clue to the producers' preference of how the public was to perceive the film could be seen when the title was briefly changed to *The Trojan War*. This title gives a much clearer impression of the film's content, covering the causes and effects of the war. It also suggests a more action-based storyline than *Troy*, a title that seems to refer to some kind of universal concept rather than to a specific set of people. But the new title lasted for only a few days before being changed back. In that time it was the focus of a flood of negative discussion on online message boards, with some of the contributors citing as the reason for their disapproval the fact that it made the film sound like a history lesson. Perhaps such an antipathy to history sounded an alarm with the film's publicity department. While stories in the press continued to refer to

Homer's poem and Schliemann's excavations, the main focus of publicity prior to release was on the film's exposure of Brad Pitt's body.

Another clue to the producers' views concerning *Troy* is in their identification with epics of the classical Hollywood period that were made after World War II rather than with more recent films. Those associated with making *Troy* were keener to point out the differences rather than the similarities between it and Ridley Scott's *Gladiator* (2000). Comparisons were bound to be made despite the Roman setting of the earlier film. Perhaps partly in an attempt to deflect such comparison, Petersen was eager to distance his own vision of the ancient world from the famous computer-generated one of *Gladiator*: "I very much wanted to go with reality . . . We haven't just built a little bit and done the rest with CG" (computer-generated imagery). Actor Eric Bana, who plays Hector, supported this strategy in referring to the film's spectacle: "You can't say we haven't seen it before – but we haven't seen it for 50 years or so."[3]

A number of reviewers have noted the Old Hollywood look and outlook of *Troy*. In what is usually called classical Hollywood, studios exerted total control over their films. Film theorists have identified a particular style of filmmaking then dominant.[4] A prominent feature is its desire to make the filmmaking process as invisible as possible and to give viewers the impression that the cinema observes the world rather than creates it. Film narrative is a key element of this practice, with both content and structure producing an onscreen world that operates by the same perceptions we bring to our own world. Prominent in this are regular laws of cause and effect, characters whose actions may be accounted for by their psychology, and stories that begin at the beginning and end at the end. All these features can be discovered in the plot of *Troy*, which uses them to create an impression of the Trojan War as historical reality and to explain mythological features like gods and heroes in human terms.

2. Linear Structure

Troy is not an adaptation of the *Iliad*, which begins in the tenth year of the siege of Troy and ends with Hector's funeral long before the end of

---

3 Both quotations are from David Eimer, "Blood, Sweat and Spears," [London] *Sunday Times* (April 25, 2004), *Culture* supplement, 5–6.
4 An extensive analysis can be found in David Bordwell, Janet Staiger, and Kristin Thompson, *The Classical Hollywood Cinema: Film Style and Mode of Production to 1960* (New York: Columbia University Press, 1985).

the war. The film shows us the events that happened before the beginning of the Trojan War (Paris and Helen in Sparta) and its end (the sack of Troy). One of the questions that faces the makers of any historical film is how much of the background they should explain to the audience. This is especially so when the subject is the ancient world, mainly because of today's decline of popular knowledge about antiquity. So events recounted in the *Iliad* that are not well known to the majority of the audience are at least put in a recognizable context. A narrative structure that commences with the cause of the war and ends with its effect makes the war the main goal of the film.

At its beginning, three texts superimposed on a map of Greece set out the main issues and participants. The first notes Agamemnon's political dominance over most of the Greek kingdoms that is about to be completed on the plains of Thessaly. The second introduces his brother Menelaus who, in contrast to the aggressive expansionism of Agamemnon, is at that moment negotiating peace with Troy, Greece's main rival. The third presents Achilles as Greece's greatest warrior and his antipathy to Agamemnon. The somewhat unwieldy quantity of written information recalls the rolling prologues found in historical epics of the post-war years which made watching the opening of a film like the opening of a history book.

These texts serve as the psychological definitions for the figures they introduce. The following scenes develop and expand the words to fit modern character types. Achilles' first appearance presents him as a modern celebrity, deep in hedonistic sleep with two naked women and surrounded by empty wine cups. Of the Trojan princes, Hector is a diplomat and Paris a romantic idealist, the knight errant who will rescue fair Helen from boorish Menelaus. Agamemnon is an arrogant and greedy tyrant, whose reaction to his brother's cuckolding is to observe that "if Troy falls, I control the Aegean." The elopement of Helen and Paris is presented as the original grievance in the story. The fact that it leads to war is explained by political expediency.

Some of the incidents described in the *Iliad* as having happened before its narrative begins are put even earlier in the film. Such reordering produces a chronologically linear narrative which is driven by regular laws of cause and effect. For instance, before Achilles joins the expedition to Troy, his mother Thetis tells him that he must choose between a long life and obscurity or a short life and glory. In Book 9 of the *Iliad* Achilles relates that Thetis has told him this, although he does not specify when she did so. The film, placing it before he even leaves home, defines his choice as the goal that will drive him. Another example is Helen's elopement, which the *Iliad* describes as a kind of flashback in Book 3.

The elopement is the ostensible cause of the war in *Troy*, to which each event may be traced back. The drive to war builds with this linear succession of causes and effects until Hector kills Menelaus to save Paris' life almost exactly halfway through the film. From now on the war is unstoppable, and the momentum built up so far propels the events to the final catastrophe. The story of Troy and of *Troy* ends in flames; of the characters introduced in the opening titles, only Paris survives.

The story ends, but its momentum still drives the history further along its linear path. Among those escaping from Troy is a youth supporting an older man. Asked for his name, he replies: "Aeneas." For those familiar with Virgil's *Aeneid*, this insertion creates the impression of another background narrative which lies outside the onscreen story and has its own dynamic. (The entire story of the fall of Troy is borrowed from the *Aeneid*, too, in adapted form.) Rather than presenting a self-contained story world which begins and ends when the film begins and ends, some of the events in *Troy* seem to have been plucked from an independently existing chronicle, part of a continuing extra-cinematic narrative. If the opening recalled the prologues of post-war epics, this strategy recalls their epilogues, which typically predicted great future events or developments. Modern audiences can thus regard themselves as the descendants of the historical figures onscreen. Our concerns are similar to or identical with theirs. In this way *Troy*, too, assures its viewers that, while it may portray ancient people, "we, not the projected past, are their real concern."[5]

3. Omissions, Additions, Alterations

Benioff's claim that *Troy* adapts the Trojan War myth "in its entirety" should not be taken literally. Rather, it selects its content from the entire myth. Some aspects are completely left out, among them the sacrifice of Iphigenia, the prophecies of Cassandra, and the grief and defiance of Hecuba. Others are altered for the sake of narrative economy. (The siege of Troy lasts weeks rather than years.) Occasionally, radical changes occur in order to fit the myth to the narrative and themes of the film. For example, in the myth Agamemnon and Menelaus survive and reappear in Aeschylus' *Oresteia* and Homer's *Odyssey*; in *Troy* both are killed. Menelaus dies at the hands of Hector almost before the war has started.

---

5   Maria Wyke, "Are You Not Entertained? Classicists and Cinema," *International Journal of the Classical Tradition*, 9 (2003), 430–445; quotation at 435.

This alteration illustrates the film's theme of fraternalism, showing how the fate of the stronger brother (Hector and Paris, Agamemnon and Menelaus) or brother-like figure (Achilles and Patroclus) is bound up with that of the weaker. Menelaus' death also marks the pivotal moment in the war. The first half of the film, with the possibility of peace, is dominated by dialogue; the second half is dominated by action and spectacle. A mass charge of the Greek armies immediately follows Menelaus' demise.

Differences between ancient Greek and modern morality provide another reason to alter the myth. An omission which reviewers frequently noted is the sexual relationship between Achilles and Patroclus. Although there is nothing in Homer concerning this, it appears in later versions of the myth. Its repeated mention in reviews is evidence for popular knowledge of it. This is one aspect where the film became an adaptation of the *Iliad* alone, for the filmmakers denied that Achilles is anything but heterosexual in the poem. Asked by reporters, Pitt said: "I found nothing in the text."[6] It has been generally assumed that this is an example of the pressures exerted by the studios to protect the image of their star actors. In fact it may be an instance where the film's departure from the ancient myth does not go far enough. With Patroclus now Achilles' young cousin and protégé, their relationship never seems close enough to present an adequate motivation for the grief-driven rage that seizes Achilles after Patroclus' death. Perhaps if Patroclus and Achilles had been actual brothers Achilles' reaction would have been more credible.

One of the most spectacular visual features in the film has its roots not in any ancient narrative but in a modern one. The Trojan night attack on the Greek ships opens with huge balls of flaming straw rolled onto the stakes that the Trojans have planted on the beach as their first line of defense. Such a scene does not appear in the *Iliad*, although attack by fire is a frequent threat. But the images of exploding balls of flame remind viewers of the burning missiles catapulted into the German army in the opening battle in *Gladiator*. This visual reiteration borrows a popularly established image of ancient warfare to give credibility to its own. Historical films are just as likely to refer to film history as to historical events.

The poetic justice demanded in the finale of the classical Hollywood film motivates some of the most radical changes from the myth in *Troy*. If it were to be true to the *Iliad* or to Greek myth and literature, those

6   Charlotte Higgins, "*Troy* Stars Speak Out at 'Futility of War'," *The Guardian* (May 14, 2004), 8.

characters functioning as villains would survive while more sympathetic characters would be dead or enslaved. But Menelaus and Agamemnon are killed off. Helen returns to her life in Sparta with Menelaus in the myth, apparently unpunished for her adultery; in the film she escapes from Troy together with Paris, Briseis, and Andromache and her infant son. This child is hurled to his death from the walls of Troy in Euripides' *The Trojan Women*, but this is a scene unlikely to appear in a Hollywood film. Despite these changes, audiences have complained that the film's moral scheme is unclear and have objected that, unlike with other action-adventure narratives, they do not know which side to be on. As Petersen has commented in an interview: "It's a very unusual – but I think very real – approach to portraying life. In reality, I think there aren't really such things as 'bad guys' and 'good guys.' "[7]

4. Free Will, Determinism, and the Gods

The most fundamental alteration in *Troy* is the absence of the gods. Myth is by nature concerned with humanity's relationship with forces that they cannot rationally explain; by contrast, *Troy* offers rational explanations for everything. It is not necessarily the demands of the epic genre that motivate this rationalism; epics like the *Star Wars* and *Lord of the Rings* trilogies have no problem with fantastic creatures, and even *Gladiator* has moments of other-worldliness. But epic films of the classical Hollywood period were overwhelmingly dominated by realist historical narratives, except for Bible films. The filmmakers' ambition to place *Troy* in the tradition of classical Hollywood epics may have imposed a rationalizing strategy on their treatment of gods. Supernatural entities like gods and monsters are out of place in a realistically presented ancient world that functions according to the physical laws of our world. Petersen has stated that "people would laugh today if you had God entering the scene and fighting and helping out." Nevertheless ancient gods previously appeared in films, especially those based on Greek mythology.

   Troy adopts a strategy that interpreters of myth have applied since antiquity, rationalizing divine motivation as human emotions and psychology. For instance, it is not Aphrodite, goddess of erotic love, who motivates Helen's elopement but Helen's own attraction to Paris

---

7   This and the following quotation are from M. E. Russell, "Helmer of Troy," *In Focus*, 4 no. 5 (May, 2004); at www.infocusmag.com/04may/petersen.htm.

in the face of her unhappy marriage to Menelaus. And actions of men may replace actions of gods. Aphrodite rescues Paris from Menelaus in the *Iliad*, but the brotherly love of Hector saves him in the film. Briseis rather than the goddess Athena stops the quarrel between Achilles and Agamemnon; she does so with the prosaic and realistic-sounding declaration: "Too many men have died today." Briseis is more important in the film than in the myth. In the *Iliad* she is the ostensible cause of Achilles' fury at Agamemnon who has seized her from Achilles as a prize; in the film, probably for the sake of narrative economy, she is transformed into a Trojan princess, Priam's niece, and a priestess of Apollo. Her religious role is significant. Briseis functions as the spiritual center of the film. She voices its anti-war morality and humanizes Achilles, the godlike hero. As a prisoner held in the enemy camp she represents the possibility of overcoming an apparently irreconcilable opposition between Trojans and Greeks. This is finally achieved when Priam persuades Achilles to return Hector's body. Here Achilles proves that he understands the common humanity of Greeks and Trojans. But other Greeks, in particular Agamemnon, are not so conciliatory. Ironically, his sneer that "peace is for women" is proved wrong at the film's climax, when none other than Briseis kills him. A further example of this rationalizing strategy shows cinema's poetic capabilities. In Book 22 of the *Iliad*, the fatal combat between Achilles and Hector ends when Athena hands Achilles back his spear, with which he deals Hector a deadly blow. In the film the climax of their combat is staged in such a way that Hector lunges at Achilles with a broken-off spear which Achilles manages to seize and with which he then fatally stabs Hector.

The removal of the gods leaves humans with full responsibility for their actions. *Troy* must follow a tricky path between free will and determinism. Classical Hollywood films relied on cause and effect to produce the impression of realism, but at the same time their characters must be free to make the right or wrong choices, depending on what kind of character they represent; otherwise there can be no praise or blame and no poetic justice. So Helen is responsible for her adultery, although we are to see it from our modern views about a woman's right to escape an unhappy marriage and are meant to forgive her. While it becomes increasingly fatalistic as the war progresses, the storyline rarely demonstrates an absolute determinism of the kind that is found in myth and that would go against the film's humanist perspective. Throughout its first half there are moments when a choice has to be made that may lead to or away from war, but those choices are always freely made. There are no gods to intervene, and when Priam's priest does invoke religion, it is to support the wrong decision, the one that brings the Wooden Horse into the city.

5. Achilles' Heel

Troy comes closest to Homer's treatment of the Trojan War myth in its focus on Achilles and the causes and consequences of his rage. The myth poses problems for film adaptations because it includes a greater number of significant characters than could be accommodated even by an epic film. Such complexity threatens the unity of the film and might confuse an audience that does not already know the story. Both the *Iliad* and *Troy* turn a potentially unwieldy narrative into the story of Achilles. The main theme of *Troy*, however, is not Achilles' rage as in the *Iliad* but his glory. Its focus is on how a man becomes something more than a man: the transformation from man to myth.

Two scenes at the beginning and end of *Troy* make this intention explicit. In his first appearance, Achilles is roused from sleep to go into single combat with the Thessalian champion Boagrius. The awestruck young boy sent as messenger expresses the mythology of the hero: "Are the stories about you true? They say your mother is an immortal goddess. They say you can't be killed." Achilles replies: "I wouldn't be bothering with the shield then, would I?" This verbal appeal to logic echoes the rationalizing strategies of the film while the boy's references to stories and hearsay explain the process of mythmaking. The scene makes it clear that myths are our own creations, stories we want to believe because they inspire us but also because they offer explanations for our own failure to achieve heroic greatness. The boy goes on to say that he would not want to fight the giant Boagrius, to which Achilles responds: "That's why no one will remember your name." The message is that legends are written because of what men do and not because of what or who they are. Achilles has earned his heroic reputation by actions as a warrior, unlike Agamemnon who simply takes the glory earned by others. "Perhaps the kings were too far behind to see," Achilles tells him after the capture of the beach at Troy. "Soldiers won the battle." Odysseus makes the same point when he tells Achilles that "war is old men talking and young men dying."

In his final scene (except for his funeral) Achilles searches for Briseis during the sack of Troy. He finds her being threatened by Agamemnon and races to her rescue. But the hero said to have been "made for killing" is now denied his natural function when Briseis beats him to the death blow. Worse still, while trying to persuade her to leave Troy with him, Achilles is struck by Paris' arrows, first in the heel and then several times in the torso. In a last heroic gesture Achilles wrenches out all the arrows except the first before he collapses. When the apparently unkillable hero is discovered dead, the only remaining arrow is in his heel. The camera then looks down on Achilles from high above and so invites us to identify with the Greek soldiers: all are staring down at Achilles' body with its apparent single wound. Our own explanation would not have been different from theirs: the remembrance that Thetis held new-born Achilles by the heel to make the rest of his body invulnerable in sacred fire.

Achilles' heel has not been previously mentioned in the film, so its unusual nature seems to derive entirely from this one incident. In this way the story of the almost invulnerable hero has its explanation in his own last actions; by leaving Paris' arrow in his heel, Achilles achieves mythic immortality. The scene shows viewers how myths can be made, giving us the evidence to explain not the inexplicable but the stories that arise from the unexpected. *Troy* frames the story of Achilles by the two scenes discussed, each of which deals simultaneously with his mortality and perceived invulnerability and reveals that the film's focus is on the mythmaking process rather than on the myth itself. More specifically, *Troy* is concerned with the retelling of myth. Odysseus opens the film: "Will our actions echo across the centuries?" He also concludes it: "If they ever tell my story . . . let them say I lived in the time of Achilles." References to the transmission of myth appear throughout, as when Odysseus attempts to persuade Achilles to join the expedition: "This war will never be forgotten – nor will the heroes who fight in it." The king of Thessaly says: "Achilles? I'll remember the name." Most specific is Thetis' prediction to Achilles: "They will write stories about your victories for thousands of years. The world will remember your name." *Troy* repeatedly reminds viewers of their own role in the telling of stories about Achilles, and we find ourselves in a continuing tradition that began with Homer's ancient audiences. The fact that the Trojan War myth in *Troy* and in the *Iliad* centers on the same character reinforces the importance of Homer's poem for creating the myth of Achilles.

Epic films usually tell their historical stories from the perspectives of often fictional individuals. Large-scale events are explained in terms of their psychology. This method gives filmmakers a great deal of latitude but also fictionalizes history. In *Troy* we can witness the reverse process. The ancient mythology surrounding the Trojan War sought to explain what was regarded at the time of its composition as historical events through the stories of individuals. But in going beyond the laws of the physical world and appealing to supernatural entities like gods and superhuman heroes, history became myth and men became legends. *Troy* explains how this might have happened because the film adapts ancient Greek tales to a modern Hollywood story and so historicizes myth. As poet and filmmaker Jean Cocteau observed: "History consists of truths which in the end turn into lies, while myth consists of lies which finally turn into truths."[8]

8   Quoted from the documentary *Jean Cocteau: Autobiography of an Unknown* (1985), directed by Edgardo Cozarinsky. – I should like to thank colleagues at the Universities of Reading and London for their comments, with special thanks to Alastair Blanshard.

CHAPTER EIGHT

The Fate of Troy

Stephen Scully

Wolfgang Petersen's *Troy* is no *Iliad*, but why should it be? Virgil's *Aeneid* is no *Iliad*, and James Joyce's *Ulysses* no *Odyssey*. Nor should they be. Petersen's primary task is not fidelity to an ancient text but to tell, as Homer does, a rousing good story. The credits say that *Troy* is "inspired by" the *Iliad*, but the title suggests that the film also intends to deviate from Homer's poem. Some of Petersen's innovations are splendid, none less so than Briseis herself killing Agamemnon. Such an idea might have sparked the envy of the ancient poets had they learned of it, even if Agamemnon's premature death at Troy would have made havoc of Aeschylus' *Oresteia* and deprived Clytemnestra of the pleasure of dispatching her disagreeable husband. Another innovation in the film, although less bold, is the attention Petersen devotes to Troy itself, the doomed city. To a far greater extent than possible in Homer's telling, Petersen's reshaping of the story makes his audience experience the pathos of a city destroyed.

To discuss that pathos, we must say something about the film's overall design, on which my view is mixed. If we judge by its opening and close, *Troy* is rather dreadful. Comparison with Ridley Scott's *Gladiator* (2000) makes the point. *Gladiator* has a terrific opening scene. It is not hampered by historical accuracy, but that hardly takes away from the thrill of the action. *Gladiator* begins with the highly mechanized Roman army poised for battle against a German horde of barbarians in a dense forest. There is little historical likelihood or even logic in all this, but the sequence made for great spectacle and set the pace for the remainder of the film. The cool efficiency of the film's hero in the hand-to-hand slaughter which follows only enhanced our sense of Rome's bloody might. It did not take much imagination to see how such a culture could turn this art of war to the pleasures of the gladiatorial games. No other civilization has made the spectacle of man-killing a commonplace sport.

The opening scenes of *Troy* pale by comparison. The film begins with an episode introducing Achilles and Agamemnon but not with the scene from the *Iliad*. In northern Greece, Agamemnon's army stands poised to do battle against the forces of a local king when the two leaders agree to spare their troops and let a duel of their champions decide the day. After the Thessalian king calls out a name, a hulk of a man comes forward amid great cheers. But when poor Agamemnon calls out Achilles' name, no one appears. His hero is back at the nearby village, sleeping after a night with two local girls. When he finally makes it to the front, he dispatches his gargantuan opponent by coming up on him on the run, soaring high in the air, and in his descent piercing his neck and shoulder blade with the point of his sword. The scene is needlessly contrived, although Achilles' balletic leap foreshadows his climactic duel with Hector. The film then cuts to Sparta, where Menelaus and Helen are hosting a Trojan peace embassy. Prospects of a successful mission quickly vanish when at a banquet steeped in medieval-looking revelry and Persian excess the pretty-faced Paris slips away to Helen who is waiting upstairs. Menelaus fails to notice his wife's indiscretions as his hands and eyes are on the dancing girls in the banquet hall, but Hector, Paris' older and socially minded brother, is more observant. When he wrinkles his brow with concern, we suspect that Paris' actions do not bode well for Troy. Both scenes smack of 1950s Hollywood sword-and-sandal stories of love and war.

Troy, to its peril, has done away with Homer's gods, although Achilles' immortal mother Thetis does make an odd cameo appearance as an aging goddess. The absence of divine machinery and its mundane dialogue keep *Troy* from achieving epic greatness. We first sense trouble when Helen greets Paris with the ponderously earnest line: "Last night was a mistake." Apparently the lovers have met like this before. For what reason? In the ancient tradition, they have been brought together by the power of the gods. Petersen is forced to concoct reasonable motivations of his own. It is not Aphrodite's bitter-sweet Eros that draws Helen to Paris but rather her desire to live a comfortable life with a man she can relate to: "I don't want a hero. I want a man I can grow old with." Nor does Paris elevate the dialogue with his comment: "Men will hurt us . . . but I will love you until the day they burn my body. I will love you." As readers of Homer since antiquity have recognized, much of the greatness of the *Iliad* lies in its speeches. But nowhere have Petersen's changes let Homer down more than in the script and the motivation of the plot. Both the dialogue and the humdrum reasons for war reduce an epic scale to the commonplace. Something other than dialogue and nuanced portrayal of character are necessary to hold our interest and attention. For me, it was anxiety for the welfare of Troy, a concern which Petersen managed to keep fresh throughout.

Nor does its closing scene enhance the film. In keeping with his excision of the gods and using another medieval symbol, Petersen first substitutes an old if elegant-looking sword for the Palladium, the ancient statue of Pallas Athena, which the Greek and Roman traditions identify with the safety of Troy. Ancient lore has it that this small wooden image of the armed goddess fell from the heavens in response to a prayer from Ilus, the founder of Troy, and secured the city as long as it was in Trojan hands. According to post-Homeric Greek sources, Odysseus and Diomedes whisked it away from Troy and so made the sack of the city possible. Romans claimed that Aeneas rescued the Palladium from the burning city and brought it to Italy, where he became the ancestor of the Romans.

Modifying an early scene from the *Iliad*, Petersen introduces the magic sword at a moment of high pathos when Priam, fearful for his son's life and for the welfare of Troy, hands it to Paris in a garden before he faces Menelaus in a duel in front of the city walls. As he hands the sword to his son, Priam tells him about its antiquity and the legend that the Trojan line will never die as long as it remains in Trojan hands. In the duel Menelaus wounds Paris in the thigh and knocks his sword to the ground. With a cowardliness almost unbearable to watch, Paris hobbles back to his brother standing nearby and falls down at his feet, but he leaves the charmed emblem of Troy's future behind. Hector saves the day by stepping in for his younger brother and killing Menelaus. Getting rid of Helen's Greek husband simplifies the story, and with this bold revision the filmmakers avoid the melodramatic encounter between Menelaus and Helen at war's end when, according to non-Homeric sources, he is ready to pierce her with his sword. Nor need they allude to the couple's resumption of their marriage and their eternal life in the Elysian Fields as forecast in the *Odyssey*. With Menelaus dead, Paris to our relief now regains a bit of his manhood and retrieves the Sword of Troy before the two armies resume combat.

Troy's talismanic sword then returns in the final scene. As the city is burning and survivors of the royal family, including Helen and Paris, sword in hand, are about to escape through a secret passageway, Paris turns to a bystander and asks him his name. "Aeneas," says the young man. In the ancient accounts, Aeneas is Paris' cousin and the legendary figure identified with continuing the Trojan line of descent as ancestor of the Romans. Here he is a new acquaintance to whom Paris hands the Sword of Troy on the spur of the moment. Heroic after all, Paris returns to the burning city, leaving Helen and her new protector to make their way to safety on their own. For those who do not know the Aeneas legend, *Troy* ends with a puzzle about the fates of Aeneas, Helen, and Paris; for those who do, *Troy* ends with a laugh.

Neither the opening nor closing scenes of *Troy* are in the *Iliad*. The film begins and ends with Paris and, in tandem with its love story about Achilles and Briseis, tells the story of a boy-lover who in a few weeks, the film's length of the Trojan War, grows up to be a man and even something of a hero. His role in *Troy* contrasts with the relative neglect of Paris in the *Iliad*. Apart from his two prominent scenes in Books 3 and 6, Paris rarely appears. From Book 7 to Book 15 there are occasional accounts of his exploits in battle, but mainly in single-line references.[1] After that, Paris, unlike Helen, disappears from the action as a major character and comes close to vanishing altogether. In the last nine books he is mentioned only five times.[2] Helen's role stands in stark contrast. She is the last woman to speak in the *Iliad* when, in a ritual lament, she mourns for Hector and her own ill fate, "for no one else in wide Troy / was gentle and dear to me, but they all bristle at the sight of me" (24.774–775).

The *Cypria*, a post-Homeric epic, indicates that Aphrodite instructed Paris to take Aeneas, not Hector, with him to Sparta, the intent being from the start to seize Helen. But unlike the *Cypria* and *Troy*, Homer says nothing about Paris' time in Sparta and only twice offers information about his return journey home.[3] Homer is equally quiet about the Judgment of Paris, alluding to it only once, when the Olympians are debating whether Hermes should steal Hector's corpse from Achilles' tent. The allusion to Paris' choice of Hera's, Athena's, and Aphrodite's gift is so oblique that Aristarchus, the leading Hellenistic critic of Homer, rejected the lines outright (*Iliad* 24.25–30).

---

1   *Iliad* 7.2, 355, 374, 388, 389, 400; 8.82; 11.124, 369, 505, 581; 13.766, 774; 15.341. All translations from the *Iliad* below are my own.
2   *Iliad* 22.115, 359; 24.28, 249, 763.
3   *Iliad* 3.443–445 and 6.289–292.

It hardly seems accidental that Homer's references to Paris appear near the beginning of the *Iliad*. His most prominent occurrence is in Book 3. Scarcely has the fighting between Greeks and Trojans begun when the two armies halt their combat, "hopeful to be rid of the sorrow of warfare" (3.112), and negotiate a truce for Paris and Menelaus to fight in single combat. The winner will take "the woman and the possessions" (3.254–255). If mortals had been able to have their way, friendship would have replaced war, and the legend of Troy would have ended almost before it began. But Aphrodite intervenes and, rescuing Paris from certain death, whisks him away to his bedchamber, where he and Helen make love. Homer elegantly dramatizes how the collective desire for peace is usurped by the eroticism which had sparked the war.[4] This scene appears here in order to cast aside the purported cause of the Trojan War for what will emerge as the true concerns of the *Iliad* and its major characters. The Olympian gods are at the center of these concerns.

Zeus especially takes great interest in the truce of Book 3. When nameless warriors on both sides pray to Zeus that he honor and oversee the peace treaty, the narrator comments that "none of this would the son of Cronus accomplish" (3.302). Even more than Hera, Athena, or Poseidon, Zeus is eager for the war to press on to its bitter end. After Menelaus defeats Paris in the duel and the Trojan War appears to be over, Zeus taunts Hera with the following words (4.14–19):

> Let us consider how these things will be,
> whether we should again stir up grim warfare and the terrible
> fighting, or make the armies friends with each other.
> If somehow this way were sweet and pleasing to us,
> the city of Priam might still be a place men dwell in,
> and Menelaus could lead Argive Helen home.

The *Iliad* never explains what Zeus finds sweet and pleasing in the destruction of Troy. His eagerness to see the city destroyed is especially curious as Zeus acknowledges that there is no city under the heavens which he more honors than Troy (4.44–47):

---

4   Cf. my "Eros and Warfare in Virgil's 'Aeneid' and Homer's 'Iliad'," in *Being There Together: Essays in Honor of Michael C. J. Putnam on the Occasion of His Seventieth Birthday*, ed. Philip Thibodeau and Harry Haskell (Afton: Afton Historical Society Press, 2003) 181–197, especially 183–184. See also Robert J. Rabel, *Plot and Point of View in the Iliad* (Ann Arbor: University of Michigan Press, 1997), 75–79.

> Of all the cities of men who live upon the earth,
> cities which dwell under the sun and starry heaven,
> none has ever been more honored in my heart than sacred Ilios
> and Priam and the people of Priam of the good ash spear.

Whatever his reasons, they certainly go beyond Paris' abduction of Helen. It seems that Zeus finds sweet something which is darker and closer to the tragedy of human existence. Our understanding of Zeus' motives may lie in how he frames his love for sacred Ilios (Troy) even as he acknowledges its doom. The city, a sacred space of civic order and stability that the Greeks considered to be mankind's highest social achievement, is set within an Olympian, even cosmic, frame (sun and stars) but recognized as mortal. Like the leaves on a tree in one of the most famous similes in the *Iliad* (6.147–149), the city is only of a season. Zeus' will that his beloved Ilios fall stems less from punishment than affirmation, the perspective that the immortals alone are free from a world of change, mutability, and death.[5]

Cutting the gods out of his film, Petersen significantly domesticates plot and motivation. His recourse is to make a story of true love on the one hand and of naked imperialism on the other. How pale compared with what Homer gave him! It is crucial to the broad canvas of epic that some force larger than human contain man. In ancient epic the gods fulfill this role, but it need not always be so. In Tolstoy's *War and Peace* history functions in much the same way. Without such framing, the hero looms too large.

Petersen has been criticized for telling two stories in one: the story of Troy from beginning to end and the story of Achilles' wrath. Alcaeus, the seventh-century lyric poet from Lesbos, managed to link the two narratives with great economy:

> As the story goes, grief came to Priam and his sons
> on account of evil deeds, a bitter grief, o Helen, from you,
> and with fire Zeus destroyed
> sacred Ilios.

---

5   Cf. Sheila Murnaghan, "Equal Honor and Future Glory: The Plan of Zeus in the *Iliad*," in *Classical Closure: Reading the End in Greek and Latin Literature*, ed. Deborah H. Roberts, Francis M. Dunn, and Don Fowler (Princeton: Princeton University Press, 1997), 23–42, at 24, and Jenny Strauss Clay, "The Whip and the Will of Zeus," *Literary Imagination*, 1 (1999), 40–60. See further my *Homer and the Sacred City* (Ithaca: Cornell University Press, 1990; rpt. 1994), 16–40 and 124–127, and "Reading the Shield of Achilles: Terror, Anger, Delight," *Harvard Studies in Classical Philology*, 101 (2003), 29–47, especially 41–44.

Not like you was the bride whom Peleus, the noble
son of Aeacus, married, inviting all the blessed gods
to the wedding, taking Thetis the delicate maiden from her
father's halls

to the home of the Centaur Chiron where Peleus loosened
the pure maiden's girdle, and his love
and the greatest of Nereus' daughters flourished;
within a year

she bore a son, the finest of the semi-gods, Achilles,
blessed driver of chestnut horses.
And for Helen's sake they perished, the Phrygians
and their city.[6]

Alcaeus' poem is often understood as a cautionary tale juxtaposing two women in order to teach adolescent girls to be good.[7] But it seems less concerned with finding a happy marriage to contrast with Helen's wretched one than with the story of two marriages converging at Troy with its deadly effect on the sacred city and its people. By postponing the phrase "sacred Ilios" to the end of the first stanza, Alcaeus stresses the heavy price of Helen's infidelity, a theme to which he returns at the end of the fourth stanza. The two marriages make a complementary pair in a divine scheme that brings on the fall of Troy. Alcaeus managed to join the marriages of Helen and Thetis in the story of Troy. Petersen did not.

Classical scholar Daniel Mendelsohn is the harshest of Petersen's critics. He quotes Aristotle's *Poetics* in his rebuke of the director:

Homer may be said to appear "divinely inspired above the [other ancient Greek poets who wrote about the Trojan War], since he did not attempt to treat the war as a whole, although it had a beginning and an end; for the plot was bound to be too extensive and impossible to grasp all at once – or, if kept to a reasonable size, far too knotty in its complexity. Instead taking up just one section, he used many others as . . . episodes with which he gives his composition diversity. But the others construct one composite action about a single man or period, as for instance the poet of the

6   My translation of Alcaeus 42 is adapted from *Greek Lyric*, vol. 1: *Sappho and Alcaeus*, ed. and tr. David A. Campbell (Loeb Classical Library; Cambridge: Harvard University Press, 1982), 256–259.

7   So Denys Page, *Sappho and Alcaeus: An Introduction to the Study of Ancient Lesbian Poetry* (Oxford; Clarendon Press, 1955; rpt. 1975), 280. For a view closer to mine cf. Anne Pippin Burnett, *Three Archaic Poets: Archilochus, Alcaeus, Sappho* (Cambridge: Harvard University Press, 1983), 190–198.

> *Cypria* and the *Little Iliad.*" . . . Petersen's *Troy* falters hopelessly for
> precisely the same reasons that those lost, bad poems did. *Troy* claims,
> in a closing credit sequence, to have been "inspired" by the *Iliad*, but
> however much it thinks it's doing Homer, the text it best illuminates is
> Aristotle's.[8]

But Petersen deserves his day in court. For Mendelsohn, the *Iliad*
"is precisely about what is proposed, in its famous opening line, as its
subject matter: the wrath of Achilles, its origins, its enactment, its
consequences." But is the *Iliad* only about this? Its title, *Ilias*, attested at
least since Herodotus, suggests otherwise.[9] It derives from Ilios, one of
the two names for Troy commonly found in Homer's poem, especially in
the formulaic phrase "sacred Ilios." Since antiquity, the *Iliad* has been
thought to be about Achilles and Hector, and it closes with Hector
(his funeral), not with Achilles (his meeting with Priam). The third-
century A.D. philosopher and Homer critic Porphyry addressed the question of Homer's title this way: "Homer wished to show not only Achilles
but also, in a way, all heroes . . . so unwilling to call it after one man,
he used the name of the city, which merely suggested the name of
Achilles."[10] There is none of this expansiveness in Mendelsohn's view of
the *Iliad*.

Petersen seems to have sensed what Alcaeus had already seen, or
at least part of it since he omits the gods. Homer's concentration on
Achilles' wrath at the opening of the *Iliad*, a wrath directed against his
fellow Greeks, initiates a process that culminates in Achilles symbolic-
ally laying waste to sacred Ilios by killing Hector, its protector. (The
name "Hector" means "holder, preserver.") The structure of the *Iliad*
precludes a direct narration of the fall of Troy, but the city's fate hovers
perpetually over the poem and at crucial moments comes to the fore in
poignant prognostications. Perhaps none is more affecting than the dirge
at the end when Troy's three most prominent women, Andromache,
Hecuba, and Helen, deliver speeches of lamentation. Hector's wife
Andromache, speaking first, addresses her dead husband and then their
son, visualizing with chilling clairvoyance the day, soon to arrive, when
"some Achaian, / in a rage because Hector killed his brother, father, or

---

8   Daniel Mendelsohn, "A *Little Iliad*," *The New York Review of Books* (June 24, 2004),
46–49, at 46.
9   Herodotus, *The Histories* 2.116.
10   Porphyry, *Homeric Questions* 1. I quote from Seth Benardete's translation of Porphyry to draw attention to his essay, "The *Aristeia* of Diomedes and the Plot of the *Iliad*,"
Agon, 1.2 (1968), 10–38; quotation at 10.

son, / will take you by the hand and hurl you from the tower, / a horrible
death" (24.734–737).

The *Iliad* may be described as one prolonged note reaching a cre-
scendo of heroism and warfare in Book 22, when Achilles and Hector
face each other in single combat. Just at the moment when the war
music is at its loudest in the climactic clash between the city-defender
and the city-destroyer "full of savage strength" (22.312–313), the
narrative becomes strangely serene. It pauses first to describe Achilles'
divine armor, which has remained largely unmentioned since Book 19
when Achilles received it (22.313–316):

> Protecting him, the shield, beautiful and elaborately wrought,
> enfolded [Achilles'] chest; he tossed his glittering four-horned
> helmet, and about it waved beautiful, golden horsehair
> plumes, which Hephaestus had set thick about the crest.

After this juxtaposition of the savage and the divine, the narrator turns
to a simile (22.317–321):

> As a star goes among the stars in the night's darkening,
> the evening star, the most beautiful of the stars set in heaven,
> such was the gleam from the keen point of Achilles' spear
> as he poised it in his right hand, devising evil against godlike Hector,
> eyeing the beautiful flesh where it might especially yield.

This sudden expansiveness, likening the death-stroke to the evening
star, has struck many readers. The image of a star bringing on night
fits Hector's movement toward death, but the simile ultimately tells us
more about Achilles and his affinities with stars mentioned in Books
18–22. Like the joyful scenes of human life among those on his shield,
the evening star is remarkably distant from the violent human drama
toward which the poem has been moving. The shield and the evening
star become symbols of death in an impersonal world that only Achilles
among mortals can gaze upon with pleasure.[11]

Clearly, this decisive moment is not only Achilles' but also Hector's,
the culmination of his civic heroism in his death at Achilles' hand.
As the narrator makes clear with his simile, the moment also comes
as close as the *Iliad* can to a dramatization of Troy's fall (22.405–
411):

---

11   I adapt this discussion of Book 22 from "Reading the Shield of Achilles," 46–47.

> So [Hector's] head was befouled in the dust; and now his mother
> tore out her hair, and ripped the shining veil from her,
> and let out a great wail as she looked upon her son.
> His dear father groaned piteously, and the townspeople around him
> were seized by wailing and lamentation throughout the city.
> It was most like what would happen, if all lowering
> Ilios had been burning top to bottom in fire.

As this last simile attests, by now the *Iliad* has journeyed far from its exclusive attention to Achilles and his wrath against the Achaeans in Book 1.

Petersen's film, even more than the *Iliad*, is about Troy, even if there are some significant omissions in his telling of the city's story. The women, who add great depth to Homer's epic, are reduced in grandeur, power, and number. Hecuba, Priam's wife and Hector's mother, makes no appearance. The speeches of Andromache and Helen are drastically cut as the two women are reduced to being little more than beauties who give in to male authority. Petersen once again domesticates Homer, this time shifting the famous scene of Hector, Andromache, and their infant son in Book 6 from the city gate to the bedroom. He has Andromache, sitting on the marriage bed behind a crib, beseech Hector not to fight the next day but to stay at home. While he replies ("You'd make a fine general, my love"), the camera pans to Astyanax gazing sweetly up at his parents. Petersen effectively makes us aware of all that will be lost when the city falls, but he loses Homer's mastery in setting a familial scene in a public place. Instead of the sentimentality of a baby smiling, Homer's Astyanax, on the city wall with his mother, shrieks in terror when his father, in full armor, reaches out to kiss him. It is the parents who laugh, moved by their son's understandable fear even as they are aware of the doom that awaits them all.

In Book 22, husband and wife once again meet in a public space. The scene begins with Andromache at home and preparing a bath for Hector when she hears the Trojan women shrieking from the city wall. Running like a madwoman from the house, she arrives at the wall in time to see Hector's corpse being dragged behind Achilles' chariot. As she falls into a faint, she hurls from her head the veil which Aphrodite had given her on her wedding day. In both scenes Homer recasts the intimate and familial as public and communal by setting the climax of a scene at or on the city wall. The walls of Troy symbolize the divide between civilization and war, a strong but precarious border which shelters women, children, and old men from rape or slaughter.

Plate 1 The ruins of Troy today (view from south). Lower city with excavation (foreground) and citadel (background). Courtesy of Troia Project, University of Tübingen.

Plate 2 Troy (view from south). From upper right to lower left: Schliemann's trench (Troy I), ramp and citadel walls (Troy II), citadel wall (Troy VI), Greek and Roman sanctuary (Troy VIII–IX), and houses of lower city (Troy VI–VII). Courtesy of Troia Project, University of Tübingen.

Plate 3   Computer reconstruction of Troy at the end of Troy VI (view from north). Courtesy of Troia Project, University of Tübingen.

Plate 4–5 Achilles and Briseis. Red-figure Panathenaic amphora by the Cleophrades Painter (ca. 490–480 B.C.). Antikenmuseum, Basel, and Collection Ludwig (inv. no. 424). Photo: Claire Niggli.

Plate 6 Achilles tending the wound of Patroclus, a scene not in the *Iliad*.
Interior of Attic red-figure kylix by the Sosias Painter (ca. 500 B.C.). Staatliche
Museen, Berlin, Germany, Archives Charmet / Bridgeman Art Library.

Plate 7 The shield of Achilles. Illustration from *Le costume ancien ou moderne* by Jules Ferrario (Milan, ca. 1820), after Angelo Monticello (1778–1837). Bibliothèque des Arts Décoratifs, Paris, France, Archives Charmet / Bridgeman Art Library.

Plate 8   The duel of Achilles and Hector. Attic red-figure volute krater attributed to the Berlin Painter (ca. 500–480 B.C.). © The Trustees of The British Museum.

Plate 9   Achilles dragging Hector's body, with Priam and Hecuba (l.) and the goddess Iris. Attic black-figure hydria attributed to the Antiope Group (ca. 520–510 B.C.). © Museum of Fine Arts, Boston, Massachusetts, USA, William Francis Warden Fund / Bridgeman Art Library.

Plate 10 Priam begging Achilles for the return of Hector's body. Red-figure Attic skyphos by the Brygos Painter (ca. 490 B.C.). Kunsthistorisches Museum, Vienna.

Plate 11   Maria Corda as Helen in the *art déco* splendor of Alexander Korda's *The Private Life of Helen of Troy*. The William Knight Zewadski Collection.

Plate 12 The Bronze-Age palace of Knossos comes to life as King Priam's palace in the Minoan Troy of Robert Wise's *Helen of Troy*. Paris, Helen, Cassandra, Hecuba, and Priam (center l. to r.) hear the Greeks' demand for the return of Helen. The William Knight Zewadski Collection.

Plate 13   On the set of Wise's *Helen of Troy*. The wooden horse inside Troy. The William Knight Zewadski Collection.

Plate 14 The model set of Troy, "the city of Paris and Helen, the city that Homer wrote about," for Robert Wise's *Helen of Troy* as seen in *Behind the Cameras*: "The Look of Troy," a promotional television program hosted by Gig Young. Warner Bros.

Plate 15   "Homer's *Iliad*, one of the greatest love stories ever written." Gig Young promoting Homer ("This book was our challenge") and Hollywood in *Behind the Cameras*: "Sounds of Homeric Troy." Warner Bros.

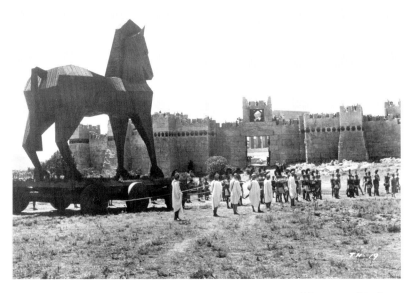

Plate 16 The wooden horse approaches a Troy protected by rugged-looking walls in Giorgio Ferroni's *La guerra di Troia*. The William Knight Zewadski Collection.

Plate 17   A strange horse enters an exotic Troy in John Kent Harrison's *Helen of Troy*. Minoan columns are by now standard for the city's look. Universal Studios.

Plate 18 A tiny Achilles before the massive walls of Troy in Wolfgang Petersen's *Troy*. Warner Bros.

Plate 19 Troy. The city's architecture is an eclectic mixture of Minoan, Egyptian, Near Eastern, and other styles.

Plate 20 Which is the face that *should* have launched a thousand ships? Rossana Podestà (r.) as Helen and a pre-stardom (but already pouting) Brigitte Bardot (L.) as her handmaid Adraste in *Wise's Helen of Troy.*

Petersen does not render this theme but dramatizes that of a city in danger in his own way. Introducing us to noble Hector at Sparta makes us fear for Troy long before we actually see the city. The Trojans' slow sea journey home helps sustain our curiosity about and concern for their city, especially when we hear Hector, surprised by the sight of Helen, severely chastising Paris for his reckless love and his indifference to Troy. By the time we first see Troy, we marvel at its high and seemingly impregnable walls, but we also think of the fate that awaits it. The early scene at Sparta may be weak in some respects, but it works well in arousing our curiosity and anxiety for Troy in peril. Petersen may have learned a trick here from the *Iliad* itself, which does not turn to Troy until Book 3.

The duel between Achilles and Hector in *Troy* is staged as if it were choreographed. Hector is a perfectly good swordsman. The problem is that his virtuosity – and his virtue – are all too human. Achilles' swordplay is of a different order. While Hector fights, Achilles dances. In the moments before the kill, with balletic leaps – perhaps Petersen's substitute for Homer's simile of the beautiful evening star – Achilles soars above Hector, then whirls upon him and pierces Hector's armor. If the film generally avoids the divine, in this scene Achilles is terrifying and demonic, more than human in his warrior's might and less than human in his animal grace.

The *Iliad* itself recognizes the ebb and flow of battle as a dance, the Greek word *stikhes* describing both a chorus and a battle line. In one of his war speeches, Hector at first contrasts the works of war and the gentler art of dance but reveals that the twists and turns of the shield are their own form of dance (7.235–241):

> Do not test me like some feeble boy
> or woman who does not know the works of war.
> I myself know well both battles and man-slayings;
> I know how to wield to the right and to the left the dry ox-hide
> shield, which for me is the shield way of fighting.
> I know how to rush into the press of fleet chariots;
> I know how in close combat to dance for the fierce war god.

In a speech before his troops, Ajax also at first distinguishes manly war from dance ("Hector did not invite you to come to dance but to fight"; 15.508) but then in a metaphor points out their underlying symmetry. What, he asks, is better than "at close quarters to mingle our hands and our strength"? (15.510) The word choice goes beyond the image of the dance and joins the intimacy of warriors to that of lovers. "Mingle" is a standard term in Greek poetry for love-making. For example, Paris reminds Helen that, returning from Sparta, he "mingled [with her] in love and the bed" on an island (3.445). Nowhere is the association of love and war stronger than when Hector reminds himself of "the gentle cooing, / the kind between . . . a maiden and a young man who dally in love-talk with each other" (22.127–128), an image of budding eroticism which comes into Hector's mind just before he faces Achilles. Not long before, Hector spoke of the "love-talk of war" (17.228) to encourage his allies to join in battle and test whether they shall live or die. The language of Homeric heroes may suggest that the true intimacies of the *Iliad* are to be found in warfare. Martial and marital imagery become inseparable. But the result is the destruction, not the creation, of civilized order.

Troy does not and cannot capture all the complexities of the Homeric poem or its imagery, but in Achilles' dance against Hector's methodical if valiant sword work we sense a warrior who has turned mortal combat and the resulting fall of the sacred city into a god-like ballet of death.

I close with a memory which Michael Herr recorded as he looked back on the Tet Offensive in the Vietnam War: "And for the next six years I saw them all, the ones I'd really seen and the ones I'd imagined, theirs and ours, friends I'd loved and strangers, motionless figures in a dance, the old dance."[12]

12   Michael Herr, *Dispatches* (New York: Avon, 1968; several rpts.), 66.

CHAPTER NINE

Helen of *Troy*

Monica S. Cyrino

"Men are haunted by the vastness of eternity. And so we ask ourselves: Will our actions echo across the centuries? Will strangers hear our names long after we're gone and wonder who we were? How bravely we fought? How fiercely we loved?"

The opening voice-over of Wolfgang Petersen's *Troy* expresses the film's self-conscious remembrance and re-creation of the glorious deeds of ancient heroes. Under the words of a smooth-voiced Odysseus the audience hears the ominous rumble of military drums punctuated by a woman's yearning song. Here is the double focus of the film's narrative: love and war, a war fought for love. The most famous war of antiquity was fought for the love of the most beautiful woman on earth, Helen of Sparta or, as she is more famously known, Helen of Troy. The distance she travels between her two names tells her story.

Early in the film, the camera pans along a steep wall of rock rising from dark blue waves, with ships anchored in the choppy waters. The viewers' eyes are drawn upward to a rough stone palace carved out of the sheer cliff face and set precariously high above the water. A title flashes on the bottom of the screen: "Port of Sparta – Greece." A cut to the interior of the palace reveals a long banquet table crowded with revelers enjoying a celebratory meal. At the center of the table, a tall, imposing man rises and addresses his guests: Menelaus, King of Sparta.

He faces two young Trojans, Hector and Paris, directly across the table: "Princes of Troy, on our last night together, Queen Helen and I salute you." At the mention of her name, the camera focuses for the first time on Helen. She is dressed in a lustrous gown of fiery red, decked in gleaming gold jewelry, and her blond mane of hair is tousled around her face and spilling down her shoulders. Paris is gazing intently at her, as if to induce her to look at him, but Helen's eyes are lowered. As her husband Menelaus continues to speak of the peace treaty between Sparta and Troy, Helen slowly looks up and fixes her kohl-rimmed eyes on Paris. They exchange a dark glance. Soon Helen steals upstairs and Paris, with a furtive peek over his shoulder, follows her.

While *Troy* claims to be "inspired" by Homer's *Iliad*, much of its action covers material narrated in lost works from the cycle of Greek epic poems on the subject of the Trojan War.[1] The narrative in the early part of the film was once told in an epic, composed after the *Iliad*, called the *Cypria*. Its title refers to the prominent role of Aphrodite, the Greek goddess of love, beauty, and sexuality, who had a major cult sanctuary on the island of Cyprus in the eastern Mediterranean Sea. The contents of the lost epic are known to us from later summaries and quotations, and by all accounts its eleven books offered a rather tedious if detailed catalogue of several events leading up to the point at which the *Iliad* begins.[2] Many of the important episodes related in the *Cypria* center on the relationship between Helen and Paris, in particular on how the star-crossed pair came to be joined together. The *Cypria* opened with the tale of the wedding of Peleus and Thetis, the mortal king and the sea goddess who became the parents of the great Greek hero Achilles. This wedding was attended by all the gods, demigods, and elite humans except one. During the banquet, Eris, goddess of discord, disgruntled over being the only one left uninvited, tossed upon the table a golden apple designated "for the fairest," causing a major quarrel to erupt among the assembled goddesses. Zeus, the supreme god, wisely wanted no part in the decision of who was the fairest and assigned the judge's task to a mortal. This was Paris, who was idling away his time as a shepherd on the slopes of Mt. Ida above the city of Troy. In the famous Judgment of Paris, the young Trojan prince passed over the goddesses Hera and Athena,

1   On the film's use of material from the lost poems of the Greek epic cycle see Daniel Mendelsohn, "A *Little Iliad*," *The New York Review of Books* (June 24, 2004), 46–49.

2   The contents of the *Cypria* are summarized by Proclus, a fifth-century A.D. philosopher, in his literary handbook *The Chrestomathy*. For the text of Proclus' summaries see *Homeri Opera*, vol. 5, ed. T. W. Allen (Oxford: Clarendon Press, 1912; rpt. 1978), 102–109. Of Proclus' six summaries of lost epics, the *Cypria* is the only anonymous one.

awarded the golden apple to Aphrodite, and so became the favorite of this dangerous goddess.[3] As a reward to her judge, and perhaps even as a bribe, Aphrodite sent Paris to Sparta, where he was to obtain Helen, the most beautiful mortal woman in the world. But Helen was already married to Menelaus.

In a manner comparable to the *Cypria*, *Troy* begins the story of Paris and Helen a few days after their first meeting in Sparta. Viewers versed in geography may wonder at the film's fanciful location of Sparta on the Greek coast, which affords the royal palace of Menelaus and Helen an enviable sea view. Ancient Sparta, however, was landlocked in the middle of the Laconian plain, without direct access to the sea. (The closest port was at Gythium, modern Gythio, located twenty-seven miles south of Sparta.) Inside the palace Menelaus entertains Paris and Hector after they have concluded a pact between their two previously hostile cities. The frank, avid gazes between Paris and Helen across the banquet table indicate that their love affair is well under way. Although the Greek epic tradition makes no mention of Hector joining his younger brother on his trip to Sparta, Hector's presence in this early scene of *Troy* emphasizes the important bond between the brothers that propels much of the plot as the film progresses. Hector is a sympathetic character throughout the film, inviting viewers to identify with him through an attractive combination of his warrior's courage, family loyalty, and strong sense of duty to his homeland. When Hector watches with worried suspicion as Paris sneaks away to join Helen, the audience follows his anxious glance and realizes how perilous the pair's erotic passion is.

Upstairs in her bedroom, a long shot frames a pensive Helen undoing her hair ornaments at her dressing table.[4] Paris slips through the door and never stops staring at her as he drives the bolt shut with a vigorous thrust, demonstrating the lithe insouciance and sexual magnetism of the legendary Trojan. In the Greek epic tradition, there are contradictory reports whether Helen and Paris consummated their passion in Sparta. The *Iliad* suggests that this occurred after their flight on the tiny island of Cranae nearby in the Laconian gulf.[5] But the *Cypria* summary notes that Paris and Helen had sexual intercourse the night before they

3   The hostility of Hera and Athena toward the Trojan race because of the insult of Paris is mentioned at *Iliad* 24.25–30.
4   On Diane Kruger, a model turned actress, and Petersen's casting of her as Helen cf. my "She'll Always Have Paris: Helen in Wolfgang Petersen's *Troy*," *Amphora*, 4 no. 1 (2005), 10–11 and 18.
5   Paris reminds Helen that they made love for the first time on the island of Cranae at *Iliad* 3.443–445.

set sail from Sparta, a much riskier place for their adulterous encounter. Like the lost epic, *Troy* dramatically puts the start of their sexual relationship in Sparta. "You shouldn't be here," Helen whispers, avoiding Paris' eyes in the knowledge that to look at him means to succumb to him. The Helen of the *Iliad* also turns her eyes away from Paris in their bedroom in Troy (3.427), perhaps both to indicate her distress and to avoid his irresistible allure. Paris counters teasingly, aware of his powerful charm: "That's what you said last night." – "Last night was a mistake," she replies. "And the night before?" – "I've made many mistakes this week." Paris approaches her from behind, and there is a close-up of Helen's face as he strokes her neck and shoulders. Her rapt expression indicates that her protests are all in vain. In response to his question "Do you want me to go?" Helen turns to him and drops her dress to the floor. The lovers embrace.

Some ancient versions of the story have Menelaus conveniently called away to the island of Crete for a family funeral while Paris is visiting Sparta, so the lovers have an easy escape.[6] *Troy* radically concentrates the time of their encounter, forcing the lovers to face the anguish of their last night together. While Menelaus is distracted downstairs with a dancing girl and Hector continues to look anxiously up the stairway, the film exposes Paris and Helen in a moment of crisis. After lovemaking Paris gives Helen a beautiful necklace of pearls "from the Sea of Propontis": the *Cypria* records that Paris bestowed many gifts upon Helen. An emotional Helen begins to weep at the thought of Paris' departure in the morning, just as she is depicted weeping in the *Iliad*.[7] She caresses her lover's face and describes what the loss will mean to her: "Before you came to Sparta, I was a ghost. I walked and I ate and I swam in the sea, but I was just a ghost." Paris responds with an impulsive invitation: "Come with me!" Helen's eyes widen in surprise; she is tempted but doubtful. "Don't play with me," she warns him. Then Paris delivers a romantic and fateful speech destined to rouse even the disconsolate heart of Helen. "If you come, we'll never be safe. Men will hunt us. The gods will curse us. But I'll love you – till the day they burn my body. I will love you." She nods, smiling through her tears. (This evokes Andromache "smiling through tears" in her encounter with her husband Hector at *Iliad* 6.484.) Here *Troy* effectively confirms the Greek

---

6   The tradition of Menelaus' absence is noted in Proclus' summary of the *Cypria* and is followed by Ovid, *Heroides* 17.160.

7   *Iliad* 3.142 and 24.773.

literary tradition of the seductive agency of Paris and Helen's willing acquiescence to her "abduction" from Sparta.

The next shot shows the royal Trojan ship under full sail on the open sea. In the Greek epic tradition Helen and Paris set sail for Troy in amorous privacy *à deux*, dallying at various stops along the way.[8] The *Iliad* alludes to the fact that Paris brought Helen back to Troy by a roundabout way via Sidon in Phoenicia. The *Cypria* also notes the stop in Sidon, which Paris, somewhat implausibly, sacked.[9] But the film takes them straight to Troy. Here Petersen follows the convention of epic cinema by emphasizing male relationships, in this case the fraternal bond between the princes. Paris, aware of his illicit act, nervously approaches Hector on deck with a genial comment about the weather. Hector's cautious nature causes him to reply with typical archaic Greek skepticism: "Sometimes the gods bless you in the morning and curse you in the afternoon."[10] Paris suddenly becomes earnest: "Do you love me, brother? Would you protect me against all enemies?" Then, below deck, Helen unwraps her hooded cloak and reveals herself to an incredulous Hector. Now comes a quick cutaway to Helen's empty bedroom and a raging Menelaus. Back on the Trojan ship, Hector also is furious and berates Paris for betraying his family and bringing certain destruction to Troy. Hector's reproach of Paris as an unwarlike woman-izer in this scene of the film echoes his disparaging speech in the *Iliad* just before Paris meets Menelaus in single combat.[11] Paris is adamant: if war is to come, he will die fighting for Helen. Paris' inexperience in military matters is well known from the ancient literary tradition, and in the film he also does not realize the political implications of his action. "I won't ask you to fight my war," he tells Hector. His brother, veteran of many armed conflicts, replies: "You already have."

In a parallel scene of fraternal relations, Menelaus next sails to Mycenae – also implausibly located by the sea – to see his brother Agamemnon, who scolds him for trusting the Trojans: "Peace is for the

8   But the *Cypria* summary notes that Aphrodite commanded her son Aeneas to sail with Paris to Sparta.

9   *Iliad* 6.289–292 alludes to their roundabout journey. The Greek historian Herodotus records the story that Helen and Paris stopped in Egypt at *Histories* 2.113–116, but he also notes that the *Cypria* has them traveling directly from Sparta to Troy in only three days (2.117). Proclus' summary records their stop in Sidon.

10   The sentiment is common in archaic Greek poetry. See, for example, Archilochus, fragment 58 (Campbell).

11   Hector calls Paris a "woman-crazy pretty-boy seducer" with no battle experience at *Iliad* 3.39–57. Here and below, translations of the *Iliad* are my own.

women . . . and the weak." Menelaus, still fuming, asks: "Will you go to war with me, brother?"[12] Later, Agamemnon expresses his delight that Helen has given him a reason to attack wealthy Troy: "I always thought my brother's wife was a foolish woman, but she's proved to be very useful." Consistently throughout the Greek epic tradition, Helen is the direct cause of the war, while the acquisition of wealth is only a secondary motive for the Greeks. The *Iliad* uses variations of the phrase "Helen and (all) the possessions" to describe the reason for the conflict; at one point, Paris says he will restore Helen's property and add some of his own but will not surrender Helen herself.[13] By contrast, from its very beginning *Troy* emphasizes that Helen is merely the official pretext for war, intended to cover up a well-orchestrated and long-desired power grab by greedy Agamemnon. An introductory text has informed viewers that Agamemnon had already brought most of Greece under his rule by conquering it, and in an earlier scene Petersen has shown us an example of how Agamemnon's ruthlessness has prevailed. Now the abduction of Helen becomes an incendiary excuse and justification for the attack on Troy by a superpower Greek force, similar to the argument about "weapons of mass destruction" in the recent American-led invasion of Iraq. (The war council in Agamemnon's palace will have reminded at least some of the American viewers of their own political leaders.) Soon after, a magnificent computer-generated shot reveals the massive Greek armada sailing at full speed to Troy. The image is clearly intended to evoke the famous phrase from Christopher Marlowe's *Doctor Faustus* describing Helen ("the face that launched a thousand ships"), but it also provides a menacing visual contrast to the earlier shot of the lone Trojan ship carrying the two lovers to their destiny.

According to the *Cypria*, Helen and Paris are married when they reach Troy. The film reflects this in an impressive sequence of their arrival at the city that is replete with wedding imagery. Petersen follows the couple's chariot with an overhead shot as it enters through the gates and proceeds through a crowd of cheering spectators. To the sounds of epic fanfare and beneath a shower of rose petals, Helen and Paris lead the procession, Hector following on horseback. Helen is dressed in a simple white gown, wearing Paris' pearl necklace, her hair smoothed down and tamed by a crown of golden leaves. Gone is the opulent wild

---

12   The brothers had also planned the expedition in the *Cypria*.
13   For the phrase see *Iliad* 3.70, 91, 285; 7.350, 400–401; 22.114. Paris offers to return Helen's property at *Iliad* 7.362–364. Herodotus, *Histories* 1.3, notes that the Greeks sought not only Helen but also reparations for her abduction.

mane of the Spartan queen. In her place the film audience now sees a pale and uneasy bride, made anxious by the stares and whispers of the Trojan matrons who watch her as she passes. As in the epic tradition, Helen's nervous demeanor suggests that she fears the censure of the women of Troy, for her relationship with Paris is not legitimate. In the *Iliad*, Helen tells Aphrodite that the Trojan women will reproach her if she joins Paris in bed.[14] While Helen looks tense and uncomfortable, Paris is beaming.

The scene shifts to the royal palace, where King Priam awaits the return of his sons. When Paris introduces Helen, her eyes lowered in shyness and respect, Priam inquires archly: "Helen of Sparta?" Paris quickly corrects him: "Helen of Troy." As in the epic tradition, a magnanimous and fatherly Priam accepts Helen without question or blame and welcomes her into his now doomed city. In the *Iliad*, Priam expressly refuses to hold Helen responsible for the war with the Greeks and always treats her with tenderness and even admiration; he blames the gods, not Helen, for the war (3.164–165). So Helen's entry into Troy with all its pomp becomes, as it were, the first strike of the Greeks, since her beauty overwhelms the Trojans and weakens their resolve to send her back. This scene will be echoed later in the film by the fateful entry of the Trojan Horse, also accompanied by a celebration of the unwitting townspeople. The moment of her transition from "Helen of Sparta" to "Helen of Troy" signals the destruction of her adopted city. Tellingly, it is none other than Paris who makes this explicit with his words to Priam.

The remainder of the film finds Helen securely behind the walls of Troy, where she also remains in the *Iliad*. Since the *Iliad* focuses primarily on the war itself and in particular on the quarrel between Agamemnon and Achilles in its final year, Helen appears only in several scenes in Book 3 and briefly in Books 6 and 24. Her name is mentioned several times, especially in the earlier books, in connection with the war's causes.[15] Helen's name is first cited in Book 2 as the motivation for destruction and warfare. She is mentioned twice as the direct cause of the deaths of many Greeks "far from their homeland" in Troy when the goddess Hera rouses Athena (161–162), who in turn rouses Odysseus (177–178), to motivate the Greeks to stay in Troy and fight rather than to grant the Trojans the glory of victory and the custody of "Helen of Argos."[16] Later in the same book, Helen is again mentioned twice as the

14 Helen worries about criticism at *Iliad* 3.411–412.
15 *Iliad* 2.161, 177, 356, 590; 4.19, 174; 7.350, 401; 9.339; 11.125; 19.325; 22.114.
16 "Argos" here refers to the general area of the Argolid plain, where Mycenae was located. Sparta is further south in Laconia.

sole reason the Greeks want to retaliate against the Trojans for "the struggles and groans" they have undergone on her behalf. The old counselor Nestor urges the army to pay back the Trojans for their suffering "on Helen's account" (356), and Menelaus is described as the one Greek who most strongly desires revenge against the Trojans because of his agony "over Helen" (590).[17] This verbal emphasis on Helen's accountability for the war in the early part of the *Iliad* corresponds to her prominence as the driving motivation of the plot in the first part of *Troy*.

Helen first appears as a character in Book 3 of the *Iliad*, and her conspicuous presence pervades much of the action in that book, which offers a kind of "flashback" to events that occurred before the war began and long before the start of the *Iliad*. Several of the adventures recorded in the *Cypria* are consistent with what we learn from the *Iliad*. Book 3 restages an earlier time by "reintroducing" Helen and the theme of her adulterous love affair with Paris for the purposes of "narrative integration."[18] At the beginning of the book, Paris, glamorously light-armed and attired in a leopard-skin, struts out from the Trojan ranks and challenges the best of the Greeks to fight him (16–20). Much to his consternation, Menelaus accepts his dare, knowing that he can easily defeat the inexperienced Paris in combat and achieve his vengeance (21–29). Although Paris is struck with fear (30–37), he agrees to face Menelaus in a duel whose outcome will end the conflict for both sides (67–75). The idea that the two men principally involved in the dispute over Helen would work out their claims in a separate and decisive battle belongs to an earlier narrative time frame and suggests the immediate aftereffects of Helen's flight from Sparta.

High above the Trojan plain, Helen is in the great hall of the palace weaving a tapestry with scenes from the war being fought "on account of herself" (125–128). From this very first image of her and throughout the *Iliad*, Helen is one of the few characters who has a sense of the larger narrative scope and purpose of the war, which is being fought, as she later tells Hector, "so that hereafter we may be subjects of song for the

---

17   On the association of Helen with violent conflict and death in the *Iliad* see Robert Emmet Meagher, *The Meaning of Helen: In Search of an Ancient Icon* (Wauconda: Bolchazy-Carducci, 2002), 29–33 (first published as *Helen: Myth, Legend, and the Culture of Misogyny* [New York: Continuum, 1995]).

18   Gregory Nagy, *Homeric Questions* (Austin: University of Texas Press, 1996), 78–79, discusses how different themes from the narrative tradition about the Trojan War are integrated into the early part of the *Iliad*.

people of the future."[19] Helen's tapestry, like the *Iliad* and even like *Troy*, is intended to be a record of the heroic trials suffered by Greeks and Trojans in the war started and waged because of her: "The work at the loom mirrors her life."[20] The goddess Iris, disguised as a Trojan woman, approaches Helen and urges her to go to the ramparts to watch the fight in which she will be the prize (130–138). Helen, suddenly filled with nostalgia for Menelaus and her home in Sparta, goes to the wall at the city gates, weeping softly (139–142). As here, an air of melancholy and regret clings to Helen in each of her appearances in the *Iliad*. In Book 3 in particular she is constantly looking back on her past and vividly drawing it into her present. This emotional characterization of Helen serves to bridge the time between the first flush of excitement inherent in the romantic events of the *Cypria* and the guilty self-awareness she feels as the *casus belli* several years later in the martial narrative of the *Iliad*.

At the tower she finds Priam and several of the Trojan elders, who whisper together about the ineffably beautiful but dangerous and ruinous woman in their midst (154–160). Here the epic offers a single specific detail about Helen's appearance, observed by the elders: "She seems strikingly like the immortal goddesses in her look" (158). Priam now greets her with affection, calling her his "dear child" as he asks her to name the various Greek leaders who are assembled beneath his city walls (161–170). The fact that Priam is unfamiliar with the Greek warriors and has to have them identified again suggests an earlier time long before the events of the *Iliad*, when the warring armies first encountered each other on the battlefield. Helen responds with similar fondness and respect for Priam, whom she calls her "dear father-in-law" (172). Yet the sight of her fellow Greeks overwhelms her with shame and self-recrimination, and she expresses her vehement wish that she had died before she left her home and family and sailed away with Paris (173–175). Nevertheless she acquiesces to Priam's request and points out Agamemnon, Odysseus, and Ajax (177–235). During the catalogue, Helen's emotions are again aroused when she fails to see her two brothers Castor and Polydeuces on the battlefield. She quickly explains their absence by surmising that they must feel humiliation over her dishonorable behavior (236–242). No one in the *Iliad* ever directly criticizes Helen except herself, and this she does with exquisite finesse and

19   *Iliad* 6.357–358. On Helen's consciousness of her literary afterlife see Mihoko Suzuki, *Metamorphoses of Helen: Authority, Difference, and the Epic* (Ithaca: Cornell University Press, 1989; rpt. 1992), 40–41.

20   Quoted from Paolo Vivante, *Homer* (New Haven: Yale University Press, 1985), 86.

severity every time she appears.[21] Helen's ability to express her pain so candidly affords her "an inner depth that projects her beyond the occasion and lets us see her as a character removed from time and space."[22] Helen's harsh self-blame together with her anxiety for her brothers highlights the epic's attribution of accountability for the war solely to her.

The duel between Paris and Menelaus is inconclusive: Menelaus is clearly the victor, but Paris is rescued from his opponent's grasp by the goddess Aphrodite and set safely down in the bedroom he shares with Helen (325–382). The power of Aphrodite here parallels her prominence in the *Cypria*. Just as she had brought Paris and Helen together in Sparta, she will now unite them again in Troy. Aphrodite finds Helen on the ramparts and appears to her disguised as an old woman whom Helen loved dearly long ago in Sparta (383–389). She urges Helen to join Paris in bed, describing his radiant charm (390–394). Helen's grim present gives way to her romantic past when a beloved figure from her former home reveals to her a captivating image of Paris as he must have appeared to her at Sparta.[23] But Helen shakes off the nostalgic mirage when she recognizes Aphrodite through her disguise (395–398), then delivers a tart and impertinent rejoinder (399–412). The bitter tone of Helen's reproach is similar to her earlier self-recriminations. Helen is condemning her own susceptibility to the erotic temptation embodied by Aphrodite.[24] "Why don't you go sit beside Paris . . . coddle him and protect him . . . Not me . . . my pain just never ends" (406–412). In that moment, however, Aphrodite asserts her divinity with a stark threat: if Helen disobeys her, "I will utterly hate you as much as I strikingly love you now" (415). Helen shudders but does as she is told. She goes quietly, unseen, just as she had left Sparta under the irresistible force of the goddess.

In their bedroom, Helen turns her disgust and scorn on Paris. Yet she also demonstrates her emotional indecision as she confronts the misery of the present war and relives the erotic adventures they had shared in the past. Averting her eyes, Helen tells Paris she wishes Menelaus had killed him on the plain (427–433), then retracts her words and urges him not to fight again "or else you'll be killed" (434–436). But Paris is

---

21   Helen reproaches herself at *Iliad* 3.161–180, 241–242; 6.342–368; 24.761–775.

22   Quoted from Vivante, *Homer*, 90.

23   On the blurring of past and present in this scene see Vivante, *Homer*, 94.

24   Helen's connection to Aphrodite, a daughter of Zeus, is highlighted in this scene by the use of two epithets to describe Helen's divine paternity: "Helen, born from Zeus" (418) and "Helen, daughter of aegis-holding Zeus" (426). On this scene see also Paul Friedrich, *The Meaning of Aphrodite* (Chicago: University of Chicago Press, 1978), 59–61.

well versed in giving a sweet reply that deflects any reproach or resent-
ment.[25] After he answers Helen with soft words, acknowledging and
soothing her anger, he leads her to bed with a seductive invitation that
again brings the past immediately into the present: "Never before has
love so filled my senses, not even the first time when I took you from
lovely Sparta and sailed away . . . as I now love you, and sweet desire
takes hold of me" (437–446). Gone are thoughts of her previous
husband and home as Helen again chooses Paris. At the end of Book 3,
their lovemaking fuses past and present into a single moment and
impresses both upon the narrative of the *Iliad*.

As noted above, much of the first part of *Troy* presents material from
Book 3 of the *Iliad* that also appears in the *Cypria*. The film echoes the
epic impulse for narrative flashback when Paris and Helen are in their
bedroom in Troy the night before the Greek fleet arrives. The film
portrays Helen as conscious of her culpability for the war even as the
audience is aware that power-hungry Agamemnon only uses her as a
pretext. As she gazes out over the sea at night, there is a somber expression of dread on her face. "They're coming for me," she whispers. When
Helen acknowledges the coming war, Paris impetuously suggests that
they run away together, just as he did once before in Sparta. Helen
answers sadly: "But this is your home," and Paris counters: "You left
your home for me." There follows a conversation that could have taken
place between them back in Sparta. "Sparta was never my home," Helen
says, ignoring the literary tradition of Helen's inheritance of that kingdom from Tyndareus, her father.[26] "My parents sent me there when
I was sixteen to marry Menelaus." In contrast to the Helen of the *Iliad*,
the film's Helen never feels any longing for her ex-husband and family
since she does not even consider Sparta her home. (*Troy* also ignores
Hermione, Helen and Menelaus' daughter. Helen mentions leaving her
child at *Iliad* 3.174–175.) But even in the face of Helen's gloominess,
Paris remains naïvely optimistic, indulging in a pastoral fantasy that
recalls his days as a shepherd on Mt. Ida: "We'll live off the land!" While
Paris is idealistic and impractical, Helen is fatalistic, knowing that
Menelaus will demand the ultimate retribution from him. "You're very
young, my love," she tells him wearily. This is the only reference in
the film to an age difference between Helen and Paris. Although never
explicitly stated in the epic tradition, an age gap is suggested by the

---

25 Compare Paris' smooth and disarming reply to Hector's reproach at *Iliad* 3.58–75.
26 The sources for this paternity, e.g. Hyginus, *Fabulae* 78, are significantly later than
the *Iliad*.

different stages of social maturity evinced by their characters. Paris is consistently depicted as a reckless young playboy, in contrast to his more serious and domestically minded elder brother Hector. This scene of the film suggests a social and emotional break between Helen and Paris that diminishes the initial optimism of their romance.

The next scene is set in the great hall of Priam, where the Trojans meet in a council of war. Paris, who still believes the war is "a dispute between two men," rashly declares: "I will challenge Menelaus for the right to Helen. The winner will take her home. The loser will burn before night-fall." As in the *Iliad*, Paris initiates the duel, although in the film he challenges his rival directly. That evening in the palace courtyard, Paris explains to Priam how much he loves Helen as the two of them sit before a golden statue of Aphrodite.[27] Like Paris, Priam considers the war to be about Helen: "I suppose fighting for love makes more sense," he tells his young son. The film portrays the similarity between Paris and Priam in their naïve belief in Troy's invincibility. Hector, a greater realist, is aware that Agamemnon has come for power and will stop at nothing short of total dominion over Troy. Even Andromache, Hector's wife, agrees with him: "Fifty thousand Greeks did not cross the sea for the Spartan queen."

But Helen still thinks she can sway the outcome of the war. In the next scene, Hector finds her running through the shadowy courtyard, covered in dark veils. When he catches her, Helen begins to weep: "I saw them burning on the pyres . . . it's my fault . . . All those widows, I still hear them screaming . . . their husbands died because I'm here." Her guilt and remorse in this scene are consistent with her characterization in the *Iliad*, but the film takes Helen one step further. "I'm going down to the ships. I'm giving myself back to Menelaus," she declares. Hector, the realist, stops her romantic and useless impulse to give herself up when it is too late: "This is about power, not love." Helen is realistic, however, about Paris' chances in the duel: "Menelaus will kill him. I won't let that happen." Hector assures her that it is Paris' decision to fight, but Helen is not satisfied: "I can't ask anyone to fight for me. I am no longer Queen of Sparta." Hector stresses that her transformation from Spartan to Trojan is irrevocable: "You're a princess of Troy now, and my brother needs you tonight." Helen nods obediently and returns to Paris.

This scene evokes the meeting between Hector and Helen in the *Iliad* (6.313–368), although it takes place at a more critical moment. In the

---

27   The statue appears to be a likeness of the Auxerre Kore in the Louvre, an early archaic limestone figure dating to ca. 640 B.C.

epic, Hector goes to the house of Paris and Helen to rouse Paris back to war after the thwarted duel with Menelaus. He finds Paris fondling his weapons while Helen sits nearby directing the work of her handmaidens. Hector scolds his brother for his idleness, and Paris answers with his characteristic charm and cheerfulness. Then Helen addresses Hector, reproaching herself in bitter terms and wishing she had been "swept away" before coming to Troy, an echo of her earlier words to Priam. She agrees with Hector about Paris' shortcomings, citing his "unhinged senses," and invites Hector to rest a while from the labor of battle, "caused by me, bitch that I am, and the madness of Paris" (354–356). Helen continues to take responsibility for starting the war. Hector replies warmly but asks her to direct Paris back to the field. In the *Iliad*, Hector responds to Helen with gentleness and in terms of close familiarity, suggesting a natural sympathy between them.[28] The film version of their meeting exaggerates Helen's emotions for dramatic effect and sets it at a more crucial juncture; it also adds a remarkable stroke when Hector sends her back to Paris, thereby mirroring the command of Aphrodite in Book 3 of the *Iliad*.

In *Troy*, however, the duel between Paris and Menelaus assumes very different contours. The camera flies from the Trojan ramparts over the armies assembled on each side. Menelaus reproaches Paris for abusing his hospitality and stealing his wife "in the middle of the night," but Paris answers blithely: "The sun was shining when your wife left you," confirming Helen's willing participation in their affair. Above on the wall, Helen, dressed in shimmering white as in Book 3 of the *Iliad*, looks anxious but smiles at Paris when he looks up at her. Priam calls to her warmly, as he does in the epic: "Helen, sit with me." On the field, Paris challenges Menelaus: "Let us fight our own battle. The winner takes Helen home." Menelaus knows she is watching and wants to prove his valor, so he asks Agamemnon to let him kill "the little peacock." Agamemnon is clear about his plan to seize Troy: "I did not come here for your pretty wife. I came here for Troy." But he agrees to let his brother avenge his honor first, so Menelaus accepts Paris' challenge. Amid sounds of Agamemnon's evil laughter and Helen's fearful gasps, Menelaus easily knocks Paris down, slashes the younger man's thigh, and holds a sword to his throat. In the *Iliad*, Paris was saved from death at this moment by Aphrodite, but in the film Paris crawls back to the Trojan ranks and cowers at the feet of Hector. Menelaus, frustrated, turns his face to the ramparts and bellows at Helen: "Is this what you left me for?" Agamemnon uses the broken pact to launch the attack as

28   On the affection between Helen and Hector see Vivante, *Homer*, 55–56.

Menelaus lunges for Paris: "Fight me, you coward!" But Hector steps forward to shield his brother with his body and kills Menelaus. As he protects Paris from certain death, Hector again assumes the function of Aphrodite. A close-up of Helen's face shows her weeping in relief.

The death of Menelaus midway through the film has elicited much dismay and criticism from viewers, since the Greek epic tradition records that Menelaus retrieves Helen after the fall of Troy and takes her back to Sparta, where they resume their lives together.[29] Yet the removal of his character at this point has a strong motivation: it effectively erases Helen's function as the reason for the war and reinforces one of the film's major themes, that the true cause of the war is Agamemnon's outrageous greed for power. As Odysseus wryly informs Agamemnon in council soon after his brother's funeral: "The men believe we came here for Menelaus' wife. He won't be needing her anymore." The loss of Menelaus also serves to diminish the dramatic necessity for Helen's character in the film. The romance between Helen and Paris begins to lose its centrality to the plot, which now transfers its romantic focus to the more complex relationship between Achilles and Briseis.

After the duel, Helen is sewing the wound in Paris' thigh as they sit on their bed together. The tending of his wound may recall the story of the Trojan nymph Oenone, Paris' unhappy first wife, who was gifted with the power of healing.[30] Paris abandoned her when he went to Sparta for Helen; at the end of the Trojan War, a jealous Oenone refuses to heal Paris' arrow wound, which soon proves lethal. In this scene in the film, Paris is so ashamed that he cannot even look at Helen and seems to detach himself from her and their fateful bond: "You think I'm a coward. I am a coward. I knew he would kill me. You were watching . . . my father . . . my brother . . . all of Troy. Shame didn't matter. I gave up my pride, my honor, just to live." Helen tries to console him: "For love. You challenged a great warrior – that took courage." Helen attempts to remind Paris of their love and, in effect, to remain relevant to the plot, but Paris is visibly moving away from her and toward some new purpose. She begs him: "I don't want a hero. I want a man I can grow old with." Paris is silent and stony-faced, and his glum expression suggests he would rather be a hero. Modern film

29   The recovery of Helen by Menelaus is told in the lost epic *Iliou Persis* (*The Sack of Troy*), summarized by Proclus. Menelaus and Helen are in their palace at Sparta in Book 4 of the *Odyssey*.

30   The story of Oenone is most vividly told by Parthenius in his *Erotika Pathemata* (*Sentimental Love Stories*) 4.

demands that its flawed male protagonists somehow find redemption, and it is no surprise to the audience that Paris later is seen practicing his archery. Although nothing in the *Iliad* suggests an obvious dissolution of the romance between Helen and Paris, the film reflects the overall reduction of its importance in the epic even as it intensifies its focus on Achilles.

Our few remaining glimpses of Helen in *Troy* continue the diminution of her importance and point to her conversion to iconic status. Before Achilles meets Hector in hand-to-hand combat, a shot from within the walls of Troy shows us Hector waiting for the gate to open. The camera pulls back to frame Hector from Helen's point of view. Hector turns to look at her as she stands watching him in perfect stillness, veiled in ethereal white like a ghost. She lowers her eyes in sadness, as if to acknowledge her culpability for his imminent death. On the ramparts, Andromache turns away and collapses against the wall. Helen runs to her and embraces her while Hector is slain by Achilles. At Hector's funeral, a wide-angle shot reveals three women seated high on a dais: Andromache in the center, flanked by Briseis and Helen. All three are dressed in black. There is an ominous image of Helen holding Astyanax, the small child of Hector and Andromache, who in the epic tradition is doomed to die after the fall of Troy.[31] In each of these appearances, Helen is a harbinger of destruction, a sinister spirit of death.

The funeral scene in *Troy* evokes the final moments of the *Iliad*. At Hector's funeral in Book 24, three royal women are also present, but they deliver mournful speeches to commemorate Hector. After the laments of his wife and mother, Helen addresses Hector; this is her last appearance in the *Iliad*. As in Books 3 and 6, Helen reproaches herself and wishes she had died before coming to Troy (762–764). She recalls Hector's constant kindness and courtesy to her during her years in Troy even when others among her Trojan in-laws justifiably blamed her for their woes (765–772).[32] Helen's comments about Hector correspond to the tenderness of their exchange in Book 6, when even Hector recognized how much she loves him (6.360). Now, however, Helen acknowledges her precarious position in Troy and ends

31   The death of Astyanax, whom the Greeks throw from the walls of Troy, is eerily foreshadowed in the lament of Andromache at *Iliad* 24.734–738. The event itself is recorded in the *Iliou Persis* and reappears in Euripides' *The Trojan Women*.

32   Helen observes: "It is now the twentieth year since I left my country" (*Iliad* 24.765–766). This may be an exaggeration, as the ten-year interval before the war is nowhere else mentioned in the *Iliad*.

her speech bemoaning her lack of friends: "everyone shudders at me."[33] Like Helen in the film, the Helen of the *Iliad* manifests herself to others as an evil omen, and she knows it.

The last section of *Troy* covers events recorded in other lost works from the Greek epic cycle. Picking up after the end of the *Iliad*, a short epic called the *Little Iliad* introduces the famous tale of the Trojan Horse and briefly describes its entry into Troy. An even shorter epic, the *Iliou Persis*, provides a few more details for the story of the wooden horse. In this version, the Trojans are suspicious and discuss what to do about the horse before deciding that it is a divine gift; thinking they are delivered from the war, they take the horse inside the city amidst great celebrations. *Troy* stages the entry of the Trojan Horse according to this epic tradition but also offers a visual recapitulation of Helen's entrance into the city. As before, a flying camera follows the progress of the horse as it rolls into Troy, surrounded by jubilant citizens. The similarity between the two scenes suggests a symbolic equation of the two events: the arrival of Helen in Troy marks the beginning of the city's downfall, just as the entry of the horse signals its final destruction. On a balcony above a broad piazza, Paris and Helen are watching the people but engage in a rather icy exchange. Paris, who earlier argued that the horse should be burned, is disgusted by the revelry so soon after Hector's funeral: "Look at them. You'd think their prince had never died." Helen responds with her customary pragmatism: "You're their prince now. Make your brother proud." Paris does not look at her but stares straight ahead. The moment emphasizes Paris' anger over the death of his brother in order to set up the film's climax. Paris will avenge Hector by killing Achilles with his arrows and thereby redeem himself after his cowardice in the duel with Menelaus. But this new motivation for Paris leaves Helen increasingly on the sidelines as the film draws to a close. The war is no longer about Helen, and neither is *Troy*.

The final sequence focuses almost entirely on the romantic and ultimately tragic reunion of Achilles and Briseis in the middle of the burning royal palace. Agamemnon has tried to seize Briseis, but she kills him with a dramatic stab to the neck. Like the death of Menelaus, the death of Agamemnon at Troy is contrary to the Greek literary tradition but justified by cinematic necessity.[34] Since the film consistently

---

33   *Iliad* 24.773–775. Compare Helen's description of herself as "chilling" at 6.344 and Achilles' words about her at 19.325: "Helen, who makes us shudder."

34   The death of Agamemnon at the hands of his wife Clytemnestra on his return to Mycenae was told in the lost epic *Nostoi* (*The Returns*), summarized by Proclus, and, most famously, in Aeschylus' tragedy *Agamemnon*.

portrays Agamemnon's ruthless greed for power as the real cause of the Trojan War, his spectacular death in the city he came to destroy affirms the modern ideal that evil is always punished. Yet one final moment presents an image of Helen as an icon both blameworthy and utterly untouchable. In a rush to save a few Trojans from the ruined city, Helen and Paris head for a secret tunnel under the palace. The newly valiant Paris urges Helen to escape without him, telling her he will stay in the city. Helen replies: "The city is dead. They're burning it to the ground." But Paris is conscious of his duty and even questions the value of their love: "How could you love me if I ran now?" She begs him not to leave her, but Paris offers her a wan assurance: "We will be together again, in this world or the next . . . we will be together." In modern cinematic terms, Paris' promise points to a lack of resolution in their relationship. His words also evoke a foreboding sense of the afterlife. According to the *Little Iliad*, Paris was already dead when the city was sacked and Helen left Troy. In the film Paris is stating the obvious, that they will only see each other again in the land of the dead. As the city blazes all around them, the last image the audience sees of Helen is her disappearing figure, holding a torch.

CHAPTER TEN

Briseis in Homer, Ovid, and *Troy*

Alena Allen

Briseis, the captive slave girl of Homer's *Iliad* and the cause of Achilles' quarrel with Agamemnon, becomes the principal heroine of Petersen's *Troy*. Her romance with Achilles eclipses even that of Paris and Helen, the legendary cause of the Trojan war. Briseis and Andromache, the wife of Hector, are the first female characters we see in the royal palace of Troy after Hector and Paris return from Sparta; they greet Briseis as their "beloved cousin." Her visual prominence and narrative importance as a member of the Trojan royal family give Briseis the ability to speak with power and authority throughout the film. As Trojan royalty, she is a far more formidable prize than the Briseis of the *Iliad*, whom Achilles captured while raiding an outlying town in the Troad. Moreover, in the film she is a priestess of Apollo. She wears white to signal her virginity, and Priam notes in her first scene that she is a source of disappointment to all the noble bachelors in Troy.

As shocking as the Briseis of *Troy* may seem to anyone familiar with classical mythology, this is far from the first time that her character has been expanded. A provocative literary change already occurred in the first century B.C. In his *Heroides*, a series of fictional love letters written by heroic women of myth, the Roman poet Ovid composed a letter that he imagines Briseis wrote to Achilles while a captive in Agamemnon's camp. She reinterprets the anger of Achilles and the entire Trojan War from her personal point of view.

Along with her prominence as Trojan royalty and her centrality in the film as Achilles' love object, *Troy* combines the character of Briseis with other female characters from the Greek tradition. Through her presentation as a priestess, the film fuses Briseis with Cassandra, the prophetess and daughter of Queen Hecuba and King Priam. After she is captured by Achilles' men in the temple of Apollo, the film's Briseis confronts Achilles with such fearless demeanor that he falls in love with her. Seeing Achilles caught by romantic love evokes the memory of yet another Trojan princess, Polyxena, whom Achilles desired and who was later sacrificed on his tomb. But the most unexpected turn comes at the conclusion of the film. Briseis stabs and kills Agamemnon, thus assuming the role of Clytemnestra, Agamemnon's vengeful wife. Although Briseis hardly appears in the *Iliad*, her significance is evident. Her seizure by Agamemnon begins his quarrel with Achilles and propels the entire plot. The prominence of Briseis implicit in the *Iliad* becomes explicit in the *Heroides* when Briseis tells her own story. She becomes even more prominent in *Troy* because she propels the plot through her words and deeds.

1. *Briseis in the* Iliad

The few appearances of Briseis in the *Iliad* are expanded by her associations with other female characters. During her speech over the dead body of Patroclus in Book 19, her only words in the epic, Briseis restates words spoken by Andromache to Hector in Book 6 and anticipates the laments that Hecuba, Helen, and Andromache will speak over the body of Hector in Book 24. Such verbal echoes make Briseis part of the larger story of women's losses and sorrows as consequences of war. This technique of verbal echoes enhances Briseis' presence in the *Iliad* despite her few appearances:

> the traditional nature of Homeric poetry allows this figure of Briseis to evoke such other figures as Helen and Andromache, thereby bringing additional richness to the scenes in which she appears . . . Briseis actually evokes multiple paradigms – prize, girl, wife, widow, and captive – because of a multiformity of traditions associated with her.[1]

In the *Iliad*, Briseis speaks only once and appears only two other times. In Book 1, she is mentioned as Achilles' prize, the counterpart of Aga-

---

1   Casey Dué, *Homeric Variations on a Lament by Briseis* (Lanham: Rowman and Littlefield, 2002), 22.

memnon's prize Chryseis. When Achilles urges Agamemnon to return Chryseis to her father in order to end Apollo's plague, Agamemnon angrily tells him: "But I shall take the fair-cheeked Briseis, your prize, I myself going to your shelter, that you may learn well how much greater I am than you" (184–186). Briseis and Chryseis are linked throughout Book 1 by being described as "fair-cheeked" (143, 184, 323, 369), "girls" (98, 111, 275, 298, 336), and "prizes" (118, 185). Briseis first appears in person when Agamemnon's heralds come to lead her away. She leaves Achilles "all unwilling" (348). Achilles then withdraws from his companions and, weeping, goes to sit by the sea.

   Briseis does not come to our attention again until Agamemnon's ambassadors come to Achilles in Book 9. At this point the Trojans have beaten the Greeks back to their ships because Achilles has refused to fight. Achilles is still furious with Agamemnon and rejects all apologies and ransom gifts, even the return of Briseis despite Agamemnon's oath that he never entered her bed. Achilles explains how important Briseis is to him:

> All the other prizes of honour he gave the great men and the princes
> are held fast by them, but from me alone of all the Achaians
> he has taken and keeps the bride of my heart. Let him lie beside her
> and be happy. Yet why must the Argives fight with the Trojans?
> And why was it the son of Atreus assembled and led here
> these people? Was it not for the sake of lovely-haired Helen?
> Are the sons of Atreus alone among mortal men the ones
> who love their wives? Since any who is a good man, and careful,
> loves her who is his own and cares for her, even as I now
> loved this one from my heart, though it was my spear that won her.[2]

Achilles makes it clear that he loves Briseis, that he regards her as a wife, and that his relationship with her is as important as that of Menelaus with Helen. By connecting Briseis with Helen, the cause of the Trojan War, Achilles elevates Briseis and the importance of their relationship. This link between Briseis and Helen is further strengthened by her own speech in Book 19. Agamemnon has returned Briseis to Achilles' camp, along with many gifts. Briseis now appears for the first time since Book 1. Now she speaks her only direct words in the *Iliad*, a lament over the dead body of Patroclus. She echoes what

---

2   *Iliad* 9.334–343; quoted from the translation by Richmond Lattimore, *The Iliad of Homer* (Chicago: University of Chicago Press, 1951; several rpts.), 207.

Andromache said earlier in Book 6, but her words also foreshadow those that Andromache, Helen, and Hecuba will speak over the body of Hector in Book 24. As she stands over the body of Patroclus, she exclaims:

> Patroklos, far most pleasing to my heart in its sorrows,
> I left you here alive when I went away from the shelter,
> but now I come back, lord of the people, to find you have fallen.
> So evil in my life takes over from evil forever.
> The husband on whom my father and honoured mother bestowed me
> I saw before my city lying torn with the sharp bronze,
> and my three brothers, whom a single mother bore with me
> and who were close to me, all went on one day to destruction.
> And yet you would not let me, when swift Achilleus had cut down
> my husband, and sacked the city of godlike Mynes, you would not
> let me sorrow, but said you would make me godlike Achilleus'
> wedded lawful wife, that you would take me back in the ships
> to Phthia, and formalize my marriage among the Myrmidons.
> Therefore I weep your death without ceasing. You were kind always.[3]

Briseis displays the formulaic characteristics of other female laments in Homer. She reveals that she had had a husband and three brothers whom Achilles killed. All her memories of dead loved ones and of her city come back to her. It is no wonder that she refers to endless evil in her life. Her hopes for a new life, married to Achilles and back in Phthia with him and Patroclus, are now shattered. When Briseis speaks about her family killed by Achilles, she echoes the words spoken by Andromache to Hector:

> I have no father, no honoured mother.
> It was brilliant Achilleus who slew my father . . .
> And they who were my seven brothers in the great house all went
> upon a single day down into the house of the death god,
> for swift-footed brilliant Achilleus slaughtered all of them . . .[4]

Through the echo of their words, Homer emphasizes the losses of both women and the plight of all women who suffer the consequences of war even on opposite sides. He connects Briseis to the most stable and loving couple in the *Iliad*, Hector and Andromache.

---

3   *Iliad* 19.287–300; Lattimore, *The Iliad of Homer*, 399–400.
4   *Iliad* 6.413–414 and 421–423; Lattimore, *The Iliad of Homer*, 164.

The lament of Briseis over Patroclus also foreshadows the laments of Hecuba, Helen, and Andromache over the body of Hector in Book 24. Just as Briseis, a captive in a foreign camp, had looked on Patroclus as a protector, so Helen says to dead Hector: "I mourn for you in sorrow of heart and mourn myself also / and my ill luck. There was no other in all the wide Troad / who was kind to me, and my friend; all others shrank when they saw me."[5] Each woman – Helen, too – thanks the man she had turned to for protection in a foreign camp.

The formulaic words of Briseis, Helen, Andromache, and Hecuba over the dead join them, as do their similar life stories. These women are "objects of love and singers of lament." They are also linked by their past and future life experiences: "Each has survived or will survive the loss of a husband in battle; each has been, is, or will be a captive woman."[6] In this way Homer expands Briseis' presence in and importance for the *Iliad*.

2. Briseis in Ovid's *Heroides*

Centuries after the Homeric epics, laments came to be expressed in the elegiac verses of Roman love poetry. Propertius and Ovid turn to Homeric heroines such as Andromache and Briseis as examples of lamenting lovers. Propertius repeatedly uses Homeric heroes and heroines as models for himself and his beloved Cynthia. In his evocation of Homeric characters, he elevates the importance of his own love affair. Propertius likens himself to Achilles and Hector and equates Cynthia with Briseis and Andromache. As he evokes these Homeric figures in the context of love elegy, Propertius moves his vision of the *Iliad* from war story to love story and presents himself as a warrior in the battles of love:

> Think of Achilles when he left Briseis' arms –
> Did Phrygians stop running from his spear?
> Or when fierce Hector rose from Andromache's bed
> Didn't Mycenae's ships fear battle?
> Those heroes could demolish barriers and fleets;
> In my field I'm fierce Hector and Achilles.[7]

5   *Iliad* 24.772–775; Lattimore, *The Iliad of Homer*, 495.
6   Both quotations are from Dué, *Homeric Variations on a Lament by Briseis*, 5.
7   Propertius, *Elegies* 2.22A.29–34; quoted from Propertius, *The Poems*, tr. Guy Lee (Oxford: Oxford University Press, 1994; rpt. 1999), 52.

By contrast, Ovid has Briseis speak for herself. In the *Heroides*, Ovid creates fictional letters that famous heroines from earlier literature could have sent to their lovers. In the third of these letters, Briseis writes to Achilles while a captive in Agamemnon's camp. Ovid portrays her longing for Achilles but at the same time angry with him for giving her up. Ovid gives Briseis a chance to present her side of the story: "The writer of each letter receives the long deferred chance to occupy center stage, possessing, as every letter writer does, the opportunity to narrate her own story from her own subjective perspective."[8] Ovid uses verbal techniques similar to Homer's in order to link his Briseis to the one familiar to his readers from the *Iliad*. Ovid's Briseis quotes directly from Homer when she lists the ransom gifts Agamemnon offered to Achilles. Several times in her letter she also echoes words spoken in the *Iliad* by Briseis and Andromache, and she refers to specific scenes of the *Iliad*.

Ovid's Briseis begins her letter with an apology for her bad Greek and refers to herself as writing in a "barbarian hand" (2).[9] Ironically, it is clear that she has no lack of education because she composes her letter in elegant elegiac couplets – in Latin, not Greek, of course. Then she turns to her main concern: "If a small complaint about you, my lord and master, is not wrong, then I lodge, respecting my lord and master, a small complaint" (5–6). After this tentative and rather tortured beginning, in which she sounds none too certain about her status relative to Achilles, she goes on to ask him why he let Agamemnon's men take her away so quickly and without any resistance. This question leads her to a literal translation of the list of ransom gifts that Agamemnon had promised Achilles in Book 9 of the *Iliad*. Ovid's Briseis continues with further complaints and pleads with Achilles to take her back. She also restates words from Briseis' lament in Homer (43–50):

> Or can it be that grim fate presses upon wretched men,
> and that once our misfortunes begin no gentler hour comes?
> I saw the city walls of Lyrnessus ravaged by your army,
> my father's land, and I its ornament.
> I saw three men share death, as they shared their birth,
> three whose mother was equally theirs, and mine.
> I saw my husband lavish upon the bloody earth his magnificent ruin,
> his chest heaving, livid with his life's blood.

---

8   Sara H. Lindheim, *Mail and Female: Epistolary Narrative and Desire in Ovid's* Heroides (Madison: University of Wisconsin Press, 2003), 31.

9   Translations of Ovid's *Heroides* are taken from Florence Verducci, *Ovid's Toyshop of the Heart: Epistulae Heroidum* (Princeton: Princeton University Press, 1985), 88–97.

Ovid, with his vivid Roman sensibilities, adds more blood to Briseis' description. But he extends her lament to include words spoken in the *Iliad* by Andromache. Briseis goes on to write: "For so many lost to me I still had only you in recompense; you were my master, you my husband, you my brother" (51–52). These words are almost a direct quotation of Andromache in her plea to Hector in Book 6. Ovid has Briseis refashion her own words from the *Iliad* as well as those of Andromache's.

Having based his Briseis on Homer's, Ovid goes on to remake her thoroughly. The new Briseis is acutely aware of her status as a prize of war and thus a slave. After her first tentative complaint to Achilles she brings up another regarding his rejection of the ransom and her return to him: "How have I deserved to be held so cheap, Achilles? Where has your love sped so quickly and lightly away?" (41–42). These words echo nothing in Homer. Briseis' is now the voice of a frustrated Roman elegiac lover.

When she has finished complaining, Briseis shifts to a call for action. She asks Achilles why he is delaying and urges him to take up his weapons and to return to the battle, but to take her back first! She contrasts the Achilles she imagines loitering around his ships with the martial Achilles she once knew. Before his quarrel with Agamemnon, she writes, Achilles respected the savagery of battle and the fame won in warfare: "Once it was not security, but brilliant deeds that pleased you, and the renown won in warfare was something you found sweet" (121–122). Briseis is upholding the epic warrior's code of conduct, which values strength, valor, killing, and action on the battlefield. Now she imagines that Achilles has changed and finds that war is dangerous and staying in bed is safer. She envisions him lounging around his camp even as she writes (115–122):

> And if someone should ask why you refuse to fight?
> Battle is fatiguing: you prefer the recreation of the zither, the night
>   and love.
> War is dangerous, too. It is safer to lie in bed, clasping a girl,
> strumming the Thracian lyre with your finger tips,
> than to take up the shield and the sharp-edged sword
> and endure the weight of the helmet that flattens your curls.
> Once it was not security, but brilliant deeds that pleased you,
> and the renown won in warfare was something you found sweet.

Briseis' description of Achilles recalls the *Iliad*, when the ambassadors from Agamemnon come to his camp and find him playing a lyre with

Patroclus beside him (9.186 and 190). In addition, Ovid evokes Homer's image of Paris.[10] There we see Paris strutting out onto the battlefield wearing a leopard skin over his shoulders and rattling his javelins. Once he sees Menelaus, however, he shrinks back among his companions. His brother Hector, disgusted at his cowardice, chides him (3.52–55):

> And now you would not stand up against warlike Menelaos?
> Thus you would learn of the man whose blossoming wife you
>   have taken.
> The lyre would not help you then, nor the favours of Aphrodite,
> nor your locks, when you rolled in the dust, nor all your beauty.

Briseis also imagines Achilles in bed with a girl. This is exactly what Paris does in the *Iliad* after Aphrodite whisks him off the battlefield and puts him in his bedroom with Helen. Paris brushes off all thoughts of war and becomes possessed by love. He tells Helen (3.441–446):

> Come, then, rather let us go to bed and turn to love-making.
> Never before as now has passion enmeshed my senses,
> not when I took you the first time from Lakedaimon the lovely
> and caught you up and carried you away in seafaring vessels,
> and lay with you in the bed of love on the island Kranae,
> not even then, as now, did I love you and sweet desire seize me.[11]

Paris is something of a failure in warfare. He freely admits to Helen that Menelaus subdued him in battle. He redirects his energy from the battle-field to the bedroom. In the erotic arena he demonstrates that he is a man of action. The sheer power of Paris' passion overcomes Helen's resistance. It is just such a passion that Ovid's Briseis longs to elicit from Achilles. Briseis remembers his lust for battle and his lust for her, but his former desire is gone. Now he is withdrawn, lingering, sulking beside his ships. Throughout her letter, Briseis contrasts the Achilles he once was with the Achilles she now imagines. He is a man of action neither on the field of battle nor on the field of love; he is no longer swift-footed, but demonstrates "slow delay" (183).

From the personal perspective of Ovid's Briseis, the Trojan War is really all about love, primarily her own love affair with Achilles but also

---

10   *P. Ovidii Nasonis Epistulae Heroidum 1–3*, ed. Alessandro Barchiesi (Florence: Le Monnier, 1992), 237, notes but does not explain the comparison between Achilles in *Heroides* 3 and Paris in Book 3 of the *Iliad*.
11   *Iliad* 3.441–446; Lattimore, *The Iliad of Homer*, 112.

the love affair between Paris and Helen, which she implicitly compares with her own. Ovid sets these two relationships alongside each other and so elevates the importance of Briseis. Ovid uses Propertius' tactic, equating his relationship with Cynthia to those of Briseis with Achilles and Andromache with Hector.

3. Briseis in *Troy*

In Petersen's film, three pairs of lovers are prominent: Hector and Andromache, Paris and Helen, Achilles and Briseis. But as the film progresses, Petersen puts Briseis and her love affair with Achilles on center stage.

The centrality of Briseis becomes visually explicit as she appears in some thirteen scenes in contrast to her three in the *Iliad*, and she speaks far more lines than her counterpart in the *Heroides*. In the film, her character also echoes more heroines from classical literature than her counterparts in Homer and Ovid. The cinematic Briseis resonates with Cassandra, Polyxena, Clytemnestra, and even the goddess Athena, besides showing certain analogies to Helen and Andromache. As *Troy* progresses, Briseis becomes tightly linked with Achilles, the hero, and their love relationship turns into the most prominent one in the story.

In her first scene Briseis appears as a member of the Trojan royal family and in the white, virginal robes and veil of a priestess of Apollo. Although she had been neither in classical texts, her appearance here evokes memories of the virgins Cassandra and Polyxena, daughters of Priam and Hecuba. Polyxena is not mentioned in the *Iliad*, but Cassandra is mentioned twice. She is the most beautiful of Priam's daughters (13.365) and "a girl like Aphrodite the golden."[12] In her first scene in *Troy*, Briseis exhibits a youthful radiance and royal grace reminiscent of Cassandra.

Although Cassandra is not specifically portrayed as a priestess or prophetess in the *Iliad*, the Greek literary tradition does describe her as such, most memorably in Aeschylus' tragedy *Agamemnon*. This play tells the story of Agamemnon's return to Argos after his victory in the Trojan War. He arrives with Cassandra, whom he took as his prize after Troy fell. After Agamemnon goes into the palace, where his wife Clytemnestra will kill him, Cassandra has a vision from Apollo, god of prophecy, in which she sees her own and Agamemnon's blood

12   *Iliad* 24.699; Lattimore, *The Iliad of Homer*, 493.

being spilled in the palace. She explains to the chorus that Apollo gave her the power of divination but cursed her by making no one believe her prophecies when she rejected his advances. Her prophecies prove to be correct when Clytemnestra stands proudly over the dead bodies of both Agamemnon and Cassandra. The other Trojan princess whom Briseis recalls in *Troy* is Polyxena, Cassandra's younger sister. In his play *Hecuba*, Euripides shows the former queen of Troy, her daughters Polyxena and Cassandra, and the other Trojan women as captives of the Greeks after the fall of Troy. The Greek army has resolved to sacrifice Polyxena on the tomb of Achilles. When Polyxena agrees to go to her death without resistance, the chorus of Trojan women prisoners observe: "Nobility – how deep and terrible its stamp / on those wellborn. And when actions enhance / a good name, it wins still greater dignity."[13] In *Troy*, the royal priestess Briseis demonstrates Polyxena's kind of bravery. Achilles, judging her by her bearing when he first encounters her, comments that she must be royalty. Briseis' regal and priestly status, her courage under attack, and her beauty all evoke Cassandra and Polyxena. When we see her veiled in the temple of Apollo in the act of making offerings to the god, Briseis becomes firmly identified as his priestess. Because the god she worships is Apollo, Briseis also suggests Chryseis, the daughter of Apollo's priest in the *Iliad*.

Briseis' next scene takes place in the hut of Achilles on the beach. Eudorus, Achilles' chief lieutenant, informs him that she is being presented to him as his prize for taking Apollo's temple and the beach. This story is consistent with the epic tradition. In the *Iliad*, Briseis says in her lament over Patroclus that she was seized by the Greeks when her city fell and that Patroclus comforted her at that time. In several scenes in the film, Achilles himself attempts to comfort her. In contrast to the Briseis of Homer and Ovid, the film's Briseis is defiant. She speaks with the authority of a princess in language reflecting her elite education. She commands Achilles' attention. She meets him as an equal, even if, at the moment, she is his captive.

This first encounter sets the tone for the developing relationship between Briseis and Achilles, a tone very different from that of the mourning Briseis in the *Iliad* or the complaining Briseis of Ovid. Immediately Briseis questions Achilles' actions, dismisses him as a killer, and tells him that Apollo, her god, will take his vengeance. Achilles, who struck

---

13   *Hecuba* 379–381; quoted from *Euripides: Hecuba*, tr. Janet Lembke and Kenneth J. Reckford (New York: Oxford University Press, 1991), 41 (translators' lines 406–409).

the head off the statue of Apollo, responds that he thinks Apollo is afraid of him and that he, Achilles, knows more about the gods than priests. Briseis goes on to ask him what he wants in Troy, stating correctly that she does not think he came for the Spartan queen. He answers: "I want what all men want. I just want it more." This could sound like a threat to a captive woman, but Briseis does not display any fear. She expresses self-confidence and courage by daring to question her captor. When Eudorus tells Achilles that Agamemnon requests his presence, Achilles reassures Briseis: "You don't need to fear me, girl. You are the only Trojan who can say that."

Achilles and Agamemnon argue about who deserves credit for taking the Trojan beach that day. The scene reminds viewers of Book 1 of the *Iliad*, when Agamemnon and Achilles quarrel over the return of Chryseis to her father. In compensation for his loss of Chryseis, Agamemnon takes Briseis away from Achilles. In *Troy*, as the argument between Agamemnon and Achilles is heating up, Agamemnon has his men bring in Briseis, whom they have seized from Achilles' tent. When Achilles, enraged by Agamemnon's insult, reaches for his sword, Briseis calls out: "Stop! Too many men have died today. If killing is your only talent, that is your curse. I don't want anyone dying for me." In the *Iliad*, Achilles draws his sword to kill Agamemnon but is stopped by the goddess Athena. Briseis takes over her function in *Troy*. By assuming the role of a goddess who can control a hero like Achilles, Briseis is empowered even further. Agamemnon recognizes this when he comments, sarcastically: "Mighty Achilles silenced by a slave girl." But as Athena is the goddess of wisdom, Briseis demonstrates in her conversations with Achilles that she possesses wisdom beyond her years.

As in the *Iliad*, after his loss of Briseis Achilles withdraws from fighting and will have nothing to do with Agamemnon. The Greeks are pushed back to their ships within a day after his withdrawal, and, in contrast to the epic tradition, Hector kills Menelaus, Agamemnon's brother. Agamemnon realizes that he cannot take Troy without Achilles and agrees to return Briseis, whom he swears he has not touched. But he has already handed her over to his soldiers: "They deserve some amusement after today." In the following scene Briseis is resisting Agamemnon's men, who are about to torture her; their shouts of "Trojan whore" suggest that they also intend to rape her. But Achilles charges in unexpectedly and vanquishes all who have their hands upon Briseis. He sweeps her up into his arms and carries her off. Although nothing like this happens in the *Iliad*, it was just such an Achilles for whom Ovid's Briseis yearned, a heroic lover who would come to her defense and take her back triumphantly for himself.

After Achilles carries Briseis back to his hut, he attempts to comfort her by cleansing her wounds and offering her food, but she initially pushes him away. They engage in a dialogue in which each challenges the other's values and life choices. Questioning and listening, Briseis encourages Achilles to reflect about the gods and their relationship to mankind. Achilles tells Briseis: "The gods envy us. They envy us because we're mortal; because any moment might be our last. Everything is more beautiful because we're doomed. You will never be lovelier than you are now. We will never be here again." Briseis realizes that Achilles is not merely a killing machine. This thoughtful Achilles recalls the Achilles in Book 9 of the *Iliad*, who gives Odysseus, Agamemnon's ambassador, several reasons for not returning to battle and talks about fate: "Fate is the same for the man who holds back, the same if he fights hard. / We are all held in a single honour, the brave with the weaklings."[14] He refers to Briseis as being like his wife (341–343) and intends to return home the next morning (357–363). In the film, Briseis understands how intelligent and articulate Achilles is: "I thought you were a dumb brute. I could have forgiven a dumb brute." What she does not yet realize is that, although she cannot forgive him for his killings, she can fall in love with him.

In the *Iliad*, Briseis and Achilles are never shown together in love. Achilles states that he loves her from his heart and that she is dear to him (9.341–343). Ovid's Briseis dreams about the kind of man she wants Achilles to be but does not reveal the emotional quality of their relationship. In both texts Briseis wishes to marry Achilles and return with him to Phthia, but in neither text does she disclose her feelings about their relationship beyond stating that she wants it to continue. *Troy* makes the intensity of the emotional bond between Briseis and Achilles visually explicit. Briseis and Achilles modify their life choices as a result of their growing love affair.

Later that night, Briseis puts a knife to Achilles' throat while he is asleep. The vengeful priestess in her has decided to put an end to his life before he slays more men. He awakens and tells her to go ahead and kill him. But she hesitates, and erotic passion overcomes them both. This is what Ovid's Briseis had been dreaming of during her long confinement in Agamemnon's camp. That night in bed, Achilles and

---

14   *Iliad* 9.318–319; Lattimore, *The Iliad of Homer*, 206.

Briseis discuss leaving Troy together. Briseis acts as the catalyst for Achilles' change of heart. He ceases to talk about immortality gained through glory in warfare. The next morning Achilles decides to go home, presumably taking Briseis with him and living out a happy but unremembered life with her. This is the wish of both Homer's and Ovid's Briseis. Achilles tells his men to prepare their ships.

Unfortunately the Trojans attack at dawn, the ships begin to burn, Patroclus is killed, and any thoughts of home are finished. When Eudorus returns with Patroclus' body, Achilles in his fury attacks him. Briseis attempts to restrain Achilles, but he seizes her by the throat and throws her to the ground. The violence of his response shows us that his anger now turns Achilles into the killer he was before. Consumed with wrath, he tosses Briseis aside like a slave.

Before Achilles goes out to meet Hector the next day, Briseis pleads with him not to fight her cousin. When he returns dragging Hector's body behind his chariot, she sits in his hut sobbing; later she asks him: "You've lost your cousin, now you've taken mine. When does it end?" Achilles replies: "It never ends." That night Priam comes to retrieve Hector's body, and Achilles tells Briseis that she is free to go, too. She hesitates. Achilles gives her the necklace which his mother Thetis gave him before he sailed to Troy. Thetis told him of his choice: a long happy life at home or a short glorious life of war. Achilles later gave the necklace to his beloved cousin Patroclus. Now he gives it to Briseis. The necklace becomes a visual symbol of the equality between Briseis and Patroclus in Achilles' affection and a sign of his love. As Briseis leaves with Priam, she looks back at Achilles as if she were none too certain that she wants to go. This scene of Briseis leaving Achilles' camp is reminiscent of the scene in the *Iliad* of Briseis leaving Achilles "all unwilling" for Agamemnon.[15]

Back in Troy, Briseis appears at the funeral of Hector, sitting with Andromache and Helen. Contrary to the funeral scene in the *Iliad*, none of the women in the film speak. We last see Briseis during the fall of the city. With Troy in flames, Briseis, wearing Achilles' necklace, runs through the citadel calling out for Andromache and Paris. Finally, she kneels in prayer before a statue of Apollo. This image strongly reconnects her with Cassandra. In the Epic Cycle, Agamemnon takes Cassandra as his prize after the fall of Troy. In the film, Agamemnon appears and seizes Briseis, threatening her with just such a future. But at this point Briseis assumes her final role change. She stabs

---

15   *Iliad* 1.348; Lattimore, *The Iliad of Homer*, 68.

Agamemnon. With this act she anticipates Clytemnestra's killing of Agamemnon. She also fulfills Achilles' threat to Agamemnon earlier in the film that he would see Agamemnon dead. As she strikes Agamemnon, Briseis uses Achilles's sweeping arm motion when he killed Boagrius and Hector. Achilles, who has been searching all over Troy for Briseis to save her yet again, rushes in and watches her kill Agamemnon. He kills the two soldiers holding on to her and picks her up in his arms as he did before. Then he desired her for himself. But by now he knows that he is doomed. (He has already sent his men home.) This time he is saving Briseis for herself so that she may survive without him. Achilles was not able to save Patroclus, but he saves Briseis.

At this moment Paris appears and kills Achilles with his arrows. In no ancient version of the story is Briseis present at Achilles' death. In the *Iliad*, the last mention of Achilles and Briseis is when they go to sleep together in Achilles' hut (24.675–676). In *Troy*, Achilles and Briseis have the opportunity to bid each other farewell before Achilles dies and Briseis flees from Troy with Paris. Achilles tells her: "You gave me peace in a lifetime of war," and then he tells her to go. There is no information in the classical tradition that reveals what happens to Briseis after Achilles' death. *Troy* implies that she will be among the few survivors whom Aeneas leads to a new home.

The final scene contains all the elements of Briseis' character expansion present throughout *Troy*. A princess, she runs through the burning city looking for her royal cousins. A priestess, she takes refuge at an altar before the statue of Apollo. There she assumes the role of Agamemnon's vengeful wife. Most importantly, she resumes her central role as a romantic heroine when she and Achilles reaffirm their love before he dies. *Troy* presents the character of Briseis in a ring composition. In her first three scenes she is seen as princess, priestess, and prize, in particular evoking Cassandra. In the middle of the film she is a romantic heroine in her love affair with Achilles, fulfilling the convention of films set in the ancient world whose heroine redeems the hero with her love.[16] She is not able to save Achilles from being a killer, but she is able to make him understand love. The ring of images closes in the final scene when Briseis is seized by Agamemnon. Here she is again princess, priestess, and prize, once more recalling Cassandra.

By killing Agamemnon Briseis achieves the equivalent of an *aristeia*, the Homeric hero's ideal of proving himself the best in battle. At the

---

16 Cf. Derek Elley, *The Epic Film: Myth and History* (London: Routledge and Kegan Paul, 1984), 88–89.

same time she asserts herself as a romantic Ovidian heroine. When she is reunited with a dying Achilles for a brief romantic moment, Achilles comforts her one last time. He cradles her face, wipes away her tears, and tells her: "It's all right." Time seems to stop during their last kiss. Their final moment in each other's arms recalls to us his words to her on their first night together: "Any moment may be our last. You will never be lovelier than you are now. We will never be here again." As Briseis flees the burning city, Achilles' words have become true.[17]

17   I would like to thank Susan Shapiro and Gregory Daugherty for their suggestions and especially Monica Cyrino for helpful comments.

CHAPTER ELEVEN

Troy and Memorials of War

Frederick Ahl

"How huge a hurricane rolled out of savage Mycenae all over
Ida's plains, what forces of destiny drove into conflict
Europe and Asia, two distinct spheres: there's a tale that the whole world's
Heard, even someone in some remote land where the waves of the Ocean's
Far side crash, or who lives in a southern zone, beyond sunlight's
Central and hottest of sky's five zones, in complete isolation."

So speaks Ilioneus, spokesman for a huge delegation that the Trojan prince Aeneas sends to the Latins when he puts ashore in Italy.[1] His claim is an outrageous exaggeration at the dramatic date of its utterance, some seven years after the fall of Troy. It was an exaggeration at the time Virgil wrote the lines, well over a millennium after the traditional date of Troy's fall in the late twelfth century B.C. And it continued to be an exaggeration for the millennium and a half following Virgil's death. Finally, however, time has leveled the arc of Ilioneus' hyperbole. Now, in the European tradition, the Trojan War is indeed the universally known (insofar as anything is universally known) archetypal clash of different cultures (or barbarisms) set within the overlapping boundaries of myth and history.[2]

1   Virgil, *Aeneid* 7.222–227; my translation.
2   Gilbert Achcar, *The Clash of Barbarisms: September 11 and the Making of the New World Disorder*, tr. Peter Drucker (New York: Monthly Review Press, 2002), marks a useful counterpoise to the traditional (and age-old) tendency to view conflicts in terms of civilization vs. barbarism, familiar vs. foreign, good vs. evil.

Over the millennia, wars have become increasingly universalized and have been fought with armies larger than the total human population of the twelfth century B.C. Poets seeking to describe the increasing brutality of war have often used the Trojan War as a vehicle for conveying their responses to the conflicts among nations in their own day, just as they have used the now less familiar mythic war between the sons of Oedipus for the throne of Thebes as their archetype of civil war. The Roman epic poet Statius gives perhaps the clearest explanation why. He wrote his *Thebaid* shortly after the "Year of the Four Emperors" (A.D. 69), which brought a new ruling house to power in a sea of blood.[3] Statius declares that he will set the House of Oedipus as the limit for his tale since he lacks the necessary skill and boldness to treat the wars of his own day. My story, he says (*Thebaid* 1.17–40), will be of a fight between two contenders for an impoverished kingdom, a fight in which all human decency failed; I haven't yet the capacity, he continues, to tell of a larger struggle whose goal is to bring the wealth and resources of the whole world under one man's control – the sort of struggle, he hints, that the Roman Empire has just undergone. He makes his parallel between the mythic civil war at Thebes and the Roman civil wars with great (and prudent) obliquity. For his current emperor, Domitian, the notorious last ruler of the Flavian dynasty, was a tyrant with well-demonstrated powers of retaliation against dissident writers. Myth, then, served as a useful allegory for current history, as it always has done.

War is often portrayed as an allegorical figure. Before the great monotheistic religions came to reframe European thinking, War was represented as the ultimate allegory, a God: Ares to the Greeks, Mars to the Romans. He was human in general appearance, one of us, in a way, all of us at certain moments, but indestructible: God in armor, angry, fierce, on occasions capable of justice but always cruel. And his name was assigned in the heavens to the planet that looks red, the color of blood. Here is how Statius imagines the palace of Mars in the *Thebaid* when Jupiter's emissary, Mercury, arrives to tell him to start the long-delayed conflict between the rival brothers and the cities they are dragging into battle behind them:

> Here is where Mars likes to live; and Mercury, looking upon it, shudders
> on seeing the lifeless forests and savage estate high upon Haemus before

---

3   I discuss this work in greater detail in "Statius' *Thebaid*: A Reconsideration," *Aufstieg und Niedergang der römischen Welt*, II.32.5 (1986), 2803–2912.

him. Forces of Rage in a thousand shapes encircle parapets plated with steel, a threshold, worn thin by gates of steel. Steel pillars support the roof's dead weight. It's a place light flees from in terror: sun's rays are not reflected by its surface but hurled back. Its hard glare gives starlight a foreboding quality. The castle's garrison seems right enough: Mindless Aggression leaps from the main gate; nearby stands Blind Atrocity. Anger glows red; terror stands blood-drained, Treachery hides its weapons. Civil War grips steel cutting two ways. In the great court, Threats quarrel noisily, and at the heart, grimmest of all, Manliness stands. Rage seems beatific sitting next to Death who, armed to the teeth, displays a face blushing with gore. The only blood in its shrines is blood of war, its lamps gleam fires raped from cities burned. Captured nations decorate temple pediments – here and there are fragments of panels from smashed city gates, warships and empty chariots, heads they've crushed. Every form of violence, every kind of wound is found. Only the screams of pain, perhaps, find no expression here. You see the Master everywhere; his face shows no trace of anything but brute; for that is how the metal-working God depicted him with heavenly skill. Not yet had Vulcan seen Mars' softer side exposed in sunlight – the adulterer penalized for his disgusting truce for lust in a bed of linked chain.

As Mercury, from more peaceful Maenalus, begins to hunt the king of all these shrines, Earth trembles, the Hebrus thunders as he stops his water's flow. Herds that crop the valley, herds used in war, gallop off in a lather over the grasslands – a sign *he* is returning. The gates of the holy place, sealed with eternal adamant, spring open as he nears the entrance with his team, handsome in German blood, bringing a change of color to the fields around. Forests and deep-drifting snow make way for his advance. Behind comes the plunder, the weeping prisoners. They are exhausted, but Bellona, dark soul of war, drives them, yoked like beasts, and hurries them with long-pointed spear, hands drenched in gore. Mercury, child of Arcadian Cyllene, froze at what he saw and, sorrowing, bowed his head. Even our father Jupiter himself would be awed, if he'd ever get close. He'd forget all his threats. He'd not order *this*.[4]

Jupiter, the poet suggests, orders Mars into action because he has never seen, close up, the full identity of the forces he is unleashing in the name of what he thinks is justice, and in response to the prayers of a single individual which were not even directed to him but to the demonic powers of Hell. Mars was a lord of hosts, if you will, but a lord of hosts whose power was limited by the presence of other gods, Sexual Love, for example, who, as Aphrodite or Venus, could seduce War from his rampage of killing long enough to bear him a child named Harmony.

4   *Thebaid* 7.32–85; my translation.

Yet War was the face of only the agent of mayhem, not of his victims. When monotheism merged the features of all gods into God, it deprived even war's divine agent of an individual face in our imagination and understanding. It became easier to depersonalize not only War but also War's victims. War became "intervention," "police action," and so forth; dead humans were "casualties," mutilated bodies were part of "collateral damage." The large number of people who, in the words of another Roman epic poet, Lucan, found war useful to their interests (*multis utile bellum*; *Pharsalia* 1.182.) didn't want War's brutal face staring out at us. It might deter us. They preferred to lure us with Glory and Fatherland, as American writer Dalton Trumbo showed in *Johnny Got His Gun*, a novel first published on the eve of World War II.

War as we know it in contemporary American usage, with its capitalized W, is hardly any longer an allegorical figure because it is something wholly "other." It happens "there," not "here," as in the World War I song that is the departure point for Trumbo's novel. While many thousands of native speakers of English know what war is from military service in other lands, few of us know war in quite the way the rest of the world knows it: as the destruction of one's home and homeland, the breakdown of law and civil order, the tramp of foreign soldiers across one's soil, the maiming of tens of thousands, even millions, the rape, the pillage, the bitter humiliation of defeat or the bitter-sweetness of victory won at an appalling price. What is missing from our culture on the whole is the ability to imagine the horrors that the victor can visit on the vanquished. Czeslaw Milosz gives us a graphic representation of the utter breakdown of what one thinks of as normal order in *The Captive Mind*.[5] One of the most poignant descriptions of the sack of another people's city is in Aeschylus' tragedy *Agamemnon*, delivered by a character who never saw it, who never even left home, and who is not male: Clytemnestra, waiting for her husband's return, determined to kill him. But Aeschylus and his audience knew the story only too well. Their own city, Athens, had been sacked by the Persians less than fifty years earlier and was still being rebuilt as he wrote. And he is clearly reminding the Athenians that they ought to be able to imagine the horrors their imperial democracy is now visiting on other cities.

In the cinema, the English-speaking world dominates the representation of wars real, mythical, and fantastical: England, last invaded (officially) in 1066 and free from civil war for about three centuries; the U.S., last

5   Czeslaw Milosz, *The Captive Mind*, tr. Jane Zielonko (1953; rpt. New York: Vintage, 1990), 25–53.

invaded in 1812 (by the English) and free from civil war for about a century and a half. So English-speakers ought to profit from what others have to say about war. They know things that we are fortunate enough not to know and arrogant enough to think not worth knowing. Wolfgang Petersen has shown, over the years, that he has something to tell us about war. Now, with *Troy*, he has given us a film in which war is presented in some unusual and disturbing ways and in which echoes of other wars, both mythical and historical, resonate. While the film is not an allegory of War, it is carefully structured to suggest that what is presented in *Troy* can be understood as a comment on other wars.

A German director must approach such topics just as cautiously as Statius did, since the scars of World War II are still raw upon its victims and their descendants even after two generations. Indeed, when his producers sought to make the war film that established Petersen's international fame as a director, *Das Boot* (1981), based on Lothar-Günther Buchheim's 1973 bestseller, they had to negotiate for film rights already held by an American who was, in the words of one of the producers, preparing to convert it into "an anti-German underwater Western."[6] For we live in a culture which inclines to extreme over-simplification. There are only "good guys" and "bad guys," "heroes" and "villains." And the appalling atrocities of World War II have made it hard for the world outside to see the Germans of the period as anything but villains: Churchill's collectivized "The Hun." Thus Petersen's achievement in this German-language film, whose protagonist is based on a real U-Boat commander, is remarkable, if unsettling.

American and British naval-action films of the 1940s and 1950s show as little sympathy for U-Boats and their commanders as other war films do for the Gestapo, and with good reason. The U-Boats took a staggering toll of Allied lives and shipping. They were the ruthless sea wolves, fearsome predators who might have turned the war in Germany's favor if the British had not broken their codes. Petersen, however, shows us that the predators were also the prey. They acquire faces; they become vulnerable; and it is the Royal Air Force that becomes the ruthlessly efficient and faceless foe of the submarine whose voyage we have accompanied. This is a very different image from that suggested in such English-language films as Guy Hamilton's *Battle of Britain* (1969), in which almost casually gallant pilots of Spitfires and Hurricanes achieve success against impossible odds, thanks to improvisation and individual

---

6   Wolfgang Petersen with Ulrich Greiwe, *"Ich liebe die grossen Geschichten": Vom "Tatort" bis nach Hollywood* (Cologne: Kiepenheuer and Witsch, 1997), 153–154.

daring rather than to careful management. The English and American mind has generally regarded efficiency as a particularly German quality. Petersen puts a human face on his sea wolf, meticulously separates him from the ugly ideology which has sent him into war, and grants him a heroism comparable with that accorded American naval commanders in English-language films about the war in the Pacific. The difference is that Petersen's commander and his vessel are eventually destroyed by the faceless efficiency of the RAF, swooping down for the kill as Japanese Zeros do in American films. And *Das Boot* informs us about the huge losses sustained by German submarines in ships and personnel.

I can't say that I shed any tears for the crews who died in the U-Boats. Indeed, I could have wished that more had died sooner. But that is not the point. Germans paid a terrible price for acquiescence in that motto we also saw proclaimed on car bumpers in America during the Vietnam War, "My country, right or wrong": some twelve million dead, the destruction and partition of their homeland, and, for decades, the unspoken loss of the right to lament, and memorialize publicly, their fallen, as peoples have done in every age. The right to grieve for one's dead, regardless of what they have done, has been sacrosanct in most cultures. Most famously, it is a central issue in Sophocles' *Antigone*, in which Antigone, the sister of the dead warrior Polynices, insists on burying her brother even though she has heard a rumor that Creon, tyrant of Thebes, may have issued a decree banning such interment. I emphasize that she is acting upon a rumor since readers tend to overlook, first, that Antigone herself says so and, second, that Creon does not make his decree until after Antigone has buried her brother. Antigone's determined defiance conflates the rumor with the actual decree, which she is not on stage to hear. Although there has been no official decree banning Germany from honoring her dead in World War II, to honor them publicly is to run the risk of being seen by others as proclaiming the justice of their cause and as belittling the suffering of their victims. Similarly, Sophocles' Creon sees Antigone's lament for Polynices as her justification of Polynices' assault on his native Thebes at the head of foreign troops. In Creon's mind, honoring the dead Polynices is tantamount to dishonoring those who died righteously, defending their homeland. But this is not at all what Antigone appears to intend. In much the same way, although no official decree has been issued to that effect, the victims of Germany's aggression incline to assume that Germans have forfeited the right to memorialize their dead. The Germans, who sense this, have approached the issue more cautiously than Antigone did. For every culture must come to terms with its own past in its own way. When the U-Boat's musician sings to the crew, his song tells us that they, too, are humans. So does Petersen's film.

The German leadership and its followers not only made the Jewish people and millions of others victims of their dangerous national myth, but they also brought hideous destruction on millions of their own citizens who embraced their policies, endured them without resistance, or opposed them in their own ways. In a sense, Germany was the victim of a kind of suicidal Armageddon, which has recently found dark expression in Oliver Hirschbiegel's film *Der Untergang* (2004), a film whose English title (*Downfall*) does not adequately convey the eerie nature of a doomed world in which the motto "Death before dishonor" crumbles into death before one is dishonored. It is perhaps worth noting that Antigone's actions and Creon's refusal to give way also lead to suicides. There are more suicides in Sophocles' *Antigone* than in all the twenty-six plays attributed to Aeschylus and Euripides combined. But these suicides seem modest in comparison with the orgy of self-destruction in Hitler's bunker.

We still don't have the necessary distance to create an epic of World War II, much less of the twentieth century, the cruelest yet in human history. In Great Britain, there remain documents sensitive enough that Prime Minister Margaret Thatcher reclassified them as secret. Now they won't be available until all children born during World War II are dead. Further, political ideologies stopped Western writers from giving the Soviet Union a fair portion of credit for the Allied victory. And while we in the English-speaking world have justifiably demonized Hitler and Mussolini, we have also carefully reworked the images of our own political leaders of that era to make them champions of democracy which, in some cases, they were not. To take but a single example: the worth of inefficient democracies as opposed to allegedly efficient dictatorships was a matter of great political debate in the 1920s and 1930s. In 1930, Otto Forst de Battaglia edited a book of essays entitled *Dictatorship on its Trial.*[7] A photograph of Mussolini, who described democracy as "merely a verbal illusion for simple-minded folk," faced the title page. Winston Churchill, the writer of the Preface, declared that democracy had "invaded the Council Chamber [and] liquidated the prestige of the House of Commons." He went on to describe the United States as a "Limited Liability Dictatorship" and concluded: "The vote given to every

---

7   *Dictatorship on Its Trial,* ed. Otto Forst de Battaglia, tr. Huntley Paterson (London: Harrap, 1930).

one has been regarded as a trifle by many, and as a nuisance by many more." To his eternal credit, Albert Einstein wrote the shortest essay in *Dictatorship on its Trial*, which I cite in full: "Dictatorship means muzzles all around." The rest of the page is blank.

Most of all, though, the sheer scale of destruction in World War II paralyzes the mind: fifty million dead, almost global desolation of cities and communities. A young American tourist can be forgiven for not grasping the scale of what happened or even that it happened at all, since much of Europe has been, like Japan, rebuilt from rubble to riches in less than fifty years. In this sense, the fall of Rome's Western empire in the fifth century A.D. was much more devastating in the breadth and duration of its consequences despite the comparatively small number of casualties that accompanied it. But by the time we have all the materials necessary to tell the tale of World War II, popular culture will have so trivialized (and Americanized) most memories of the war in its efforts to accommodate the least discerning members of its audiences that truth will be a matter of indifference. Perhaps that is why Petersen, who has expressed his love for really big stories, went back to the classics for *Troy*, although the Greek and Latin authors had not been among his favorites when he read them as a schoolboy. Significantly, he makes this tale of war with a predominantly British cast and in English, not German. He is bringing his "take" on war to an audience that has never seen its own cities sacked and that increasingly inclines to view wars in terms of a simplistic opposition between "good" and "evil."

Probably the greatest difference between the ancient epic or tragic "hero" and the stereotypical modern "hero" is that the ancient hero is not invariably a "good guy." Nor are his opponents always "bad guys." With only one exception, there is no ancient epic of "good" versus "evil." In Greek antiquity, a hero is a man of divine descent who has much greater strength or power than most others around him. He may save his kingdom and his family from a tyrant, as Heracles does in Euripides' play *Heracles*, but then he goes mad and butchers his family. Yet he is still a "hero." Such a hero has much in common with the protagonist of the Western film, whose prowess at killing is his vice as much as his virtue.[8]

There have been far too many wars over the centuries for anyone to recall. American writer Kurt Vonnegut, who survived the Allied bomb-

---

8   On this cf. Martin M. Winkler, "Classical Mythology and the Western Film," *Comparative Literature Studies*, 22 (1985), 516–540, and "Homer's *Iliad* and John Ford's *The Searchers*," in *The Searchers: Essays and Reflections on John Ford's Classic Western*, ed. Arthur M. Eckstein and Peter Lehman (Detroit: Wayne State University Press, 2004), 145–170.

ing that annihilated Dresden, graphically depicted in his novel *Slaugh-terhouse Five*, proposed in *The Sirens of Titan* that all events between the birth of Christ and the present day be summarized as a "universal period of adjustment." And that's why myth is the mind's substitute for history. Myth is compact memory; it removes the framework of time that separates events in a historical narrative and allows them to collapse randomly like a scattered deck of cards, creating a new but asymmetrical pattern. The myth of Troy has come to define, and to be defined by, all subsequent wars. And because the Trojan War is mythic, it can be recalled in infinitely different ways and retold through all kinds of memories of wars, recent or remote. Indeed, the varying ancient traditions of the Trojan War suggest that even the earliest versions have merged several different conflicts into one. And with each new experience of the clash of cultures, the mythic model invites modification. As Andrew Erskine points out in his study of ancient treatments of the Trojan myth: "The meaning of the Trojan War changed constantly, adapting to time and place."[9] Most mythic narrators have personal reasons for telling their tale in a particular manner.[10]

The rewriting of myth isn't simply a matter of an author's preference for one predecessor's version over another's, as scholars tend to assume. Poets take, and politicians abuse, a freedom scholars don't have (or shouldn't have): the right to generate their own versions of myth. That's why we won't get any real sense of *Troy* if we play the classics teacher and "correct" Petersen's "errors," as if he were a wayward schoolboy, against the canonical version of Homer's *Iliad* or some handbook of mythology. Nor should we be deluded by a publisher who now markets a translation of the *Iliad* with the inscription "as seen in *Troy*" on the cover into believing that Petersen is simply translating Homeric epic into epic film. For *Troy* has a distinct touch of those ideas about war that we can see in *Das Boot*. It also has a great deal of Roman color. It is indebted to Virgil's *Aeneid* and Ovid's *Heroides* for some of its perspectives and characters, and there are also remarkable, if probably unintentional, refractions of Lucan.

Like Lucan, Petersen removes the entire divine apparatus of Greco-Roman heroic epic from *Troy*. Cuts, of course, have to be made when poetic epic is translated into an epic film. Unless one resorts to a miniseries,

9   Andrew Erskine, *Troy between Greece and Rome: Local Tradition and Imperial Power* (New York: Oxford University Press, 2001), 258.
10   I discuss some of these issues in "Homer, Vergil, and Complex Narrative Structures in Latin Epic: An Essay," *Illinois Classical Studies*, 14 (1989), 1–31.

as television directors have done, an epic film is closer in running time to a couple of the shorter Greek tragedies than to the recital time of the *Iliad* or *Aeneid*. A one-minute shot may be worth a thousand words of a novel since most novels present us with a largely self-contained world and provide the information the reader needs to understand all but the subtlest references. Ancient epic and tragic poets did nothing of the kind. They assumed (safely, on the whole) that their contemporary audiences and readers were familiar with the characters, cultures, and scenarios of Trojan or other myths. What individualized their own poetic treatments was the way they restructured their audiences' imagined prior "knowledge." Homer's Helen tells Telemachus, for instance, that she disclosed Odysseus' identity to no one after she recognized him as a spy in Troy. Hecuba, in Euripides' *Hecuba*, says that Helen told her and no one else about it. In the *Odyssey* there is no mention that Odysseus has children by the goddesses Calypso and Circe, whereas elsewhere in Greek literature we find numerous traces of other children, most notably of his son by Circe, Telegonus, who accidentally kills Odysseus and goes on to marry his father's widow, Penelope, while Telemachus marries his father's mistress, Circe. Thus Telemachus and Telegonus end up simultaneously as one another's stepfathers and stepsons. That, we know, is the plot of Sophocles' lost play *Odysseus Acanthoplex*.[11] In comparison with Sophocles, Petersen is downright modest in his modifications.

Petersen obviously faced a dilemma about what to exclude. Although he probably assumed that the largest segment of his audience would know little, if anything, about Troy, he had to be aware that he was addressing many who were familiar with the tale and that some of his reviewers would be classical scholars. Such critics tend to confuse deliberate change with ignorance, and dissatisfied reviews could and did discourage both some of the less and some of the more learned audiences from seeing the film. This was especially the case in the United States, where any film based on Greek myth is likely to be regarded either as too highbrow for ordinary tastes or as a witless travesty of the text it's based on. And it was the reviewers, not Hollywood, that failed the American public on *Troy*. While the preponderance of French, English, and German reviewers knew that Petersen had studied Latin and ancient Greek at school, the American press was generally negative and often downright dismissive, chiefly because, it was supposed, of Petersen's mishandled mythic detail.

11   For the fragments of this play see Dana Ferrin Sutton, *The Lost Sophocles* (Lanham: University Press of America, 1984), 90–94, and my discussion in *Sophocles' Oedipus: Evidence and Self-Conviction* (Ithaca: Cornell University Press, 1991), 229.

Petersen's trimming away of classical gods is not the result of ignorance but of choice, and of a choice governed at least as much by considerations of tone and focus as of time management. English-language films, after all, have a venerable tradition of representing Greek gods on screen. Several of Don Chaffey's Olympians in *Jason and the Argonauts* (1962) and those in Desmond Davis' *Clash of the Titans* (1981) were themselves the "gods" of British stage and screen.[12] But these deities, and the superb monsters Ray Harryhausen created for both productions, propel the films into the world of fantasy and science fiction. Petersen did not want echoes of these works in his film. Yet the Homeric gods do not vanish altogether. In numerous places Petersen, like Lucan, gives us a glimpse of what I would call the shadows of a divine presence. Achilles' mother Thetis is shown as woman in late middle age, wading in the sea and gathering shells that have an unreal, gem-like sparkle. She is not the eternally youthful sea-goddess of Homer who consults with Zeus and arranges for her son to be provided with divine armor. Petersen is reminding the more learned in his audience of Thetis' traditional godhood and also hinting that he is aware of what he has not included. And Achilles is not, as Greek myth sometimes suggests, immortal unless wounded in the only mortal part of his body, his heel. Petersen cleverly alludes to that tradition by having Achilles shot in the heel by Paris but actually killed by the arrows that strike him once he is down.

Aside from such allusions, there are no warring gods at all in the world of *Troy*, only unresponsive if abundant statuary in the city of Troy. Petersen does not have Apollo send plagues on the Greeks for their desecration of his shrine. He keeps the plague but suppresses the divine agent. When the Greeks feign their departure and leave the Wooden Horse behind, Priam is told not to get close to the Greek corpses lying there because they show signs of plague. The only "Judgment of Paris" is Paris' decision to smuggle Helen away on his vessel as he and Hector return home.[13] The Greek leaders, throughout, have little but contempt for the whole notion of religion. Only the occasional soldier, Briseis, and King Priam place any trust in the divine. Indeed, Priam's religiosity is ruinous for Troy. He makes a number of disastrous decisions based on what his seer tells him, among them that of bringing the

12   Cf. my "Classical Gods and the Demonic in Film," in *Classics and Cinema*, ed. Martin M. Winkler (London: Associated University Presses, 1991), 40–59.

13   Curiously, they leave from what the film identifies as the Port of Sparta. Either Petersen thought that a city in Laconia actually on the sea, such as Gythcion, would be too obscure to mention by name, or that no one would mind a Sparta moved a few dozen kilometers south. His Mycenae is also a coastal city. In Oliver Stone's *Alexander* (2004), this kind of cavalier geography sets Macedonian Pella on the coast and places Babylon in Persia.

Wooden Horse into Troy. Hector or Paris urge him not to take these steps in each instance, but neither challenges him when he persists. Priam routinely ignores the advice of his warrior generals.

Removal of the gods not only saves Petersen from the diminished illusion of reality which comes with representing gods as personages in film, but it also allows him to let the ultimately ruinous denouement of the film emerge from the complex interactions of his entire cast. Lucan did much the same in his Roman epic without gods. In what is perhaps his most famous line, he declares: "the conquering cause pleased the gods, but the conquered cause pleased Cato" (*Pharsalia* 1.128). Approval by Cato, the just human, carries more moral value than the approval of gods. Indeed, once gods are introduced as guiding and controlling forces, the winning side appears to have been granted divine approval and thus to be justified unless, like an Old Testament prophet, you suggest that the enemy's victory is God's way of punishing his special people for some transgression. Lucan's Cato is the only fully moral hero of ancient epic. Forst de Battaglia understood Lucan and his Cato to be major intellectual stumbling blocks in the case he was making for the desirability of dictatorship. The glamor of success and power, he argued, "makes the triumphant ideology accepted as their own by the vast majority. A victorious cause is pleasing not only to the gods, but also to the masses, and a difficulty overcome is approved by the Catos."[14] Lucan's Caesar restates his poet's editorial comment about the gods in a somewhat different way when he addresses his troops before their most critical battle in a civil war fought all over the Mediterranean: "The outcome will decide whether we are guilty or innocent. If we win we are innocent. If we lose we are guilty" (*Pharsalia* 7.259–260). He understands that no effective judicial mechanism exists for holding the victor to account. Two millennia later, there still is none.

But here Lucan and Petersen part company. For while Petersen has no gods, neither does he have an *immediate military victor*. And there's no whiff of a Cato. There isn't a right side or a wrong side in *Troy*. One side makes more tactical mistakes than the other because its leader won't take advice from his best general. And the most efficient killing machine on either side, Achilles, loses his life because he has started to exhibit compassion instead of cynical indifference. He succumbs to an impulse to save Briseis during the sack of Troy and dies at the hands of the only warrior in the film who shows cowardice, Paris.

14 *Dictatorship on its Trial,* 374.

Petersen demands the right to surprise us, to compel us to follow his *Troy*, not someone else's, not even Homer's. Part of the film's power lies in Petersen's refusal to confirm the more learned segment of his audience in its prior "knowledge" of the myth. In this he is exercising his artistic right to shape inherited myth, as writers of mythic texts from Homer to Beverley Cross, the well-read classicist who scripted both *Jason and the Argonauts* and *Clash of the Titans*, had done: to make us look at the world through his eyes and with his focus. He writes the myth as much as the myth writes him. Thus our "knowledge" that Helen will be taken home by Menelaus and that her sister Clytemnestra will kill or abet in the killing of Agamemnon on his return to Mycenae proves illusory. It is stripped away by Hector's killing of Menelaus and by Briseis' killing of Agamemnon. The single major Greek warrior Petersen allows to survive is Odysseus, whose voice provides the final narrative overlay. On the Trojan side, Hector is, apart from Priam, the only major casualty. Thus the killing of Menelaus makes the huge mobilization of troops by a negligent husband to retrieve his wife come to nothing, especially since Paris does not die. Agamemnon's death reduces the Greek triumph over Troy to a pointless imperial victory won for an already deceased monarch.

Troy seems to be telling us, as it refashions and trims the myth, that Agamemnon and Menelaus don't matter once the war is over. Even in ancient accounts, the Trojan War is the high point of their attainments. Return to Greece brings only death to Agamemnon and a prosperous but non-heroic life to Menelaus. Besides, Petersen needs to have some casualties of note in his film besides Patroclus, Hector, Achilles, and Ajax since he does not include most of Homer's extensive cast of warriors on either side. For Petersen does not leave Troy's destruction and Achilles' death out of his narrative, as the *Iliad* does. He seems more concerned with emphasizing something that is only the faintest of allusions in Homer: that in the world of mainstream epic the future lies with the conquered Trojans, not with the conquering Greeks. Hector's widow, Andromache, appears to escape with her son and to save herself from her usual slavery and him from his traditional death of being hurled from the walls of Troy. And there will be a Trojan, Aeneas, to ensure the generation of a New Troy in Italy – Rome.

The significance of Petersen's last-minute introduction of Aeneas must elude those unfamiliar with the myth and leave those familiar with it baffled. A youth is supporting at his side, rather than on his shoulders, an elderly, apparently unconscious man. Paris asks the youth who he is. The young man surprises us by telling Paris that he is Aeneas, thereby conveying the strange impression that these two cousins have never met previously, something rather anomalous in a script that places almost as much emphasis on relationships among cousins as on those among brothers. Petersen's Paris obviously knows who Aeneas is, even if he has not met him before. He even corrects Aeneas' pronunciation of his own name and gives him the symbolic Sword of Troy, which in his own hands had been a rather dysfunctional Excalibur. So, if Priam's observations about its power are correct (which does not necessarily go without saying), Troy will live on, provided that a Trojan wields it. This Arthurian touch suggests that Troy is an idea rather than a specific city in a precise location. Its current site has been devastated, and thousands of its faceless citizens have been killed. In short, this Trojan War is a far cry from Statius' image of War and its suffering victims. It is, rather, a testament to the validity of Caesar's cynical observation to his mutinous troops in Lucan's *Pharsalia* that "the human race lives for the benefit of a few" (*Pharsalia* 5.343) – a point which one could only wish were not just as true in the realm of *Realpolitik* today.

At this point we may want to reflect upon what drives the various princes to take part in the war. Agamemnon has an insatiable lust for power, which he advances by deploying others' desires and ambitions to his advantage. Petersen has given us a villain with no redeeming qualities at all and, sadly, with little depth. He is more like Aeschylus' Agamemnon than Homer's, although in Aeschylus' play the elders of Agamemnon's city are equally awed and shocked by his deeds and power. They respect him as much as they despise Aegisthus, the pompous idiot Clytemnestra replaces him with. Petersen's Achilles yearns for eternal fame and declines a fight only if he thinks the moment isn't quite right. He refrains from killing Hector when he has the chance, in his first action at the temple of Apollo, because he doesn't have the audience he needs to earn the greatest possible glory. This is a witty coincidence of interests for protagonist and director. It's far too early in the film to have the decisive duel! Petersen's foppish, selfish, and unthinking Paris has no desire for war at all but is, with occasional moments of conscience, prepared to have and keep Helen regardless of the larger consequences. Helen is the forlorn wife of a brutish husband prepared to run the risk of death just to escape him. Odysseus is an opportunist, last onto the beaches, deferential to authority to secure his advancement, yet curiously candid about his wiliness. Menelaus is the brutish unlovely husband prepared to recapture his wife at whatever cost. Patroclus wants to be able to share Achilles' glory. Briseis is the only prisoner of war, male or female, shown in the whole film. She is brutally treated by everyone except Achilles, but she is ready to strike back with a dagger when opportunity arises. Ajax just enjoys a fight. Priam engages in war because under the circumstances he can think of no alternative and because he loves his sons. And Hector, the family man, fights because his sense of honor and his respect for and obedience to his wrong-headed superstitious father compel him to go forth into what he knows will be a fatal duel with Achilles.

Notably absent from the Greeks' motives for war is any ideology or religion or the lust for gold or plunder. In a sense, as I have suggested, Troy itself is the idea. So to add any other ideology would be superfluous. Yet it is very hard to think of a war in which neither religious or political ideology on the one hand nor greed on the other have played a part. These absences alone make *Troy* a curiously unimpassioned oddity in the world's tales of war. We get only a rare glimpse of what makes Agamemnon's army of 50,000 interested in going to war – Eudorus' unquestioning but abstract loyalty to Achilles, for example.

The common soldier finds only one brief voice in Homer's *Iliad*, that of Thersites in Book 2. But it is at least an independent voice of dissent, however quickly it is pummeled into silence by Odysseus, the master of words, lies, and long narratives. While Homer and his successors include some anonymous deaths in their epics, they usually take time to name, and often to provide short biographies of, the lesser warriors who get cut down. They are not at all a faceless multitude, no collateral damage in the egotistical battles of princes and military officers. They are from different cities and cultures, sometimes, like Homer's Ethiopian Memnon, of different races. They have individualized armor and weapons which identify their origins or their claims to distinction, and they have parents who will lament their deaths. All this is gone in *Troy*. With few exceptions, Petersen's uniformed and helmeted combatants move into battle like the masked storm troopers of the *Star Wars* films. They have no individualized devices on their shields and no plumes on their helmets. Only Hector and Paris wear elaborate armor. We are thus lured into accepting their destruction as casually as if they were computer-generated, virtual beings in a video game – which is precisely what most of them are. And this is why *Troy* fails to convey a convincing "feel" of ancient epic in its battle scenes. In Statius' *Thebaid*, for instance, Jocasta, the mother of the two fighting brothers, goes to the camp of one, the exiled Polynices, but finds herself surrounded by helmeted soldiers and cannot tell which of them is her son. Tears spill through his visor as he comes up to her. And as he embraces her, he crushes her against the metal of his armor (*Thebaid* 7.470–559). In the *Iliad*, Hector's infant son is terrified by the plumes on his father's helmet (6.491–510). Petersen leaves his always plumeless Hector without even a helmet to terrify his son. The strong sense of the confusing and terrifying masks of war in Homer or Statius Petersen restricts to one incident. He shows us the masking nature of armor when what appears to be Achilles comes out to fight Hector. Petersen cleverly adapts his original so that no one unfamiliar with myth will realize that it isn't Achilles until Hector mortally wounds his adversary and pulls up his helmet to disclose Patroclus. In general, however, Petersen knows, and we know, that there aren't real people beneath most of the masks of his warring armies.

For this I fault him and the film very strongly. I find the indifference to the deaths of ordinary folk in *Troy* unsettling, especially since Petersen resolutely emphasizes the large armies arrayed on either side. Homer, in contrast, though he tells of a thousand ships, doesn't impress upon us the number of combatants. Since the *Iliad* identifies who is fighting whom and since the Greek and Trojan princes, unlike modern generals or heads of state, bear the brunt of the hand-to-hand combat themselves, war in Homer is not the kind in which ordinary people are losing their lives to advance the interests of the wealthy or powerful who stay far away from the front. Whatever the inequities of the ancient aristocracy, the mythic princes, like medieval knights, were expected to be in the front lines of battle themselves. Aristocratic privilege had its price. Petersen has placed Homer's warring noblemen in a context suggestive of modern soldiers, even if they are wearing ultimately retro combat fatigues and carry antiquish weapons. The chaotic melees of battle in Homer turn into some complex military tactics and maneuvers, though it's never made clear who has planned them. In short, Petersen takes what he did in *Das Boot* one step further. There he reversed the paradigm of the Anglo-American war film by depriving the Allied foe of its individual faces as he offered us his perspective on a German military unit. In *Troy*, he is more even-handed. He deprives the soldiers and civilians on both sides of their individual faces. The huge backdrop of computerized armies emphasizes that his focus is on the elite. The human race is living (and dying) for the benefit of the few who do not even live to reap those benefits. But there are only the sparsest hints of any brutal behavior toward ordinary troops or non-combatants. We see the butchered bodies of Apollo's priests, the violence against Briseis, and Achilles' brutal treatment of Hector's corpse. But we don't see Odysseus beating up Thersites or promising the spy Dolon his life and then having him killed. Nor do we see Achilles bringing human sacrifices to the funeral pyre of Patroclus. The Trojans commit no atrocities at all.

Troy stands in sharp contrast to one of the most puzzling of all war films, Robert Aldrich's *The Dirty Dozen* (1967), in which the Allies send twelve condemned criminals on a commando raid into occupied France. One of the Americans, a psychotic killer of "loose women," murders a German woman looking for her lover. Later, the commandos lock German officers and the women who have fled with them into a basement, pour gasoline through the vents, drop hand-grenades, and cremate them. I have never been sure what the producers thought we would make of this unconscionable atrocity. Are we to feel reassured because the surviving commandos will be let loose again on their own society? Similarly, in *Troy*, I am left bewildered by the curious isolation in which the warrior princes function. This is a sanitized epic that gives us a sanitized view of war. It is neither ancient-epic war nor modern war. Perhaps the idea of Troy is what really matters, though what that is remains unclear. Given the presence of Aeneas, it appears to be the survival of whatever Troy represents as an imperial reality in some other time and possibly some other place.

In casting Brad Pitt in the role of Achilles, Petersen gave us a mature man, not the often childlike youth of the *Iliad*. Achilles now is a warrior at the peak of his abilities, ready to make his play for eternal glory before age starts slowing him down, not as a rather pretty young man who had been dressed as a girl at a girls' school until lured into shedding his disguise by Odysseus. Petersen's Achilles is an experienced and cynical killer who forbids his cousin Patroclus, who looks about the right age for a Homeric Achilles, from prematurely engaging in combat. And, as almost every critic has pointed out, there is not the slightest trace of any sexual relationship between the two cousins. In Achilles' first action, a duel with a gigantic opponent, the myth evoked is that of David and Goliath rather than anything Greek. Achilles, running, closes with his opponent. He soars into the air like a bird and strikes him, samurai-style, with his sword. The encounter is over in seconds. We know beyond doubt that this man is invincible in combat. Indeed, the helmeted Achilles, in numerous close-ups, has a distinctly birdlike appearance, suggesting not so much an eagle as the more ominous owl, a symbol of death and not a flocking bird but a solitary, cold-eyed bird of prey. (I'm thinking of the *aegolius funereus*, the Boreal or Tengmalm's owl.) Achilles even hunches himself up to look like a perched bird, runs in birdlike fashion, and strikes in battle with his characteristically bird-like swoop, just as his Myrmidons, scurrying forth, move and look like the ants that their name implies.

Achilles stands in vocal contrast to most of the other male characters, whose enunciation is distinctly British, with Irish and Commonwealth overtones and in Odysseus' case with those of the down-to-earth Yorkshireman. This detail is not usually significant in Hollywood movies since consistency of accent has never been much of a priority to filmmakers. But I suspect that it does matter here. After all, we know that in most American-produced movies the British can't win anything without American help and that they can be replaced by Americans for operations in Burma, breaking the Enigma code, or escaping from Colditz. When Achilles is first called by Agamemnon to fight on his behalf, it is clear that Agamemnon can't win without him unless he puts his entire force at risk. In his thirst for glory, Achilles allows himself to be used by the king he despises, who is more the expansionist politician than the warrior. Yet in most respects he is a kind of ancient Westerner, a loner apart from the crowd, a supreme but until the death of Patroclus dispassionate killer – a very American reluctant individualist with his own ethical code and appropriately played by an American actor.

Otherwise, Petersen studiously avoids suggesting any major distinction between Greeks and Trojans, though Hector and Paris have darker hair and are not nearly as stout as the ruddier Agamemnon and Menelaus. The latter have the look, attire, and manners of over-aged, overweight piratical Vikings or degenerate Highland clansmen, even if they use copies of genuine Mycenaean cups at their banquets. And the only blond male is Achilles. The Greeks, not the Trojans, are the barbarians in *Troy*. The Trojans live in an elegant world that suggests an advanced civilization. Their city is full of visual echoes of Knossos, Sardis, Bogazköy, Karnak, and, at times, imperial Rome and Constantinople. In short, the "Greek vs. barbarian" theme prominent in Euripidean tragedy is reversed. A modern American director would surely not have resisted including Homer's valiant Ethiopian Memnon. But aside from the faintly Asiatic dancers in Menelaus' palace, the faces are all European, but in costumes and settings that defy precise definitions of era and location.

Our sense that these people have somehow, to use Vonnegut's phrase, "come unstuck in time" is enhanced by reference to the Greek naval expedition of a thousand vessels as "the largest ever." And for almost three thousand years it was. The scale of the assault has sometimes suggested parallels between the Trojan War in *Troy* and the recent Anglo-American assaults on Iraq. I am not at all persuaded by anything in the film that such was the director's design. For all the scale of the operations, Iraq was hardly a formidable military opponent that could be defeated only by cunning ruses and its own incompetent leadership. The common ethnicity of both sides also argues against any conscious parallelism. True, mythic Troy was attacked twice, first by Heracles when Priam was only a child. Heracles did not destroy the city but established Priam on his throne. Similarly, the first invasion of Iraq stopped short of sacking what remained of Baghdad after the bombing and left its modern brutal Priam in power. The second attack on Iraq in response to alleged threats posed by evidence of non-existent weapons of mass destruction does not even have a justification on the level of Helen's rape by Paris. That would require a scenario more like that in Euripides' tragedy *Helen*, in which Helen did not elope with Paris but was whisked away by the gods to Egypt and replaced by a fake. The second invasion of Iraq came in response to terrorist attacks on the United States, planned and executed mostly by Saudis but including no Iraqis. It was as if Margaret Thatcher had ordered an attack on Venezuela in response to the Argentine seizure of the Falkland Islands in 1982. That such a parallel can even cross one's mind bears witness to the degree to which Petersen's film shows sympathy for the defenders rather than the aggressors. The closest ancient approximation is the attack on Greece by Persian king Xerxes in 480 B.C.[15] The Greeks, however, deployed a fleet of their own against Xerxes, and the most famous battle of the war was a naval engagement between the two sides off the coast of Salamis. The odd feature about Troy, given its location near the coast, is its lack of any navy whatsoever, both in the ancient tradition and in this film.

More persuasive than these historical speculations is one suggested by the film's visual echoes of Darryl Zanuck's production *The Longest Day* (1962) and Steven Spielberg's *Saving Private Ryan* (1998) about the Allied naval assault on Normandy on June 6, 1944, the largest single-day naval invasion ever. It dwarfed, by about five to one, the thousand ships launched against Troy. Like Troy, the German-held coast had no naval protection against invasion. Without (the American) Achilles, (the British) Agamemnon would have no hope of victory. Achilles with his Myrmidons storms ashore first and occupies the temple of Apollo, destroying its statuary, butchering its priests, and making Briseis his prisoner.

15   Cf. also the aborted expedition by Knud den Helig (Canute the Holy) of Denmark against recently established William the Conqueror in England a millennium and a half later. Knud's invasion fleet, reported as some 1,660 ships, dispersed when the peoples south of the Danish border seized the opportunity to revolt and forced Knud to leave and put down the insurrection. See Palle Lauring, *A History of Denmark* (Copenhagen: Høst and Søn 1986), 64–66. Does recollection of this incident perhaps contribute a touch to the Viking-like manner of Petersen's Greeks, or is the tale known only to frustrated Danish imperialists?

Even if the parallel between the Greek attack on Troy and the D-Day invasion of Europe is only a cinematic allusion thematically unconnected to the rest of Petersen's film, its resonances are disturbing. For in this scenario, the inversion of the Anglo-American view of World War II is taken a large step further. Now the invaders, particularly the English, are the barbarians; and the world controlled by the confused ruler of the beleaguered continental Europeans, who brings defeat on his realm by taking bad advice and overriding his generals, represents civilization. This is despite Hitler's documented claim that it is the Germans who are the barbarians and have a moral obligation to be barbarians.[16] In Petersen's scenario, the absence of any divine force which makes Troy's fall appear as destiny makes the city's survival possible, as it is not in Homer or Virgil. But what undermines such a possibility is not the savagery of Achilles but the unquestioning loyalty of Hector to his brother and to his leader, which he sets above his own judgment. His courage and his determination to fight for his military honor, even though he knows he will be defeated by Achilles, make him act against his own and his city's best interests. Like the captain in *Das Boot*, he is a noble man in the service of a noble military tradition under an incompetent commander-in-chief. This is the mindset celebrated in Tennyson's *Charge of the Light Brigade*: "Theirs not to reason why, theirs but to do and die." They try to do what they think is their duty, and they try to survive. They are not the officers, troops, and kapos of Auschwitz remorselessly and brilliantly depicted by Tadeusz Borowski though, depending on their breaking point, they could be.[17]

Such loyalty indeed has a sinister side. Without it there would be no tyrants. It recalls what Lucan describes as "loyalty to one's military duty" (*militiae pietas*; *Pharsalia* 4.499) above and beyond one's larger sensibilities as a citizen and as a human being. Lucan sees it as one of the roots of the problems in the last days of the Roman republic.[18] It is not far apart from the way the word "patriotism" is currently misunderstood. Laelius, one of Julius Caesar's centurions and winner of the highest military award available to someone not a commanding general, the "civil oak" (*quercus civilis*, the Roman equivalent of the Victoria Cross,

16   Hermann Rauschning, *Gespräche mit Hitler* (1940; rpt. Vienna: Europa Verlag, 1973 [first complete edn]), 78 ("Ja! Wir sind Barbaren. Wir *wollen* es sein") and 79, reports Hitler's statement and its context.

17   Tadeusz Borowski, *This Way for the Gas, Ladies and Gentlemen; and Other Stories*, selected and tr. by Barbara Vedder (New York: Penguin, 1967; several rpts).

18   I discuss this idea in my *Lucan: An Introduction* (Ithaca: Cornell University Press, 1976), 119–121 and 200–201.

Congressional Medal of Honor, or Iron Cross), shows the extremes to which that kind of loyalty may go: "if you were to order me to bury my sword in my brother's heart, my father's throat, or the womb of my pregnant wife, I would do all this even if my right hand proved unwilling" (*Pharsalia* 1.376–378). A man who will do such atrocities in the name of loyalty will do anything. It takes greater courage to break the pattern of obedience to one's ruler. Although facing almost certain death in either case, the soldier does not want to die dishonored by his own community. No one would have given the U-Boat captain a medal for rebelling against Hitler. Both sides would have regarded him as a traitor.

Here, I think, is the heart of Petersen's dilemma with *Troy*. It is the eternal dilemma of heroic soldiers, especially those fighting for a losing – and therefore, in Caesar's terms, guilty – cause. Like Lucan, Petersen suggests that military victory is somehow morally worse than defeat, as Lucan did: "it was worse to be the winner" (*vincere peius erat*; *Pharsalia* 1.126–7). Now I am not trying to suggest that *Troy* in its entirety is an allegory for World War II. But there are overtones. The same script, updated, could work for a film set in Europe between June 1944 and May 1945.

As a meditation on war mythically framed, however, *Troy* does not reach the level of Michael Cacoyannis's masterpiece *Iphigenia* (1977) because there is no strong sense in *Troy* of the presence of people outside the elite. Cacoyannis uses the army, superbly manipulated by Odysseus, as a potent visual analogy to Euripides' original. Once the soldiers surround Agamemnon's headquarters, it no longer lies in his power to save his daughter. Petersen's armies are only a backdrop. His film would have been better if they were not there at all, for concentration on spectacle takes away time from the details that provide all the little touches that make a film come alive – like the toddler Orestes in *Iphigenia*, who is worth thousands of computerized soldiers. Petersen has chosen not to probe the inner drives and conflicts that propel a man to such a pitch of ambition that he is ready to kill his own child to win glory. He trims away Iphigenia, Clytemnestra, and Orestes from his presentation of Agamemnon and thus bypasses an opportunity to underscore the price Agamemnon is prepared to pay for what he seeks. Perhaps Petersen could not trust that enough of his audience would know that Agamemnon sacrificed his daughter to secure favorable winds for his expedition.

As it is, Petersen's Briseis has to stand in for Clytemnestra, Iphigenia, and Cassandra, the prophetic daughter of Priam whom Agamemnon brought home as a slave. Petersen does not develop the female characters adequately to counterbalance the loss of femininity occasioned by his removal of the gods. I found myself lamenting the absence of Hecuba, who is as much the symbol of doomed Troy as is Priam. Further, there is no sense of any strained relationships between Helen and the women of Troy, and Petersen's Helen does not convey a sense of being the ultimate *femme fatale*. I admit to some prejudice here since in my mind no one is ever likely to surpass Irene Papas' Helen in Cacoyannis's *The Trojan Women* (1971) any more than her Clytemnestra in *Iphigenia*. For my mental pictures of them indelibly bear her features and voice. This is what a good film can do. It can superimpose itself on one's prior mental images and thus become a part of the myth's evolution. Petersen has done this for me with his Hector and Achilles and in much else.

Petersen knows that controlling a myth brings with it some possibility of changing peoples' perspectives on that myth and on the historical events it assimilates and reflects. His Agamemnon is right to tell Achilles that history will remember victorious kings rather than the warrior princes who fought for them. But the strength of Homeric myth is that it can elevate Achilles over his commander, as history would not do. The *Iliad* centers on the wrath of Achilles, not on Agamemnon. The *Odyssey* focuses on Odysseus and gives the island of Ithaca its only claim to glory. The great cities of Athens and Corinth, on the other hand, get short shrift from Homer. That's Homer's triumph, in a way, over history. He could make the vanquished no less important than the victors. This is what makes conquerors eager to appropriate myth.

Petersen, it seems to me, focuses attention on what we find as a persistent theme in ancient myth: that the Trojan War is the last hurrah for the victors rather than for the vanquished. So, granted that the city is destroyed, who, if anyone, has won? In *Troy*, the answer, I have suggested, is that Troy has not died but lives on as an idea through Aeneas. This is a particularly Roman version of the tale of Troy, most notably that of Virgil's *Aeneid*. If Petersen's education followed the typical European pattern, his first encounter with an ancient version of the Trojan War would have been in Virgil, not Homer. In his film, the sequence of events from the construction of the Wooden Horse to the scenes of the sack of Troy recalls the *Aeneid* rather than the *Iliad*. Julius Caesar and his dynasty claimed descent from Aeneas, and it was rumored that Caesar and his successor Octavian (Augustus), out of family piety, contemplated rebuilding Troy and perhaps even putting the capital of their empire there.[19] The idea is not as preposterous as some scholars have argued. After all, Alexander had maddened the Macedonians by

---

19   Suetonius, *Julius* 79; Lucan, *Pharsalia* 9.950–960.

moving his capital to Babylon. And Rome did, some three centuries later, re-found the ancient city of Byzantium, just up the Bosporus from Troy, as its new capital, Constantinople. Over mythical expanses of time, ideas can regenerate almost infinitely. For the new Latin Troy was dominantly Greek-speaking. Ironically, the inhabitants called themselves Romans (*Romaioi*) and the Italians Latins.

The wealth of Constantinopolitan Troy lured Italian crusaders from Venice to sack it some nine hundred years after its foundation. A couple of centuries later they were followed by Mehmet II, who separated the new Troy from its Greco-Roman past and subjected Greece to Ottoman rule for almost four centuries. His model was Alexander the Great. He had his personal copy of Arrian's biography of Alexander read to him daily and ordered his own biography to be written in Greek, in the same format, and even on the same kind of paper.[20] Finally, in the aftermath of World War I, the liberated Greeks pursued their *megali idea*, their "great idea" of a new empire centered in Troy-Constantinople. But they met catastrophic defeat as the city of their dreams became unalterably Istanbul.

Not only Mediterranean peoples sought to capture for themselves the idea of Troy. So, too, did the Celtic Britons. Geoffrey of Monmouth argues in his *History of the Kings of Britain* that Pryd (in Latin, Brutus), the mythic ancestor of the Britons, came to Britain (Prydain) after the fall of Troy. Similarly, Petersen may have included overtones of the world's most terrible war to date in his retelling of Troy as a proclamation of European culture's revival from the ashes and rubble of war, of the re-establishment of civilization after utter pillage and destruction. That is, perhaps, the price the Allies have paid for playing Creon and suppressing, however tacitly, for half a century the need of the vanquished to lament their dead, regardless of what cause they were serving as they died. For the vanquished have emerged, like the Phoenix, from the ashes of its destruction. If that means the revival of *militiae pietas*, even of the kinder, gentler sort we find in Hector, it is still a dreadful prospect, one likely to take us down the same path with more terrible consequences. It reminds us that *militiae pietas* and dreams of empire die hard. They are a sure recipe for the Armageddon of the religious fanatic's dreams. I prefer, therefore, to understand Petersen's *Troy* as a warning to us not to make the same mistakes again, as Sophocles' *Antigone* was to his fellow Athenians.

20   Philip Mansel, *Constantinople: City of the World's Desire, 1453–1924* (1995; rpt. New York: St. Martin's, 1996), 6.

CHAPTER TWELVE

The Realist Politics of *Troy*

Robert J. Rabel

Many readers of Homer, anticipating the pleasure of becoming viewers of Homer, have been disappointed by *Troy*. The film departs from the *Iliad* in numerous ways and makes no claim to being a literal adaptation of Homer. For example, patriotism and allegiance to one's country as shown in *Troy* are modern concepts that rest uncomfortably in an ancient Greek context. But the film deserves our attention for addressing modern concerns while simultaneously engaging in a dialogue with the *Iliad*. I am here concerned with the politics of *Troy*: the Trojan War and the wrath of Achilles as manifestations of contemporary realist politics. I agree with M. I. Finley that all art dealing with the past should properly be viewed as a dialogue between present and past, but I disagree with his conclusion that "it can only be a dialogue in the present, about the present."[1] Rather, popular art as *Troy* represents it is best thought of as a dialogue with the past about the present.

Richard Ned Lebow calls political realism "the dominant paradigm in international relations for the last fifty years," although its dominance has been challenged.[2] The roots of realist thought extend back to the

1 M. I. Finley, "Introduction: Desperately Foreign," in his *Aspects of Antiquity: Discoveries and Controversies*, 2nd edn (New York: Viking, 1977; several rpts.), 11–15; quotation at 15.
2 Richard Ned Lebow, *The Tragic Vision of Politics: Ethics, Interests and Orders* (Cambridge: Cambridge University Press, 2003), 14. Contrast Jeffrey W. Legro and Andrew Moravcsik, "Is Anybody Still a Realist?" *International Security*, 24 (1999), 5–55.

Greek historian Thucydides, who has sometimes been called the found-
ing father of realism.[3] Modern realists have also borrowed much from
the works of Machiavelli, Hobbes, Nietzsche, and others.[4] Yet realism as
a systematic school of thought and self-conscious political ideology came
about only after World War I in the groundbreaking work of E. H. Carr.[5]
It received its classic expression in America in the writings of Reinhold
Niebuhr, Hans J. Morgenthau, and Kenneth Waltz.[6] Four core principles of realism shape the plot of *Troy* and give it significant coherence:
first, domestic and international relations are two manifestations of
the same phenomenon, the universal struggle for power; second, the
untamed nature of the struggle for power, resulting most notably in
the evil of war, can best be explained by the presence of evil in human
life since human nature is at least partly evil or flawed; third, only a
precarious balance of power can achieve or maintain a modicum of
peace and the rule of law in domestic and international relations; and,
finally, political ideology is only a fiction designed to disguise the true
nature of power politics and the evil inherent in mankind. As a consequence of this set of beliefs, realists adopt a tragic outlook on history
and a pessimistic attitude regarding the possibility of solving the major
social and political problems plaguing mankind, for in their view – one
that also underlies many of the ancient Greek tragedies – human
life cannot be creative without being destructive. I will examine these
four principles in order and trace their presence in *Troy*. The film conforms to the tragic view of history as espoused by the major proponents
of realism.

3   Lebow, *The Tragic Vision of Politics*, 20.

4   Jonathan Haslam, *No Virtue Like Necessity: Realist Thought in International Relations
Since Machiavelli* (New Haven: Yale University Press, 2002), provides an insightful history
of various strands of realist thought. He thinks of realism as a tradition rather than a
philosophy, "a spectrum of ideas of various hues from light to dark" (249).

5   Edward Hallett Carr, *The Twenty Years' Crisis, 1919–1939: An Introduction to the Study
of International Relations* (1939; rpt. New York: Perennial, 2001).

6   I draw mainly upon the principles of the modern American version of realism, concentrating on Niebuhr and Morgenthau rather than on Waltz, who differs from his
predecessors in a number of significant ways. Niebuhr views the desires of individuals
and groups as rooted in the instinct for survival, the will to live only later translated
into the will to power, while Morgenthau views the will to power as the primary impulse.
Campbell Craig, *Glimmer of a New Leviathan: Total War in the Realism of Niebuhr, Morgenthau,
and Waltz* (New York: Columbia University Press, 2003), distinguishes between traditions and ideas associated with realism and the philosophy of Niebuhr, Morgenthau, and
Waltz.

1. Struggles for Power

Realists define politics as the sum of human relations involving authority and the use of power. "Politics," Morgenthau says, "is a struggle
for power over men."[7] Realism views this irrational and never-ending
struggle as the engine that drives human social and political life, domestic as well as international. Hence realism takes a stand in opposition
to Marxist and liberal attitudes about politics and society. Niebuhr places
the Marxist belief that "justice will be established because weakness will
be made strong through economic forces operating with inexorable logic
in human history" in the "category of romantic illusions."[8] According to
Morgenthau, who argues against Marx, "historic evidence points to the
primacy of politics over economics."[9] Morgenthau criticizes liberal and
rationalist modes of thought for their optimistic belief that the most
serious problems of war and peace are amenable to solution through
the use of reason.[10] The idea of the importance of the struggle for power
is ultimately derived from Friedrich Nietzsche's well-known idea of
the will to power, which trumps even the human instinct for self-
preservation.[11] In one of his earliest writings, Morgenthau expressed in
the strongest possible language the strength of the will to power as the
fundamental human drive:

> the selfishness of man has limits; his will to power has none. For while
> man's vital needs are capable of satisfaction, his lust for power would be
> satisfied only if the last man became an object of his domination, there
> being nobody above or beside him, that is, if he became like God.[12]

---

7   Hans J. Morgenthau, *Scientific Man* vs. *Power Politics* (Chicago: University of Chicago
Press, 1946; rpt. 1974), 195.

8   Reinhold Niebuhr, *Moral Man and Immoral Society: A Study in Ethics and Politics* (New
York: Scribner's, 1932; several rpts.), 155 and 164. For the sake of accuracy, however, it
should be noted that Niebuhr is not critical of all aspects of Marxist thought, for he sees
Marx as having provided an admirable analysis of the contradictions inherent in bour-
geois democracy. Cf. Kenneth N. Waltz, *Man, the State, and War: A Theoretical Analysis*
(New York: Columbia University Press, 1959; rpt. 2001), 30.

9   Hans J. Morgenthau, *Politics Among Nations: The Struggle for Power and Peace*, Brief
Edition, ed. Kenneth W. Thompson (Boston: McGraw-Hill, 1993), 63. This edition contains the complete first ten chapters of Morgenthau's book with all of his basic principles.

10   Morgenthau, *Scientific Man* vs. *Power Politics*, 2–6.

11   So Craig, *Glimmer of a New Leviathan*, 10–11. Morgenthau himself is not nearly as
candid in acknowledging his influences.

12   Morgenthau, *Scientific Man* vs. *Power Politics*, 193.

In *Politics Among Nations*, his classic book on international relations, Morgenthau was less hyperbolic and poetic but remained committed to the belief that politics cannot be divorced from considerations of power. One of his basic principles held that the tendency to seek and exercise power is a significant element of all human associations.[13]

Morgenthau's analysis provides us with a precise definition of the concept of power that will aid our understanding of the nature of power politics in *Troy*. Morgenthau dissociates the idea of power from the potential or actual employment of force, which is only one manifestation of power. In his philosophy as in realism in general, war appears to be the natural human state of affairs.[14] Morgenthau defines power as "anything that establishes and maintains the control of man over man."[15] Power is primarily a psychological and not a physical relationship between those who exercise it and those over whom it is exercised.[16] Thus personal charisma must be taken into account as an independent element in determining relationships of power.[17] From the definition of power as essentially a psychological phenomenon it follows that seeking to enhance one's prestige – or, as it is put in *Troy*, seeking to win glory – is an important aspect of the universal struggle for power, since prestige gives one power over others:

> The individual seeks confirmation, on the part of his fellows, of the evaluation he puts upon himself. It is only in the tribute others pay to his goodness, intelligence, and power that he becomes fully aware of, and can fully enjoy, what he deems to be his superior qualities.[18]

The policy of prestige is just as central an element in the relationships among nations.[19] Perhaps the best way to distinguish power as it

13   Morgenthau, *Politics Among Nations*, 37. Such recognition of the nature and importance of power politics goes back at least to Thucydides; cf., for example, A. Geoffrey Woodhead, *Thucydides on the Nature of Power* (Cambridge: Harvard University Press, 1970), 104: "Power consists, after all, in having the ability to ensure that others are prepared to do what you want them to do."

14   Cf. Craig, *Glimmer of a New Leviathan*, 28.

15   Morgenthau, *Politics Among Nations*, 11.

16   Cf. Morgenthau, *Politics Among Nations*, 30. As Thomas Hobbes, *Leviathan*, ed. Richard E. Flathman and David Johnston (New York: Norton, 1997), 48, phrased the same point: "Reputation of power, is Power; because it draweth with it the adhaerence of those that need protection."

17   Cf. Morgenthau, *Politics Among Nations*, 32.

18   Morgenthau, *Politics Among Nations*, 85.

19   Cf. Morgenthau, *Politics Among Nations*, 84.

manifests itself in the potential or actual use of force from power as prestige is to observe a distinction implicit in the work of the classical realist thinkers but made explicit only recently in the writings of Joseph S. Nye. This is the distinction between "hard power," the potential or actual use of force, and "soft power." Soft power is "the ability to get what you want through attraction rather than coercion or payments."[20] Soft power depends for its success upon an audience well disposed to appreciate its allure.[21] As regards international politics, *Troy* portrays the Trojan War as motivated solely by Agamemnon's quest for greater and greater power gained through the use of force. The theft of Helen is a mere pretext, and economic considerations of the sort that Marxists judge to be significant are nowhere taken into account as an additional incentive for making war against Troy. Similarly, domestic Greek politics is portrayed as an arena in which the hard power of Agamemnon is pitted against the soft power of Achilles, his only serious rival. The Greek and Trojan armies and the major protagonists, Agamemnon and Achilles, pay little heed to considerations of morality as they go about the business of conducting politics and waging war.

According to the controversial views of Bruno Snell and, later, Arthur Adkins, Homeric Greeks lacked the idea of the self as a moral agent and hence the proper modern – that is, Kantian – conception of oneself as a being with responsibilities defined in terms of one's sense of duty.[22] This view has frequently been challenged.[23] Still, it has some application to *Troy*, at least insofar as it pays little attention to the morality of individual or collective behavior in political decisions. There are only two explicit, if fleeting, references to character judgments in terms of moral standards, both made about Priam, king of Troy. During the banquet celebrating the conclusion of a peace treaty between the Spartans and Trojans early in the film, Menelaus speaks of Priam as "a good king, a good man." Near the end of the film, as Priam prepares to return to Troy with the corpse

20   Joseph S. Nye, Jr., *Soft Power: The Means to Success in World Politics* (New York: Public Affairs, 2004), x. Nye speaks of former American Secretary of State Colin Powell's use of soft power in securing the welfare of the United States.

21   Cf. Nye, *Soft Power*, 6–16.

22   Cf. the chapter entitled "Homer's View of Man" in Bruno Snell, *The Discovery of the Mind: The Greek Origins of European Thought*, tr. Thomas G. Rosenmeyer (1953; rpt. New York: Dover, 1982), 1–22 and 310–311 (notes). According to A. W. H. Adkins, *Merit and Responsibility: A Study in Greek Values* (1960; rpt. Chicago: University of Chicago Press, 1975), 2, Homeric Greeks lacked the Kantian sense of duty and hence the modern sense of moral responsibility.

23   See, for example, Bernard Williams, *Shame and Necessity* (Berkeley: University of California Press, 1993; rpt. 1994), 21–49.

of his son Hector, Achilles commends him for being "a far better king than the one leading this army." Otherwise, we observe all political life to be conducted in terms of interest defined as power. Nevertheless, this autonomy of the political in *Troy* does not justify the conclusion that the characters do not recognize any moral standards. Nor should realists be taken to reject the validity of such principles. As Morgenthau argues:

> The realist defense of the autonomy of the political sphere against its subversion by other modes of thought does not imply disregard for the existence and importance of these other modes of thought.[24]

One of these other modes of thought is morality, for humans are moral as well as political creatures. Therefore the absence of the language of morality from most of *Troy* does not preclude the audience from making moral judgments about individuals whose behavior they witness. Indeed, in the course of the film both Achilles and Hector will emerge as good men according to Niebuhr: capable of being and doing good.

In his conduct of political affairs, Agamemnon is heedless of the importance of influencing others through a policy of prestige; that is, he pays no regard to the critical importance of soft power. The exercise of hard power alone, the use of force, offers him control over the fledgling Greek nation, a control that he desires to increase by the conquests of Thessaly and Troy. The depth of Agamemnon's greed for world domination is made clear in the film's opening sequence. Over a map of the Aegean world we read: "After decades of warfare Agamemnon, King of Mycenae, has forced the kingdoms of Greece into a loose alliance." This alliance is then referred to as "an emerging nation." Thessaly alone remains unconquered, and the film begins with Agamemnon's invasion of it. As the Greek army and the army of Thessaly are facing each other before combat, Agamemnon holds a parley with Triopas, the Thessalian king, who complains: "You can't have the whole world, Agamemnon. It's too big, even for you." This remark, prophetic of Agamemnon's death, elicits the first of many laughs we hear from Agamemnon, all in celebration of his power and its further extension. The Agamemnon of *Troy* conforms perfectly to Hobbes' description of Man in the first part of *Leviathan*: "He never laughs but with a feeling of pleasure in his own power and in the weakness of others."[25] Agamemnon later laughs

---

24   Morgenthau, *Politics Among Nations*, 15.
25   So K. R. Minogue, "Hobbes and the Just Man," in *Hobbes and Rousseau: A Collection of Critical Essays*, ed. Maurice Cranston and Richard S. Peters (New York: Doubleday, 1972), 66–84, at 67–68.

heartily when Menelaus, his brother, fights a duel with Paris. When the tide of battle turns against the Greeks because of Achilles' withdrawal, Agamemnon flies into a rage, fearing that the Trojans are now laughing at him. "Empires," Agamemnon insists in conversation with Nestor, "are forged by war. The gods protect only the strong." Like the Agamemnon of Thucydides, the Agamemnon of *Troy* employs fear as a weapon to maintain and enlarge the empire that he is attempting to extend through the use of hard power.[26]

When a disaffected Achilles decides to return home, Odysseus seems to speak for the Greeks in general when he defends his own decision to remain. His home island of Ithaca, he says, cannot afford an enemy like Agamemnon. "Fear," he counsels Achilles, "is useful." Achilles, however, refuses at any point to submit to Agamemnon's power over the Greek army and nation. Agamemnon remarks about Achilles even before he defeats the Thessalian champion: "Of all the warlords loved by the gods, I hate him the most." Achilles, who refuses to convey Triopas' scepter to Agamemnon, signals his refusal to recognize Agamemnon as his over-lord. Achilles alone challenges Agamemnon's supremacy. In the words of Morgenthau quoted above, Agamemnon's "lust for power would be satisfied only if the last man became an object of his domination, there being nobody above or beside him, that is if he became like God." Achilles embodies the threat represented by that last man. He prevents Agamemnon's assumption of god-like status, competes with him for power over the army, and by stubborn self-assertion threatens his long-term goals for the extension of his empire. In the end, Agamemnon's quest for power ends in his death, ironically during the sack of Troy, his most famous achievement. He suffers the ill effects of what Hobbes has called the "perpetuall and restlesse desire of Power after power, that ceaseth onely in Death."[27] This change from the well-attested story that Agamemnon returned home after the Trojan War appropriately emphasizes the realist concept that death alone terminates the quest for power.

If we understand power in *Troy* in realist terms as a psychological rather than a physical phenomenon, Achilles emerges as a "power politician" fully equal to Agamemnon, although he conducts politics exclusively by personal charisma or soft power. Achilles gets what he wants through attraction rather than, like Agamemnon, by coercion or fear. "I want what all men want," Achilles tells Briseis. "I just want it more."

26   Thucydides, *History of the Peloponnesian War* 1.9; cf. my "Agamemnon's Empire in Thucydides," *The Classical Journal*, 80 (1984), 8–10.

27   Hobbes, *Leviathan*, 55.

Agamemnon's primary concern is to extend his power geographically; Achilles wants power extended over time. Agamemnon is ultimately unsuccessful, but Achilles wins for himself the immortality that he promised his Myrmidons as they prepared to land on the shores of Troy. As the film concludes, Odysseus, who acts as narrator, expresses a wish that future generations will tell his story and say that he lived in the time of Hector, tamer of horses, and of Achilles. Pointedly excluding Agamemnon from this honor roll, the film may be taken to endorse the ultimate effectiveness of soft over hard power.

The audience disposed to be moved psychologically by Achilles' charisma consists not only of the Myrmidons whom he commands but also of the whole Greek army and, of course, the film's audience. Agamemnon's army parts as the Red Sea did before Moses when Achilles rides in to face the Thessalian champion, cheering "Achilles, Achilles!" The soldiers never cheer Agamemnon, whom they obey out of fear. Achilles' heroism on landing at Troy incites others to emulate him and confirms his power over their minds and actions. Achilles and his men are the first to land, and Ajax, sailing behind, exclaims: "Look at him. Look!" Ajax is spurred on to become the second commander to storm the beach and after a battle with the guards of Apollo's temple pays proper respect to Achilles for his power: "You're as fearless as the gods. I'm honored to go to war with you." Later, when Achilles sends his troops home, his lieutenant Eudorus parts from him with the words: "Fighting for you has been my life's honor, my lord." *Troy* accords honor only to soft and never to hard power.

Odysseus, the film's pragmatist, serves as go-between in the power struggle waged by Agamemnon and Achilles. Morgenthau's analysis of the privileged position occupied by the individual who stands aloof from a given battle for power helps us understand Odysseus' role:

> The deeper the individual is involved in the power struggle, the less likely he is to see the power struggle for what it is . . . The more removed the individual is from a particular power struggle, the more likely he is to understand its true nature.[28]

Odysseus understands the true nature of the animosity between Achilles and Agamemnon. In the face of their unrestricted ambitions he tries, with varying success, to harness the energies of both in the interest of achieving the narrower but immediate goal of sacking Troy. Odysseus is

28 Morgenthau, *Politics Among Nations*, 99–100.

acknowledged to be famous for his tricks, the first of which he plays on Achilles when he tries to persuade the younger hero to join the expedition against Troy: "Let Achilles fight for honor," Odysseus urges. "Let Agamemnon fight for power." This clever argument depends for its validity on the premise that questions of honor can be separated from considerations of power, an argument that seems specious in light of the realist logic underpinning political life in the film. Odysseus later encourages Achilles to "avoid the politics." Since politics is the struggle for power and power is the goal of all politics, Achilles cannot remain aloof from Greek politics and at the same time serve his personal interests. Although famous for his tricks, Odysseus can also be quite forthright when the situation requires blunt speech. After Hector kills Menelaus, Odysseus demonstrates his understanding of a truth so far voiced only by Agamemnon and in private conversations: the theft of Helen was a mere pretext for war. "The men believe we came here for Menelaus' wife," Odysseus says to Agamemnon. "We won't be needing her anymore."

If the quarrel between Achilles and Agamemnon is about the acquisition and maintenance of power, the same may be said of the Trojan War, although for reasons to be discussed below this truth is by no means self-evident to all. For example, Priam, repeatedly acknowledged to be a good man, wrongly thinks that the war is about love, specifically the love of his son Paris for Helen. He tells Hector upon the latter's return from Sparta:

> I've fought many wars in my time. Some were fought for land, some for power, some for glory. I suppose that fighting for love makes more sense than all the rest.

Hector, however, has a better understanding than his father of the war's true nature and sees through the public cause, the abduction of Helen. When Helen tries to flee from Troy and return to the Greeks to end the war, Hector restrains her: "This is about power, not love. Do you think Agamemnon cares about his brother's marriage?"

2. Power and Human Nature

The second core principle of realism holds that struggles for power, ultimately and frequently leading to war, can be traced to qualities inherent in human nature. Political theorists and historians traditionally locate the causes of war in three areas. One is psychology: wars arise because of imperfections or evils inherent in human nature. Sociologically based beliefs trace wars back to the behavior of states. This is a more optimistic school of thought, one that realists might call liberal. Marxists, for example, believe that peace may eventually be achieved and war abolished after an internal reorganization of the state. Others, moving still further from considerations of human nature, locate the cause of war in the condition of anarchy that characterizes the state system at large.[29] Morgenthau and Niebuhr opt without reservation for the first view. Morgenthau declares that imperfections in the world are the result of forces inherent in human nature and unambiguously speaks of "the inevitability of evil."[30] "Man," he says, "cannot hope to be good but must be content with being not too evil."[31] There is no possibility of escape either from the power of evil or from the evil of power. As a theologian, Niebuhr approaches the question of the evil in man from the Christian perspective of mankind's sinful nature while recognizing the potential of the individual for both willing and doing good. "How can man be 'essentially' evil," he asks, "if he knows himself to be so? What is the character of the ultimate subject . . . which passes such devastating judgments upon itself as object?"[32] Niebuhr's view is concisely expressed in the title of his book *Moral Man and Immoral Society*. Individuals, he argues, contain within themselves the capacity for doing good as well as evil, although they are morally obliged to do good. But when they form groups or associations of any kind, the flaws in their individual characters are exponentially magnified. Groups, therefore, cannot be expected to conduct social and political life according to the standards expected of individuals. In order to validate their actions, groups are given to formulating moral justifications for their behavior that appear manifestly hypocritical when viewed objectively.[33] Niebuhr, like Morgenthau, views much of political ideology as a cloak that nations use to conceal the base motives for their actions. "The moral obtuseness of human collectives," he says, "makes a morality of pure disinterestedness impossible."[34]

29   Cf. Waltz, *Man, the State, and War*.
30   See Morgenthau, *Politics Among Nations*, 3; the quotation is from *Scientific Man vs. Power Politics*, 191.
31   Morgenthau, *Scientific Man vs. Power Politics*, 192.
32   Reinhold Niebuhr, *The Nature and Destiny of Man: A Christian Interpretation*, vol. 1: *Human Nature* (1941; rpt Louisville: Westminster John Knox Press, 1996), 2.
33   Cf. Niebuhr, *Moral Man and Immoral Society*, 9.
34   Niebuhr, *Moral Man and Immoral Society*, 272.

Two of the principal ways in which individual goodness may manifest itself in relation to the selfishness of the group are in the actions of the patriot and of the idealist. About the patriot Niebuhr states: "Altruistic passion is sluiced into the reservoirs of nationalism with great ease." In his theory of the psychological origins of patriotism he claims that patriotic feelings arise when an individual sentimentally reflects on appealing scenes of his environment and the enchantments of his youth. His imagination then "transmutes the universal beneficences of nature into symbols of the peculiar blessings which a benevolent nation bestows upon its citizens," and so he becomes a patriot.[35] Patriotic sentiments are often exploited by the group in the interest of bad causes. On the other hand the idealist, whose patriotism is circumscribed or negated by allegiance to a transcendent cause or causes, proves his worth by standing in opposition to the selfish interests of the group or nation in which he lives.[36]

These realist descriptions of the patriot and idealist conform closely to the characters of Hector and Achilles in *Troy*, a film in which human nature reveals itself more in action than in speech. Even so, characters occasionally give voice to the pessimistic realist perspective that war is an inevitable result of human nature and has nothing to do with the corruption of the state or the political anarchy rampant in the film's portrayal of the Aegean world. Men are simply born to fight. Nestor, arguing for the need to enlist Achilles in the war against Troy, says that Agamemnon has no need to control his one major antagonist; he need only unleash him: "That man was born to end lives." Odysseus, enlisting Achilles in the campaign, says: "Your business is war, my friend." When Achilles threatens to desert the Greek army, Odysseus adds to this sentiment: "Stay, Achilles; you were born for this war." Achilles himself shares this outlook. When Briseis asks why he chose the life of a warrior, he responds: "I chose nothing. I was born, and this is what I am." After the death of Hector Briseis asks Achilles when the killing will finally stop, and he answers: "It never ends." This blunt declaration of the realist perspective on war is immediately followed by a quiet scene in which Briseis is sitting alone at night and watching the sea pound the shore. We may regard the constancy of the waves as a symbol of the realist view that war and violence are inevitable in human life.

Hector is the exemplary patriot, a moral man willing to give up his life for the group, an immoral society of Trojans acting in the interest

---

35   The quotations are from Niebuhr, *Moral Man and Immoral Society*, 91 and 92.
36   Cf. Niebuhr, *Moral Man and Immoral Society*, 94.

of a bad cause, the theft of a Greek king's wife. "This is my country," Hector at first tells Priam, "and these are my countrymen. I don't want to see them suffer so my brother can have his prize." Nevertheless, Hector fights when called upon. His patriotism, in Niebuhr's phrase already quoted, "is sluiced into the reservoirs of nationalism with great ease." This exemplary Trojan hero wins our esteem for his sentimental attachment to family and country, which *Troy* idealizes. He even indulges briefly in the kind of fond recollection of his youth that Niebuhr sees as characteristic of the patriot. On the boat smuggling Helen from Sparta to Troy, Paris approaches his older brother and asks for protection from his enemies. Hector interrupts his carving of a toy lion for his little son and answers: "The last time you spoke to me like this you were ten years old and you'd just stolen father's horse." Niebuhr sounds just the note that captures the essence of Hector's character: he is given to transmuting "the universal beneficences of nature into symbols of the peculiar blessings which a benevolent nation bestows upon its citizens." Hector personifies his country as the truest and most important form of family. As the Greeks pour ashore onto the Trojan beach, he tells his warriors that all his life he has lived by a simple code: "Honor the gods, love your woman, and defend your country." Hector expresses his allegiances according to the typical Homeric scale of ascending affection. Here, country comes above all else, for to Hector it is the truest form of family. "Troy is mother to us all," he tells his troops. "Fight for her." And: "No son of Troy shall ever submit to a foreign ruler."[37]

Achilles, on the other hand, represents the realist's conception of the idealist, one who is good because he steadfastly opposes the immorality of the group. In this case the group is a fledgling Greek nation led by a ruthless tyrant who is seeking total control over the Aegean world. "Don't waste your life following some fool's orders," Achilles advises Patroclus. Achilles deserves a large measure of our regard simply for his hostility toward Agamemnon. "What are you doing in thrall to that pig of a king?" he asks Odysseus. Achilles' allegiance transcends the concrete political interests of the group; it is directed toward fulfilling the dictates of an abstract code of ethics predicated on the need to win glory and

---

37   The fact that Homeric heroes typically catalogue their loyalties in ascending order of affection was first pointed out by Johannes Th. Kakridis, *Homeric Researches* (1949; rpt. New York: Garland, 1987), 19–20 and 152–164. The Hector of *Troy* proclaims a different ascending three-part scale of affection from that of Hector in the *Iliad*. Homer's Hector places the citizens of Troy lowest, then family, and his wife Andromache highest (*Iliad* 6.450–454). On this see my *Plot and Point of View in the Iliad* (Ann Arbor: University of Michigan Press, 1997), 99.

attain a kind of immortality that surpasses in worth even what the gods themselves enjoy. "The gods envy us," Achilles tells Briseis. "Everything's more beautiful because we're doomed . . . We will never be here again." According to Niebuhr, idealists, whose patriotism is qualified by loyalties that transcend devotion to the state, must always remain a minority.[38] In *Troy*, this is a minority of one.

3. Balance of Power

Since the struggle for power knows no limits and human nature is in some measure evil, peace and social and political stability can be achieved only by a fragile balance of power. The idea of the balance of power can be found as early as the writings of Thucydides and Polybius.[39] It became a principle of international relations in early modern Europe and a central tenet of realism in the twentieth century.[40] What brings about a balance of power is the existence of a number of independent states that wish to remain independent. Balance, Waltz says, "is not so much imposed by statesmen on events as it is imposed by events on statesmen."[41]

According to Morgenthau, only power can check and limit the growth of power. Two main patterns exist in any particular instance where a balance of power prevails. One is the pattern of direct opposition. A may embark upon an aggressive policy to B, and B may counter A with a policy to preserve the status quo or with an aggressive policy of its own. The other pattern, that of competition, involves a fluid and dynamic interchange among three entities. The power of A to dominate C is balanced by the power of B, while in turn B's power to dominate C is balanced by A's.[42] Wherever the rule of law is not supported by the mutual interests of the powers involved, the balance of power in domestic and international contexts remains precarious.[43]

The politics of *Troy* reveals the operation of both patterns. In each case, power serves to limit power, and a modicum of peace and cooperation is achieved as long as a balance serves to limit the aspirations of the parties involved. In the antagonism between Agamemnon and Achilles in Thessaly and at the banquet celebrating the peace treaty between

38   Cf. Niebuhr, *Moral Man and Immoral Society*, 94.
39   Cf. Waltz, *Man, the State, and War*, 198–199.
40   Cf. Haslam, *No Virtue Like Necessity*, 90.
41   Cf. Waltz, *Man, the State, and War*, 209.
42   Cf. Morgenthau, *Politics Among Nations*, 188–192.
43   Cf. Morgenthau, *Politics Among Nations*, 117–118.

Sparta and Troy, equilibrium in the distribution of power brings a measure of stability. But when one element in the struggles for power attempts to gain ascendancy over the other, in each case by the theft of a woman, balance breaks down. This breakdown in turn leads to the film's tragic conclusion.

In the pattern of competition, Agamemnon's power to employ the military services of the Greeks in his plan for conquest is checked only by the power of a recalcitrant Achilles. Achilles' power to dominate and establish his pre-eminence as a hero is in turn balanced by Agamemnon's hard power as a king who is maintaining a tense equilibrium in relation to the soft power of Greece's greatest warrior. Agamemnon requires the services of Achilles in order to extend his empire first to Thessaly and then to Troy. Achilles needs Agamemnon's military resources to provide him with a theater of operations on a scale so vast and unprecedented that his glory will never be forgotten. This balance of power leads to a quick and almost bloodless victory over the forces of Thessaly when Achilles dispatches the Thessalian champion with a single blow. However, later events prove the truth of the expository narration. Indeed Agamemnon leads only a loose and fragile alliance. Alliances founded on a balance of power are by nature precarious. The fragility of the Greek alliance is fully exposed during the Trojan War when Agamemnon encroaches upon Achilles' right to the possession of Briseis, a Trojan priestess whom Achilles has captured in a raid and with whom he falls in love. Achilles' earlier refusal to convey the scepter of Triopas to Agamemnon – "He's not my king," Achilles said to Triopas on that occasion – reveals to us the balance of power then existing in the Greek army. After the first successful day of fighting at Troy, however, Triopas will personally present this scepter to Agamemnon. At that moment Agamemnon will disturb the balance of power with his theft of Briseis.

Immediately after the Greek victory over the Thessalians, the scene shifts to Sparta and introduces us to the pattern of direct opposition. The expository narration again provides us with necessary information: "Agamemnon's brother Menelaus, King of Sparta, is weary of battle. He seeks to make peace with Troy, the most powerful rival to the emerging Greek nation." We are left to infer that Sparta and, given Agamemnon's imperialist nature, the rest of the Greek world have been pursuing an imperialist policy toward Troy. The Trojans seem to have countered with a policy of preserving the status quo, as we may infer from Hector's observation to Paris that their father Priam has for many years been working for peace. Troy and Sparta have finally reached a state of equilibrium in which peace serves the mutual interests of two powers involved in a struggle for international supremacy. This balance is almost immediately disrupted when Paris steals Helen.

4. The True Nature of Power

Political ideology is only a pretext that disguises the true motives according to which states act.[44] The human mind, Morgenthau says, "in its day-by-day operations cannot bear to look the truth of politics straight in the face."[45] Therefore ideological disguises and slogans make power politics psychologically and morally acceptable.[46] Morgenthau's belief that humans and states are essentially evil raises the question why people, themselves as evil as states, should require ideological disguises for the actions carried out by the latter. Niebuhr shares Morgenthau's belief in the illusionary nature of political ideology, but in his view individuals are ethically and morally superior to states. So he is able to provide an explanation for ideological pretense: political ideology arises from mankind's inability to conform collective life to individual ideals.[47] Moral man requires ideological pretexts to shield him from recognizing the evil carried out by immoral society.

Troy fully dramatizes the realist concept that ideology is a pretext. After Paris' abduction of Helen, Menelaus comes to Mycenae to seek his older brother's help. Agamemnon promises to lead an expedition against Troy to avenge the insult to his brother, but as the two embrace Agamemnon looks off into the distance, as if he were contemplating the true reason for the coming war. He later acknowledges to Menelaus before the latter's duel with Paris: "I didn't come here for your pretty wife. I came here for Troy." As we already saw, Hector, Agamemnon's chief adversary, is aware that the theft of Helen is only a pretext to make

---

44   This core principle finds realism at its weakest. Winston Churchill noted in a speech entitled "Anglo-American Unity," delivered September 6, 1943, at Harvard University on receiving an honorary degree: "The empires of the futures are the empires of the mind." Quoted from *Winston S. Churchill: His Complete Speeches 1897–1963*, ed. Robert Rhodes James, vol. 7: *1943–1949* (New York: Chelsea House, 1974), 6823–6827; quotation at 6826. Alister McGrath, *The Twilight of Atheism: The Rise and Fall of Disbelief in the Modern World* (New York: Doubleday, 2004), xi, who slightly misquotes Churchill's words, interprets him to mean that the great powers after World War II would not be nation states but ideologies. Recent events surrounding the rise of hostility between much of the Islamic world and the West seem to confirm the truth of Churchill's observation.

45   Morgenthau, *Politics Among Nations*, 16.

46   Morgenthau, *Politics Among Nations*, 102–105.

47   Cf. Niebuhr, *Moral Man and Immoral Society*, 9.

the war morally and psychologically acceptable to the Greeks. In *Troy*, ideology is a hypocrite's means to bridge the gap between the moral behavior of the individual and the immoral behavior of society. The film celebrates the fight for honor on the part of the individual. But revenge for an insult to the honor of the entire group serves only as a duplicitous pretext to disguise the hard truth of power politics resulting in war.

To Niebuhr, this inability of society to conform collective life to the moral ideals of the individual represents "one of the tragedies of the human spirit."[48] Morgenthau, too, came to regard tragedy as an inherent quality of human existence rather than a creation of Greek and later Western art.[49] Much of Greek tragedy juxtaposes human achievement and human transgression; the two are inseparable. Similarly, *Troy* transforms Homeric epic into tragedy. At its conclusion the film juxtaposes the horror of the destruction of Troy, seen through King Priam's eyes, with the claims to heroic achievement that Odysseus pronounces at the funeral of Achilles:

> If they ever tell my story, let them say that I walked with giants. Men rise and fall like the winter wheat, but these names will never die. Let them say that I lived in the time of Hector, tamer of horses. Let them say that I lived in the time of Achilles.

---

48 Niebuhr, *Moral Man and Immoral Society*, 9.
49 So Lebow, *The Tragic Vision of Politics*, 308.

CHAPTER THIRTEEN

The Trojan War on the Screen: An Annotated Filmography

Martin M. Winkler

The first part of this filmography traces the chronology of big-screen adaptations of the Trojan War myth and briefly comments on individual films. Like Wolfgang Petersen's *Troy*, these films are not faithful adaptations of Homer but are based on or "inspired" by the *Iliad* and, in most cases, by Book 4 of Virgil's *Aeneid*, the most famous and influential ancient account of the fall of Troy. Films adapting Homer's *Odyssey* are not included here except where a brief reference is appropriate. Such films also tend to show or at least refer to the city's fall, mainly because the end of the Trojan War provides a convenient point of departure for the story of Odysseus' return and because filmmakers understandably cannot resist showing off the Trojan Horse.

The filmography's second part lists some noteworthy television productions or series episodes. Part 3 samples some oddities and otherwise amusing or remarkable items to indicate the variety that references to ancient myth can take on large and small screens. This part is by no means comprehensive; it is intended to whet readers' appetites to look for additional items on their own. Annotations in all three parts occasionally reveal the writer's preferences.

The listings exclude filmed or taped adaptations of classic stage plays on Trojan-War themes like Shakespeare's *Troilus and Cressida*, Jean Racine's *Hermione*, Heinrich von Kleist's *Penthesilea*, or Jean Giraudoux's *La Guerre de Troie n'aura pas lieu*. It also omits films with modern settings that contain names of mythical characters in their titles or plots. Television documentaries, which often contain film excerpts or staged scenes, are excluded as well.

Not all of the silent films listed survive or are accessible. Reliable information can be scarce or non-existent, and sources may contradict each other concerning credits, running times, and release dates. The same is true for some of the sound films. The Italian epics of the 1950s and 1960s, for instance, were often retitled and recut (usually shortened) for export to the United States or for broadcasts on commercial American television. Many of them are available today only in poorly dubbed videos of bad to atrocious quality. Their colors are faded, their images scratched or jumpy, and their widescreen compositions (in a 2.35:1 or similar aspect ratio) ruined by panning and scanning (1.33:1) for 16mm transfers, the basis of television broadcasts. A considerable part of their low standing among film critics and classicists is due to the fact that these films rarely if ever can be watched in the way they were intended to be watched.

In the present listings credits have been omitted except for the names of directors, given for purposes of identification, and brief discussions of actors when warranted. Information about credits, plots, or both is available from various sources. The Internet Movie Database (www.imdb.com) is the most extensive and usually reliable electronic film guide. The following books also provide first orientations:

De España, Rafael. *El Peplum: La antigüedad en el cine*. Barcelona: Glénat, 1998.

Elley, Derek. *The Epic Film: Myth and History*. London: Routledge and Kegan Paul, 1984.

Lucanio, Patrick. *With Fire and Sword: Italian Spectacles on American Screens 1958–1968*. Metuchen: Scarecrow Press, 1994.

Le péplum: L'antiquité au cinéma. Ed. Claude Aziza. CinémAction 89. Condé-sur-Noireau: Corlet/Télérama, 1998.

Sinemythologia: Oi ellênikoi mythoi ston pankosmio kinêmatografo. Ed. Michalis Dêmopoulos. Athens: Politistikê Olympiada, 2003.

Smith, Gary A. *Epic Films: Casts, Credits and Commentary on Over 250 Historical Spectacle Movies*. Jefferson: McFarland, 1991.

Solomon, Jon. *The Ancient World in the Cinema*. 2nd edn. New Haven: Yale University Press, 2001.

1. Cinema

1902

Le jugement de Paris (The Judgment of Paris)
France. Director: Georges Hatot. Hatot worked with Louis Lumière and made short films on biblical topics. His *Néron essayant des poisons sur un esclave* ("Nero Trying Out Poisons on a Slave," 1896) was the earliest film about the cinema's favorite Roman emperor.

1908

La caduta di Troia (The Fall of Troy)
Italy. Director: Luigi Maggi. Maggi was one of the pioneers of epic films set in antiquity. He is best known today for *Gli ultimi giorni di Pompeii* (*The Last Days of Pompeii*, 1908) and *Nerone* (*Nero, or The Burning of Rome*; also known as *Nero, or the Fall of Rome*; 1909).

1910–1911

La caduta di Troia (The Fall of Troy)
Italy. Directors: Giovanni Pastrone (under the pseudonym Piero Fosco) and Romano Luigi Borgnetto. The first important film on its subject, with a running time of *c.* 35 minutes. Pastrone later wrote and directed *Cabiria* (1914), one of the most spectacular, famous, and influential epics in film history, set during the Second Punic War.

1924

Helena. Part 1: *Der Raub der Helena* ("The Rape of Helen"); Part 2: *Der Untergang Trojas* ("The Fall of Troy").
Germany. Director: Manfred Noa. Long lost monumental epic made at the height of German silent film production but overshadowed by Fritz Lang's *Die Nibelungen* (also in two parts). With a cast of thousands, Noa filmed in Bavaria on a scale rivaling that of the historical epics made at the Ufa studios in Berlin. His gigantic set of Troy was said to have been built so sturdily that it could withstand even storm winds. Spectacular highlights were a chariot race, Helen's welcome to Troy, land and sea battles, a still impressive Trojan Horse, and a huge conflagration. The film was restored in 2001 to a length of 204 minutes.

1927

The Private Life of Helen of Troy (Helen of Troy)
U.S. Director: Alexander Korda. British (originally Hungarian) producer-director Korda's attempt to set foot in Hollywood around the time of the transition from silent to sound films. Two-thirds of its footage are lost. The screenplay was based on John Erskine's 1925 novel of the same name and resembles some of the witty drawing-room comedies of the 1920s (despite the presence of a character with the forcedly unfunny name of Malapokitoratoreadetos). At the end, Helen tries out her wiles even on Ulysses. Korda gave the title part to his wife, actress Maria Corda. Korda later made *The Private Life of Henry VIII* (1933) and *Rembrandt* (1936), both famous and accomplished films which provide us with examples of his "upstairs-downstairs" perspective on history. In 1937 he began production of *I, Claudius* with director Josef von Sternberg and with Charles Laughton as Claudius, but the film was never completed.

1931

La regina di Sparta (The Queen of Sparta)
U.S./Italy. Director: Manfred S. Noa. This low-budget 80-minute mini-epic produced in Hollywood for an Italian company amazes by its free-wheeling approach to plot material from the *Iliad*. The dysfunctional family relations among Priam, Paris, and Helen are in a class of their own. Classical scholars who tear their hair over *Troy* should take a look at this film.

1953–1954

Loves of Three Queens (The Love of Three Queens, Eternal Woman, The Face That Launched a Thousand Ships)
France/Italy. Directors: Marc Allegret and Edgar G. Ulmer. Screen siren Hedy Lamarr, who had been the first film actress to appear in a nude scene (in Gustav Machaty's *Extase* of 1932) and who had played the titular seductress in Cecil B. De Mille's *Samson and Delilah* (1949), produced this star vehicle for herself. She plays a modern woman who is undecided about what costume to wear to a ball and asks three men for advice. They suggest Helen of Troy, Empress Josephine, and Geneviève of Brabant. The film had a complicated and ill-fated production history; it is said to have been originally over three hours long (and unfinished).

In the classical episode, Venus and Jupiter make appropriate onscreen appearances. Ulmer later directed *Hannibal* (1960).

1956

Helen of Troy
U.S. Director: Robert Wise. The chief model for *Troy* almost four decades later and produced by the same studio, this was the first widescreen epic on the Trojan War. It was advertised on *Behind the Cameras*, the studio's television series to promote upcoming releases, as both archaeologically sound and reverent of Homer's *Iliad* ("this book was our challenge"). It is, however, a rather impersonal effort on the part of director Wise. The cast of famous British, French, Italian, and American actors appears a bit lost in the sets. This is most obviously the case for the Helen of twenty-one-year old Rossana Podestà, who did not speak English. Wise chose her over Elizabeth Taylor, Ava Gardner, and Lana Turner. Podestà had played Nausicaa in Mario Camerini's *Ulisse* (*Ulysses*) the year before. That same year she had given an excellent performance in Valerio Zurlini's *Le ragazze di San Frediano* (*The Girls of San Frediano*). Neither Podestà nor Jacques Sernas as Paris – billed as "Jack Sernas," presumably to make his first name more easily pronouncible to American audiences – nor the overall persuasiveness of the film were helped by the presence of a pre-stardom Brigitte Bardot as Helen's handmaid. (Perhaps if Bardot had played Helen . . .) But the city of Troy, closely patterned on the palace at Knossos on Crete, looks impressive. Wise was assisted on some of the mass scenes and action sequences by one experienced and one future director, Raoul Walsh and Sergio Leone, both uncredited.

1957

The Story of Mankind
U.S. Director: Irwin Allen. The future "master of disaster" here produced, directed, and co-wrote a different kind of disaster: an all-star episodic history of mankind based on the best-selling novel by Hendrik Willem Van Loon. Ronald Colman in his final role is the Spirit of Man who fights the devil (Vincent Price) for the survival of mankind before a heavenly tribunal. Classical antiquity is represented by Hippocrates (a fatherly Charles Coburn), Caesar, Cleopatra (Virginia Mayo!), Nero (Peter Lorre!!), and, of course, Helen of Troy (glamor starlet Dani Crayne; Hedy Lamarr this time around is Joan of Arc). Footage from Wise's *Helen of Troy* and Howard Hawks's *Land of the Pharaohs* (1955) is used to give

the film a modicum of visual appeal. French filmmaker Georges Méliès had long before pioneered this approach to history with *La civilisation à travers les ages* ("Civilization across the Ages," 1908).

1962

La guerra di Troia (The Trojan War, The Trojan Horse, The Wooden Horse of Troy, The Mighty Warrior)
Italy/France. Director: Giorgio Ferroni. Loosely based on the *Aeneid*, this film is one of the better Italian muscleman epics set in antiquity. Its hero is Aeneas, played by Steve Reeves; its theme the end of the Trojan War and the surviving Trojans' escape to Italy. In Troy, Aeneas' is the voice of reason against a reckless Paris. Ferroni's style, especially his hand-ling of the widescreen format, overcomes obvious plot limitations. The scene of the Trojan Horse being dragged across the plain toward Troy and entering the city is superior to Wise's. American bodybuilder Reeves is most famous for having been Hercules in Pietro Francisci's *Le fatiche di Ercole* (*Hercules, The Adventures of Hercules*; 1958) and *Ercole e la regina di Lidia* (*Hercules Unchained, Hercules and the Queen of Lydia*; 1959). Ferroni previously made *Le Baccanti* (*The Bacchantes*, 1961), an epic based on Euripides' tragedy, and directed two quasi-historical Roman films in 1964. Cf. also below.

1962

L'ira di Achille (Fury of Achilles, Achilles)
Italy. Director: Marino Girolami. This unusual film reveals a greater familiarity with the *Iliad* than all other films, opening with shots of the famous ancient marble bust of Homer while a narrator introduces the story. The plot is set in motion when the Greeks capture Chryseis, Briseis, and an invented Xenia (added as soon-to-be lover of Patroclus). A number of famous scenes from the *Iliad* duly appear on screen, if in condensed form: the plague sent by Apollo, the quarrel between Agamemnon and Achilles (with Athena momentarily appearing to the latter), Thetis' epiphany to Achilles, the forge of Hephaestus (Achilles' divine armor is golden; his shield, however, does not display scenic decorations and is not round), and Hector's farewell from his family (and the Trojans). Priam's visit to Achilles contains a surprising twist. As does the *Iliad*, the film excludes Achilles' death and the fall of Troy. More surprisingly, there is no Helen. American bodybuilder Gordon Mitchell, although too old for the part, is a gaunt Achilles, a doomed dealer of death fully aware

of his own end. The interiors of Troy sport Minoan columns, but the exteriors with their crenellated towers and walls look quasi-medieval.

1965

Il leone di Tebe (The Lion of Thebes; Helen, Queen of Troy)
Italy/France. Director: Giorgio Ferroni. Muscleman epic that takes Euripides' tragedy *Helen* as its starting point. After the Trojan War, Helen and Menelaus are returning to Sparta, but a shipwreck off the Egyptian coast separates them. Helen and the eponymous hero, her faithful defender, are brought to the pharaoh's court. Since Helen is played by Yvonne Furneaux, it is understandable that the pharaoh is instantly smitten with her. Various palace intrigues ensue, but Helen's bodyguard saves the day.

1972

The Trojan Women
Greece/United Kingdom/U.S. Director: Michael Cacoyannis. Second of three adaptations of Euripidean tragedy by a distinguished Greek writer-director, with an international cast of famous actresses. Irene Papas stands out as a fearless and smart Helen who also radiates a mature eroticism (and knows it). Cacoyannis found the location for Troy after the fall in the ruins of a walled city in Spain, minimally dressed with pillars to evoke classical antiquity. He had previously filmed *Electra* (1962), with Irene Papas in the title role, and would complete his trilogy in 1977.

1973

Elena si, ma . . . di Troia (Helen, Yes . . . Helen of Troy)
Italy. Director: Alfonso Brescia. An erotic parody of the myth, with a former Miss Austria in the title role and footage from Ferroni's *La guerra di Troia*. Brescia later directed three other ancient epics, among which *La rivolta dei pretoriani* (*Revolt of the Praetorians*, 1964) is the only big-screen spectacle set at the time of Emperor Domitian.

1977

Iphigenia
Greece. Director: Michael Cacoyannis. Adapted from *Iphigenia in Aulis*, Cacoyannis's third film of Euripides is the culmination of film adaptations

of Greek tragedy in the realistic mode. Irene Papas as Clytemnestra and a young Tatiana Papamoschou in the title role are stand-outs in a uniformly accomplished cast. The memorable score is by Mikis Theodorakis, who had also written the music for Cacoyannis's earlier adaptations.

1996

Achilles
United Kingdom. Director: Barry Purves. In eleven minutes, this "Claymation" (i.e., clay animation) short narrated by Derek Jacobi tells the homoerotic love story of Achilles and Patroclus during the Trojan War and the deaths of both. Their love is not in the *Iliad* but is first attested for Aeschylus' lost trilogy about Achilles (*The Myrmidons, The Nereids*, and *The Phrygians* or *Hector's Ransom*).

2004

Troy
U.S. Director: Wolfgang Petersen. The most expensive and longest Trojan-War epic made to date, unlikely to be rivaled in the foreseeable future. Many of its strengths are not obvious on a first viewing; some of its weaknesses are. The wooden horse is almost too beautiful to be menacing or mysterious.

2004

Singe den Zorn ("Sing the Wrath")
Germany. Directors: Matthias Merkle and Antje Borchardt. A dramatic staging of the *Iliad* in 96 minutes. In the ruins of Troy at Hisarlık, a cast of fourteen recites and enacts about 4,000 lines of Homer in the translation by Johann Heinrich Voss, the best-known German version.

2. Television

1953

"The Fall of Troy (1184 B.C.)"
U.S. Director: Sidney Lumet. Episode in series *You Are There*, a half-hour program on great moments in history presented in the manner of live news broadcasts and hosted by Walter Cronkite. Lumet also directed the episode "The Return of Ulysses" the following year. Other episodes

involving classical antiquity dealt with the deaths of Socrates, Caesar, and Cleopatra.

1955

"The Iliad"
U.S. Adaptation for series *Omnibus*, a cultural production hosted by Alastair Cooke. Other episodes on classical themes dealt with Salome and Brutus. An adaptation of Sophocles' *Oedipus the King*, featuring Christopher Plummer, aired in 1957.

1965

"The Myth Makers"
United Kingdom. Director: Michael Leeston-Smith. Episode in cult series *Doctor Who*, in which the eponymous doctor and his crew time-travel to the Trojan War. "Having initially dismissed the famous wooden horse as a fiction of Homer's, the Doctor is eventually driven to 'invent' it himself, thereby giving the Greeks the means to defeat the Trojans" (BBC website). "The Romans," another classical episode from the same year, is set during the time of Nero.

1966

"The Revenge of the Gods"
U.S. Director: Sobey Martin. Episode in short-lived science-fiction series *The Time Tunnel*, in which two modern scientists are deposited at various moments of history when the eponymous machine malfunctions. Here they land in the Greek camp during the last year of the Trojan War and are promptly mistaken for gods. To emphasize the wooden horse, the script makes Ulysses, not Agamemnon or Achilles, the most prominent among the Greek leaders. But at least Epeius, the craftsman who built the horse, receives a screen appearance. Footage from Wise's *Helen of Troy* and Rudolf Maté's *The 300 Spartans* (1962) cannot prevent another disaster perpetrated by producer Irwin Allen.

1967

Le Troiane ("The Trojan Women")
Italy. Director: Vittorio Cottafavi. One of Cottafavi's highly acclaimed adaptations of Greek tragedy for Italian public television. Cottafavi had

previously directed several quasi-ancient mythological and historical films, among them *Ercole alla conquista di Atlantide* (*Hercules Conquers Atlantis, Hercules and the Captive Women*; 1961), regarded by cinema cognoscenti as the best of all muscleman epics.

1971

L'Eneide ("The Aeneid")
Italy/Yugoslavia. Director: Franco Rossi. Rossi's follow-up to his *Odissea* of 1968. This six-hour version of Virgil's epic for public television is the only screen adaptation worthy of serious consideration vis-à-vis its model. The most memorable performance is by Greek actress and singer Olga Karlatos as Dido, queen of Carthage, to whom Aeneas recounts the fall of Troy. The discovery of the Trojan Horse in Rossi's *Odissea* is, however, a more accomplished sequence and boasts the screen's eeriest wooden horse ever.

1979

"Of Mycenae and Men"
United Kingdom. Director: Hugh David. Half-hour comic oddity, written by Frederick Raphael and Kenneth Macleish, on "what might have happened to Helen of Troy after the Trojan War" (BBC website). Curvaceous Diana Dors plays Helen; Freddie Jones is Menelaus, and Bob Hoskins is Mr. Taramasalatopoulos.

1995

"Beware Greeks Bearing Gifts"
U.S. Director: T. J. Scott. Episode in series *Xena, Warrior Princess*. The eponymous lady and her sidekick take part in the Trojan War to help Xena's friend Helen. The Trojan Horse, here made of bamboo, plays a large part in the plot. In a later episode called "Ulysses," Xena encounters and falls in love with an Ithaca-bound Odysseus. (The episode's German title translates as "What Homer Could Not Know." Quite so.) Originally a character in the television series *Hercules: The Legendary Journeys*, Xena became an equally successful series heroine, traversing space and time from pre-Trojan War Greek myth down to Roman history and on to Norse mythology – all without aging, of course.

1997

Crayola Kids Adventures: The Trojan Horse
Canada/U.S. Director: Michael Kruzan. Songs and slapstick humor liven up this retelling of the Trojan War story from the Judgment of Paris to the fall of Troy. Intended for children ages 7–11. The cast are children wielding toy weapons.

1999

Hercules: Zero to Hero
U.S. Director: Bob Kline. Animated direct-to-video sequel to Disney's theatrical release *Hercules* of the same year. Helen of Troy is just one of the characters from Greek myth that are brought into the story of Hercules, although their mythology is unconnected with his.

2003

Helen of Troy
U.S. Director: John Kent Harrison. Three-hour television epic that profited from the anticipated theatrical release of *Troy*. Unusually, it features Theseus of Athens as a major character in the story of Helen before the Trojan War. Achilles, by contrast, is a minor character, most notable for being the kind of "brute" that Petersen's Achilles turns out not to be. (Harrison's Achilles sets up Hector for a treacherous kill.) Agamemnon is murdered in his bath by a Clytemnestra who unexpectedly appears in Troy after its fall.

3. Miscellanea

1913

König Menelaus im Kino ("King Menelaus at the Movies")
Austria. Director: Hans Otto Löwenstein. A parody in which the director plays Helen of Troy.

1937

Nothing Sacred
U.S. Director: William A. Wellman. Classic screwball comedy that briefly features famous women from myth and history: Helen of Troy, Salome,

Lady Godiva, and Catherine the Great. The last-mentioned is played by one Elinor Troy.

1951

Sköna Helena (Helen of Troy)
Sweden. Director: Gustaf Edgren. Operetta after Jacques Offenbach's *La belle Hélène*. Eva Dahlbeck, best known internationally for her work with Ingmar Bergman, plays the title role.

1960

La regina delle Ammazzoni (Love Slaves of the Amazons, Queen of the Amazons, Colossus and the Amazons, Colossus and the Amazon Queen)
Italy. Director: Vittorio Sala. Glaucus, the strongest Greek after the Trojan War, and his friend Pyrrhus are engaged in adventures among the Amazons. The film is one of many examples of how loosely the plots of muscleman films may be related to Greek myth.

1961

The Three Stooges Meet Hercules
U.S. Director: Edward Bernds. At the height of the sword-and-sandal films, the eponymous trio put in their two drachmas' worth of parody by time-traveling to tenth-century-B.C. Ithaca and meeting assorted mythical characters. These include Ajax, Ulysses, Achilles, and Helen. No relation to actual myth is intended. The humor is for aficionados only.

1962

La leggenda di Enea (War of the Trojans, The Avenger, Legend of Aeneas, The Last Glory of Troy, Conquering Heroes)
Italy/France. Director: Giorgio Rivalta. In a condensation of the second half of Virgil's *Aeneid*, Aeneas, again played by Steve Reeves, fights over a new homestead in Italy for the survivors of the Trojan War. The film is a sequel to Ferroni's *La guerra di Troia*, footage of which is used when Aeneas remembers the fall of Troy. His reminiscence is prompted when he sees wall paintings of the fall, a very loose adaptation of a famous moment in Book 2 of the *Aeneid*.

1967

Doctor Faustus
United Kingdom. Directors: Richard Burton and Nevill Coghill. Adaptation of Christopher Marlowe's *The Tragedy of Doctor Faustus*, with Burton as Faustus and Elizabeth Taylor, the star of Joseph L. Mankiewicz's *Cleopatra* four years earlier, as Helen of Troy. The Faust legend has been filmed numerous times.

1968

"Elaan of Troyius"
U.S. Director: John Meredyth Lucas. Episode in the original *Star Trek* series, whose plot is somewhat patterned after the origin of the Trojan War, as the pseudo-Greek names indicate. The eponymous lady belongs to the nobility of the planet Elas, which has been engaged in wars against the planet Troyius for centuries. To ensure peace, she is given to the leader of Troyius as a bride but proves destructive. Another occasionally Helen-like character is the half-human and half-alien Deanna Troi in *Star Trek: The Next Generation*, who in the episode "Ménage à Troi" is abducted and who appears in pseudo-ancient garb in "Hollow Pursuits" (both 1990).

1981

Der Schatz des Priamos ("The Treasure of Priam")
West Germany. Director: Karl Fruchtmann. Three-hour television biography of Heinrich Schliemann.

1981

Das Liebeskonzil ("Council of Love")
Austria. Director: Werner Schroeter. Film version by independent filmmaker Schroeter, based on the controversial play by Oskar Panizza and his blasphemy trial and imprisonment in 1895. Helen, Salome, and Agrippina as well as Mary and Jesus are among the play's and film's ancient characters. The subject is syphilis; the attack is on religious hypocrisy. Schroeter's adaptation had to battle courts and censors.

1996

Hamlet
Director: Kenneth Branagh. Act II, Scene 2 of the play contains a recital of Achilles' son Pyrrhus slaughtering Priam. Branagh's full-text adaptation contains a visual enactment, with John Gielgud as Priam and Judi Dench as Hecuba.

2001

The Pharaoh Project
U.S. Director: Brad Tanenbaum. Science-fiction adventure in which modern characters bear names that evoke figures from various periods of history, including Ramses, Alexander the Great, and Genghis Khan. The modern Helen Trajen parallels, of course, Helen of Troy. For addicts only.

2004

The Trojan Women
U.S. Director: Brad Mays. Adaptation of Euripides' tragedy by a stage director with a modern twist: the story is presented as if for television news, complete with a newscaster and on-scene reporter. Mays had adapted Euripides' *Bacchae* to film in 2001.

Bibliography

Achcar, Gilbert. *The Clash of Barbarisms: September 11 and the Making of the New World Disorder.* Tr. Peter Drucker. New York: Monthly Review Press, 2002.

Adkins, A. W. H. *Merit and Responsibility: A Study in Greek Values.* Chicago: University of Chicago Press, 1975; first publ. 1960.

Ahl, Frederick. "Homer, Vergil, and Complex Narrative Structures in Latin Epic: An Essay." *Illinois Classical Studies,* 14 (1989), 1–31.

——. *Lucan: An Introduction.* Ithaca: Cornell University Press, 1976.

——. *Sophocles' Oedipus: Evidence and Self-Conviction.* Ithaca: Cornell University Press, 1991.

——. "Statius' *Thebaid*: A Reconsideration." *Aufstieg und Niedergang der römischen Welt,* II.32.5 (1986), 2803–2912.

Allen, Richard. "Representation, Illusion, and the Cinema." *Cinema Journal,* 32 (1993), 21–48.

Allen, T. W. (ed.). *Homeri Opera.* Vol. 5. Oxford: Clarendon Press, 1912; rpt. 1978.

Arnold, Frank. "Wolfgang Petersen: Keine Welt in Schwarz und Weiss." *Kölner Stadtanzeiger* (May 14, 2004); http://www.ksta.de/artikel.jsp?id=1084203219381.

Aziza, Claude (ed.). *Le péplum: L'antiquité au cinéma.* CinémAction 89. Condé-sur-Noireau: Corlet/Télérama, 1998.

Barchiesi, Alessandro (ed.). *P. Ovidii Nasonis Epistulae Heroidum 1–3.* Florence: Le Monnier, 1992.

Bazin, André. *What Is Cinema?* Tr. Hugh Gray. Vol. 1. Berkeley: University of California Press, 1967; rpt. 1974.

Benardete, Seth. "The *Aristeia* of Diomedes and the Plot of the *Iliad*." *Agon*, 1.2 (1968), 10–38.

Bierl, Anton; Arbogast Schmitt, and Andreas Willi (eds.). *Antike Literatur in neuer Deutung*. Munich: Saur, 2004.

Bluestone, George. *Novels into Film*. Berkeley: University of California Press, 1961. First publ. 1957.

Boller, Paul F., and Ronald L. Davis. *Hollywood Anecdotes*. New York: Morrow, 1987.

Bolzoni, Francesco, and Mario Foglietti. *Le stagioni del cinema: Trenta registi si raccontano*. Soveria Mannelli: Rubettino, 2000.

Borchardt, Antje. "Singe den Zorn: Homers Ilias in Troia." *Pegasus-Onlinezeitschrift*, 4 no. 3 (2004), 65; http://www.pegasus-onlinezeitschrift.de/agora_3_2004_borchardt.html.

Bordwell, David; Janet Staiger, and Kristin Thompson. *The Classical Hollywood Cinema: Film Style and Mode of Production to 1960*. New York: Columbia University Press, 1985.

Borowski, Tadeusz. *This Way for the Gas, Ladies and Gentlemen; and Other Stories*. Selected and tr. by Barbara Vedder. New York: Penguin, 1967; several rpts.

Brady, James. *The Marines of Autumn: A Novel of the Korean War*. New York: St. Martin's, 2000.

Brandau, Birgit; Hartmut Schickert, and Peter Jablonka. *Troia – Wie es wirklich aussah*. Munich: Piper, 2004.

Briley, Ron. "Reel History: U.S. History, 1932–1972, as Viewed through the Lens of Hollywood." *The History Teacher*, 23 (1990), 215–236.

Bullock, Marcus, and Michael W. Jennings (eds.). *Walter Benjamin: Selected Writings*. Vol. 1: *1913–1926*. Cambridge: Belknap Press/Harvard University Press, 1996.

Burgess, Jonathan S. *The Tradition of the Trojan War in Homer and the Epic Cycle*. Baltimore: Johns Hopkins University Press, 2001; rpt. 2004.

Burnett, Anne Pippin. *Three Archaic Poets: Archilochus, Alcaeus, Sappho*. Cambridge: Harvard University Press, 1983.

Burns, Walter Noble. *Tombstone – An Iliad of the Southwest*. Garden City: Doubleday, Page, 1927.

Buxton, Richard (ed.). *From Myth to Reason? Studies in the Development of Greek Thought*. Oxford: Oxford University Press, 1999.

Byrd, Max. "The Month That Was." *The New York Times Book Review* (April 22, 2001), 25.

Campbell, David A. (ed. and tr.). *Greek Lyric*. Vol. 1: *Sappho and Alcaeus*. Loeb Classical Library. Cambridge: Harvard University Press, 1982.

Cardullo, Bert (ed.). *Bazin at Work: Major Essays and Reviews from the Forties and Fifties*. New York: Routledge, 1997.

Carr, Edward Hallett. *The Twenty Years' Crisis, 1919–1939: An Introduction to the Study of International Relations.* New York: Perennial, 2001; first publ. 1939.

Clay, Jenny Strauss. "The Whip and the Will of Zeus." *Literary Imagination,* 1 (1999), 40–60.

Craig, Campbell. *Glimmer of a New Leviathan: Total War in the Realism of Niebuhr, Morgenthau, and Waltz.* New York: Columbia University Press, 2003.

Cranston, Maurice, and Richard S. Peters (eds.). *Hobbes and Rousseau: A Collection of Critical Essays.* New York: Doubleday, 1972.

Crowdus, Gary. "Dramatizing Issues That Historians Don't Address: An Interview With Oliver Stone." *Cinéaste,* 30 no. 2 (2005), 12–23.

Cyrino, Monica S. "She'll Always Have Paris: Helen in Wolfgang Petersen's *Troy*." *Amphora,* 4 no. 1 (2005), 10–11 and 18.

Danek, Georg. *Epos und Zitat: Studien zu den Quellen der Odyssee.* Vienna: Verlag der Österreichischen Akademie der Wissenschaften, 1998.

"David Benioff . . . Web Access." www.bbc.co.uk/print/films/webaccess/david_benioff_1.shtml.

De España, Rafael. *El Peplum: La antigüedad en el cine.* Barcelona: Glénat, 1998.

de Jong, Irene J. F. (ed.). *Homer: Critical Assessments.* 4 vols. London: Routledge, 1999.

——. *Narrators and Focalizers: The Presentation of the Story in the* Iliad. 2nd edn. Bristol: Bristol Classical Press, 2004.

Dêmopoulos, Michalis (ed.). *Sinemythologia: Oi ellênikoi mythoi ston pankosmio kinêmatografo.* Athens: Politistikê Olympiada, 2003.

Dué, Casey. *Homeric Variations on a Lament by Briseis.* Lanham: Rowman and Littlefield, 2002.

Eckstein, Arthur M., and Peter Lehman (eds.). *The Searchers: Essays and Reflections on John Ford's Classic Western.* Detroit: Wayne State University Press, 2004.

Edwards, Mark W. *Homer: Poet of the* Iliad. Baltimore: Johns Hopkins University Press, 1987; rpt. 1990.

——. *The Iliad: A Commentary.* Vol. 5: *Books 17–20.* Cambridge: Cambridge University Press, 1985.

Eimer, David. "Blood, Sweat and Spears." [London] *Sunday Times* (April 25, 2004), *Culture* supplement, 5–6.

Eisenstein, Sergei. *Film Form: Essays In Film Theory.* Ed. and tr. Jay Leyda. San Diego: Harcourt Brace Jovanovich, 1977. First publ. 1949.

——. *The Film Sense.* Ed. and tr. Jay Leyda. New York: Harcourt Brace Jovanovich, 1975. First publ. 1942.

Elley, Derek. *The Epic Film: Myth and History.* London: Routledge and Kegan Paul, 1984.

Epstein, Daniel. "David Benioff's Epic Adaptation, TROY: Interview by Daniel R. Epstein." www.ScreenwritersUtopia.com.

Erskine, Andrew. *Troy between Greece and Rome: Local Tradition and Imperial Power.* New York: Oxford University Press, 2001.

Fagles, Robert (tr.). *Homer: The Iliad.* New York: Viking, 1990; several rpts.

Finley, M. I. *Aspects of Antiquity: Discoveries and Controversies.* 2nd edn. New York: Viking, 1977; several rpts.

Fitton, J. Lesley. *The Discovery of the Greek Bronze Age.* London: British Museum Press, 1995; rpt. 2001.

Fittschen, Klaus. *Der Schild des Achilleus.* Archaeologia Homerica II.N.1. Göttingen: Vandenhoeck and Ruprecht, 1973.

Forst de Battaglia, Otto (ed.). *Dictatorship on Its Trial.* Tr. Huntley Paterson. London: Harrap, 1930.

Fowler, Robert (ed.). *The Cambridge Companion to Homer.* Cambridge: Cambridge University Press, 2004.

——. "Herodotos and His Contemporaries." *Journal of Hellenic Studies,* 116 (1996), 62–87.

Frazer, J. G. *Pausanias's Description of Greece.* 2nd. edn. Vol. 1: *Translation.* London: Macmillan, 1913.

Frazer, Richard M., Jr. (tr.). *The Trojan War: The Chronicles of Dictys of Crete and Dares the Phrygian.* Bloomington: Indiana University Press, 1966.

Friedrich, Paul. *The Meaning of Aphrodite.* Chicago: University of Chicago Press, 1978.

Gelmis, Joseph. *The Film Director as Superstar.* Garden City: Doubleday, 1970.

Genette, Gérard. *Palimpsests: Literature in the Second Degree.* Tr. Channa Newman and Claude Dubinsky. Lincoln: University of Nebraska Press, 1997.

Giakoumis, Pantaleon (ed.). *Homer, Hellas und Europa.* Aachen: Verlag Mainz, 2004.

Goethe, Johann Wolfgang von. *Goethes Werke* (Weimar Edition). Vol. 35 (1892): *Tag- und Jahres-Hefte.* Rpt. Munich: Deutscher Taschenbuch Verlag, 1987. Vol. 40.

Graves, Robert. *The Greek Myths.* New York: Penguin, 1993. First publ. 1955.

Griffin, Jasper. "The Epic Cycle and the Uniqueness of Homer." *Journal of Hellenic Studies,* 97 (1977), 39–53.

——. *Homer.* 2nd edn. Bristol: Bristol Classical Press, 2001.

Grossardt, Peter. "Ein Echo in allen Tonlagen: Der *Heroikos* von Flavius Philostrat als Bilanz der antiken Troia-Dichtung." *Studia Troica,* 14 (2004), 231–238.

Hainsworth, J. B. *The Idea of Epic.* Berkeley: University of California Press, 1991.

——. *The Iliad: A Commentary.* Vol. 3: *Books 9–12.* Cambridge: Cambridge University Press, 1993.

Hardie, Philip R. *Virgil's* Aeneid: *Cosmos and Imperium.* Oxford: Clarendon Press, 1986.

Hardin, Stephen L. *Texian Iliad: A Military History of the Texas Revolution, 1835–1836.* Austin: University of Texas Press, 1994.

Haslam, Jonathan. *No Virtue Like Necessity: Realist Thought in International Relations Since Machiavelli.* New Haven: Yale University Press, 2002.

Herr, Michael. *Dispatches.* New York: Avon, 1968; several rpts.

Hertel, Dieter. *Troia: Archäologie, Geschichte, Mythos.* Munich: Beck, 2001.

Heubeck, Alfred; Stephanie West, and J. B. Hainsworth. *A Commentary on Homer's Odyssey*. Vol. 1: *Introduction and Books I–VIII*. Oxford: Clarendon Press, 1988; rpt. 1990.

Higgins, Charlotte. "*Troy* Stars Speak Out at 'Futility of War'." *The Guardian* (May 14, 2004), 8.

Hobbes, Thomas. *Leviathan*. Ed. Richard E. Flathman and David Johnston. New York: Norton, 1997.

Hofmann, Heinz (ed.). *Antike Mythen in der europäischen Tradition*. Tübingen: Attempto, 1999.

Howard, Patricia. *Gluck: An Eighteenth-Century Portrait in Letters and Documents*. Oxford: Clarendon Press, 1995.

Hunter, Virginia. *Past and Process in Herodotus and Thucydides*. Princeton: Princeton University Press, 1980.

James, Robert Rhodes (ed.). *Winston S. Churchill: His Complete Speeches 1897–1963*. Vol. 7: *1943–1949*. New York: Chelsea House, 1974.

Jakobson, Roman. *Selected Writings*. 2nd edn. Vol. 2: *Word and Language*. The Hague: Mouton, 1971.

Jameson, Fredric. *Signatures of the Visible*. New York: Routledge, 1990.

Johnson, Samuel. *Lives of the English Poets by Samuel Johnson, LL. D.* Ed. George Birkbeck Hill. Vol. 3: *Swift–Lyttleton*. Oxford: Clarendon Press, 1905.

Kakridis, Johannes Th. *Homeric Researches*. New York: Garland, 1987; first publ. 1949.

King, Katherine Callen. *Achilles: Paradigms of the War Hero from Homer to the Middle Ages*. Berkeley: University of California Press, 1987.

Kirk, G. S. *Myth: Its Meaning and Function in Ancient and Other Cultures*. Berkeley: University of California Press, 1970; several rpts.

Kniebe, Tobias. "Homer ist, wenn man trotzdem lacht: 'Troja'-Regisseur Wolfgang Petersen über die mythischen Wurzeln des Erzählens und den Achilles in uns allen." *Süddeutsche Zeitung* (May 11, 2004); http://www.sueddeutsche.de/kultur/artikel/607/31576/print.html.

Korfmann, Manfred; Joachim Latacz, and David Hawkins. "Was There a Trojan War?" *Archaeology*, 57 no. 3 (May–June, 2004), 36–41.

Kullmann, Wolfgang. "Oral Poetry Theory and Neoanalysis in Homeric Research." *Greek, Roman and Byzantine Studies*, 25 (1984), 307–323.

Latacz, Joachim. *Achilleus: Wandlungen eines europaischen Heldenbildes*. Stuttgart: Teubner, 1995.

——. *Homer: His Art and His World*. Tr. James P. Holoka. Ann Arbor: University of Michigan Press, 1996; rpt. 1998.

——. *Kampfparänese, Kampfdarstellung und Kampfwirklichkeit in der Ilias, bei Kallinos und Tyrtaios*. Munich: Beck, 1977.

——. *Troy and Homer: Towards a Solution of an Old Mystery*. Tr. Kevin Windle and Rosh Ireland. Oxford: Oxford University Press, 2004.

Lattimore, Richmond (tr.). *The Iliad of Homer*. Chicago: University of Chicago Press, 1951; several rpts.

Lauring, Palle. *A History of Denmark*. Copenhagen: Høst and Søn, 1986.

Leavis, F. R. *Mass Civilisation and Minority Culture*. Cambridge: Minority Press, 1930.

Lebow, Richard Ned. *The Tragic Vision of Politics: Ethics, Interests and Orders*. Cambridge: Cambridge University Press, 2003.

Lee, Guy (tr.). *Propertius: The Poems*. Oxford: Oxford University Press, 1994; rpt. 1999.

Lefkowitz, Mary R. *The Lives of the Greek Poets*. Baltimore: Johns Hopkins University Press, 1981.

Legro, Jeffrey W., and Andrew Moravcsik. "Is Anybody Still a Realist?" *International Security*, 24 (1999), 5–55.

Lembke, Janet, and Kenneth J. Reckford (trs.). *Euripides: Hecuba*. New York: Oxford University Press, 1991.

Leprohon, Pierre. *The Italian Cinema*. Tr. Roger Greaves and Oliver Stallybrass. New York: Praeger, 1972.

Lindheim, Sara H. *Mail and Female: Epistolary Narrative and Desire in Ovid's Heroides*. Madison: University of Wisconsin Press, 2003.

Logue, Christopher. *All Day Permanent Red: The First Battle Scenes of Homer's Iliad*. New York: Farrar, Straus and Giroux, 2003.

Lombardo, Stanley (tr.). *Homer: Iliad*. Indianapolis: Hackett, 1997.

Lorimer, Hilda Lockhart. *Homer and the Monuments*. London: Macmillan, 1950.

Lucanio, Patrick. *With Fire and Sword: Italian Spectacles on American Screens 1958–1968*. Metuchen: Scarecrow Press, 1994.

Mack, Maynard. *Alexander Pope: A Life*. New York: Norton/New Haven: Yale University Press, 1985.

Mansel, Philip. *Constantinople: City of the World's Desire, 1453–1924*. New York: St. Martin's, 1996; first publ. 1995.

McFarlane, Brian. *Novel to Film: An Introduction to the Theory of Adaptation*. Oxford: Clarendon Press, 1996.

McGrath, Alister. *The Twilight of Atheism: The Rise and Fall of Disbelief in the Modern World*. New York: Doubleday, 2004.

McMurtry, Larry. "His True Love Is Politics" (review of Bill Clinton, *My Life* [New York: Knopf, 2004; rpt. 2005]). *The New York Times Book Review* (July 4, 2004), 1 and 8–9.

McNally, Richard J. *Remembering Trauma*. Cambridge: Belknap Press/Harvard University Press, 2003.

McWilliams, John P., Jr. *The American Epic: Transforming a Genre, 1770–1860*. Cambridge: Cambridge University Press, 1989.

Meagher, Robert Emmet. *The Meaning of Helen: In Search of an Ancient Icon*. Wauconda: Bolchazy-Carducci, 2002. First publ. as *Helen: Myth, Legend, and the Culture of Misogyny*. New York: Continuum, 1995.

Mendelsohn, Daniel. "A Little Iliad." *The New York Review of Books* (June 24, 2004), 46–49.

Milosz, Czeslaw. *The Captive Mind*. Tr. Jane Zielonko. New York: Vintage, 1990; first publ. 1953.

Miola, Robert S. *Shakespeare and Classical Tragedy: The Influence of Seneca*. Oxford: Clarendon Press, 1992.

Monaco, James. *How to Read a Film*. 3rd edn: *The World of Movies, Media, and Multimedia: Language, History, Theory*. New York: Oxford University Press, 2000.

Morgenthau, Hans J. *Politics Among Nations: The Struggle for Power and Peace*. Brief Edition, ed. Kenneth W. Thompson. Boston: McGraw-Hill, 1993.

——. *Scientific Man* vs. *Power Politics*. Chicago: University of Chicago Press, 1946; rpt. 1974.

Nagy, Gregory. *Homeric Questions*. Austin: University of Texas Press, 1996.

——. *Homer's Text and Language*. Urbana: University of Illinois Press, 2004.

Naremore, James (ed.). *Film Adaptation*. New Brunswick: Rutgers University Press, 2000.

Nestle, Wilhelm. *Vom Mythos zum Logos: Die Selbstentfaltung des griechischen Denkens von Homer bis auf die Sophistik und Sokrates*. 2nd edn. Stuttgart: Kröner, 1941; rpt. 1975.

Newman, John Kevin. *The Classical Epic Tradition*. Madison: University of Wisconsin Press, 1986.

Niebuhr, Reinhold. *Moral Man and Immoral Society: A Study in Ethics and Politics*. New York: Scribner's, 1932; several rpts.

——. *The Nature and Destiny of Man: A Christian Interpretation*. Vol. 1: *Human Nature*. Louisville: Westminster John Knox Press, 1996; first publ. 1941.

Novick, Sheldon M. (ed.). *The Collected Works of Justice Holmes: Complete Public Writings and Selected Judicial Opinions of Oliver Wendell Holmes*. The Holmes Devise Memorial Edition. Vol. 3. Chicago: University of Chicago Press, 1995.

Nye, Joseph S., Jr. *Soft Power: The Means to Success in World Politics*. New York: Public Affairs, 2004.

Oliva, Gianni (ed.). *Interviste a D'Annunzio (1895–1938)*. Lanciano: Rocco Carabba, 2002.

O'Sullivan, Neil. *Alcidamas, Aristophanes, and the Beginnings of Greek Stylistic Theory*. Stuttgart: Steiner, 1992.

Page, Denys. *Sappho and Alcaeus: An Introduction to the Study of Ancient Lesbian Poetry*. Oxford: Clarendon Press, 1955; rpt. 1975.

Païsl-Apostolopoulou, Machı (ed.). *Eranos: Proceedings of the Ninth International Symposium on the Odyssey*. Ithaca: Centre for Odyssean Studies, 2001.

Pasinetti, P. M. "*Julius Caesar*: The Role of the Technical Adviser." *Film Quarterly*, 8 (1953), 131–138.

Petersen, Wolfgang, with Ulrich Greiwe. *"Ich liebe die grossen Geschichten"*: Vom *"Tatort" bis nach Hollywood*. Cologne: Kiepenheuer and Witsch, 1997.

Pierrot le Fou: A Film by Jean-Luc Godard. Tr. Peter Whitehead. New York: Simon and Schuster, 1969.

Quaresima, Leonardo, and Laura Vichi (eds.). *La decima musa: il cinema e le altre arte/The Tenth Muse: Cinema and the Other Arts*. Udine: Forum, 2001.

Quintus of Smyrna. *The Trojan Epic: Posthomerica*. Ed. and tr. Alan James. Baltimore: Johns Hopkins University Press, 2004.

Rabel, Robert S. "Agamemnon's Empire in Thucydides." *The Classical Journal*, 80 (1984), 8–10.

——. *Plot and Point of View in the Iliad*. Ann Arbor: University of Michigan Press, 1997.

Ramelli, Ilaria, and Giulio Lucchetta. *Allegoria*. Vol. 1: *L'età classica*. Milan: Vita e pensiero, 2004.

Rauschning, Hermann. *Gespräche mit Hitler*. Vienna: Europa Verlag, 1973 (complete ed.); first publ. 1940.

Roberts, Deborah H.; Francis M. Dunn, and Don Fowler (eds.). *Classical Closure: Reading the End in Greek and Latin Literature*. Princeton: Princeton University Press, 1997.

Röhl, Wolfgang. " 'Menschen hauen sich die Köpfe ein'." *Stern* (April 19, 2004); http://www.stern.de/unterhaltung/film/index.html?id=522904&q= petersen%20menschen.

Roland, Charles Pierce. *An American Iliad: The Story of the Civil War*. 2nd edn. Lexington: University of Kentucky Press, 2004.

Rothstein, Edward. "To Homer, Iraq Would Be More of Same." *The New York Times* (June 5, 2004), Section B (*Arts and Ideas*), 9.

Russell, M. E. "Helmer of *Troy*," *In Focus*, 4 no. 5 (May, 2004); at http://www.infocusmag.com/04may/petersen.htm and http://www.infocusmag.com/04may/petersenuncut.htm.

Scherer, Margaret R. *The Legends of Troy in Art and Literature*. 2nd edn. New York: Phaidon, 1964.

Schmeling, Gareth (ed.). *The Novel in the Ancient World*. Leiden: Brill, 1996.

Scully, Stephen. *Homer and the Sacred City*. Ithaca: Cornell University Press, 1990; rpt. 1994.

——. "Reading the Shield of Achilles: Terror, Anger, Delight." *Harvard Studies in Classical Philology*, 101 (2003), 29–47.

Shanower, Eric. *Age of Bronze: Behind the Scenes*. Image Comics of Orange, California, 2002.

——. *Sacrifice*. Image Comics of Orange, California, 2004.

——. *A Thousand Ships*. Image Comics of Orange, California, 2001.

Shay, Jonathan. *Achilles in Vietnam: Combat Trauma and the Undoing of Character*. New York: Atheneum, 1994.

——. "Achilles: Paragon, Flawed Character, or Tragic Soldier Figure?" *The Classical Bulletin*, 71 (1995), 117–124.

Silk, Michael. *Homer: The Iliad*. 2nd edn. Cambridge: Cambridge University Press, 2004.

Sinyard, Neil. *Filming Literature: The Art of Screen Adaptation*. New York: St. Martin's, 1986.

Slatkin, Laura M. *The Power of Thetis: Allusion and Interpretation in the* Iliad. Berkeley: University of California Press, 1991.

Small, Jocelyn Penny. *The Parallel Worlds of Classical Art and Text*. Cambridge: Cambridge University Press, 2003.

Smith, Gary A. *Epic Films: Casts, Credits and Commentary on Over 250 Historical Spectacle Movies*. Jefferson: McFarland, 1991.

Smith, Murray. "Film Spectatorship and the Institution of Fiction." *The Journal of Aesthetics and Art Criticism*, 53 (1995), 113–127.

Snell, Bruno. *The Discovery of the Mind: The Greek Origins of European Thought*. Tr. Thomas G. Rosenmeyer. New York: Dover, 1982; first publ. 1953.

Solomon, Jon. *The Ancient World in the Cinema*. 2nd edn. New Haven: Yale University Press, 2001.

Stanley, Keith. *The Shield of Homer: Narrative Structure in the* Iliad. Princeton: Princeton University Press, 1993.

Steiner, George (ed.). *Homer in English*. London: Penguin, 1996.

Sutton, Dana Ferrin. *The Lost Sophocles*. Lanham: University Press of America, 1984.

Suzuki, Mihoko. *Metamorphoses of Helen: Authority, Difference, and the Epic*. Ithaca: Cornell University Press, 1989; rpt. 1992.

Tatum, James. *The Mourner's Song: War and Remembrance from the* Iliad *to Vietnam*. Chicago: University of Chicago Press, 2003.

Taylour, Lord William. *The Mycenaeans*. 2nd edn. New York: Thames and Hudson, 1983; rpt. 1990.

Thibodeau, Philip, and Harry Haskell (eds.). *Being There Together: Essays in Honor of Michael C. J. Putnam on the Occasion of His Seventieth Birthday*. Afton: Afton Historical Society Press, 2003.

Thomas, Carol G., and Craig Conant. *The Trojan War*. Westport: Greenwood Press, 2005.

Thomas, Rosalind. *Oral Tradition and Written Record in Classical Athens*. Cambridge: Cambridge University Press, 1989.

Troia: Traum und Wirklichkeit (essay collection). Stuttgart: Theiss, 2001; rpt. 2002.

Verducci, Florence. *Ovid's Toyshop of the Heart: Epistulae Heroidum*. Princeton: Princeton University Press, 1985.

Vivante, Paolo. *Homer*. New Haven: Yale University Press, 1985.

Vöhler, Martin; Bernd Seidensticker, and Wolfgang Emmerich (eds.). *Mythenkorrekturen: Zu einer paradoxalen Form der Mythenrezeption*. Berlin: de Gruyter, 2004.

Wace, Alan J. B., and Frank H. Stubbings (eds.). *A Companion to Homer*. New York: Macmillan, 1974. First publ. 1962.

Waltz, Kenneth N. *Man, the State, and War: A Theoretical Analysis*. New York: Columbia University Press, 1959; rpt. 2001.

Warner, William. "The Resistance to Popular Culture." *American Literary History*, 2 (1990), 726–742.

Wees, William C. "Dickens, Griffith and Eisenstein." *The Humanities Association Review / La Révue de l'Association des Humanités*, 24 (1973), 266–276.

Weil, Simone. *The Iliad or The Poem of Force: A Critical Edition*. Ed. James P. Holoka. New York: Lang, 2003.

West, M. L. (ed. and tr.). *Greek Epic Fragments from the Seventh to the Fifth Centuries B.C.* Loeb Classical Library. Cambridge: Harvard University Press, 2003.

——. *Hesiod: Theogony.* Oxford: Clarendon Press, 1966.

Wiethoff, Tobias. "Interview mit dem Regisseur Wolfgang Petersen: 'Ich gehe dahin, wo der Stoff ist'." *Westdeutsche Zeitung* (May 7, 2004); http://www.wz-newsline.de/seschat4/200/sro.php?redid=58942.

Williams, Bernard. *Shame and Necessity.* Berkeley: University of California Press, 1993; rpt. 1994.

Winik, Jay. *April 1865: The Month That Saved America.* New York: HarperCollins, 2001.

Winkler, Martin M. "Altertumswissenschaftler im Kino; oder: *Quo vadis, philologia?*" *International Journal of the Classical Tradition,* 11 (2004), 95–110.

—— (ed.). *Classical Myth and Culture in the Cinema.* New York: Oxford University Press, 2001.

——. "Classical Mythology and the Western Film." *Comparative Literature Studies,* 22 (1985), 516–540.

—— (ed.). *Classics and Cinema.* London: Associated University Presses, 1991.

——. "*Dulce et decorum est pro patria mori?* Classical Literature in the War Film." *International Journal of the Classical Tradition,* 7 (2000), 177–214.

—— (ed.). *Gladiator: Film and History.* Oxford: Blackwell, 2004.

——. "Homeric *kleos* and the Western Film." *Syllecta Classica,* 7 (1996), 43–54.

——. "Neo-Mythologism: Apollo and the Muses on the Screen." *International Journal of the Classical Tradition,* 11 (2005), 383–423.

Wolf, Christa. *Cassandra.* Tr. Jan van Heurck. New York: Farrar, Strauss and Giroux, 1984.

Wood, Michael. *In Search of the Trojan War.* 2nd edn. Berkeley: University of California Press, 1996; rpt. 1998.

Woodford, Susan. *Images of Myths in Classical Antiquity.* Cambridge: Cambridge University Press, 2002; rpt. 2003.

——. *The Trojan War in Ancient Art.* Ithaca: Cornell University Press, 1993.

Woodhead, A. Geoffrey. *Thucydides on the Nature of Power.* Cambridge: Harvard University Press, 1970.

Wyke, Maria. "Are You Not Entertained? Classicists and Cinema." *International Journal of the Classical Tradition,* 9 (2003), 430–445.

——. "Classics and Contempt: Redeeming Cinema for the Classical Tradition." *Arion,* 3rd ser., 6.1 (1998), 124–136.

Young, Philip H. *The Printed Homer: A 3,000 Year Publishing and Translation History of the* Iliad *and the* Odyssey. Jefferson: McFarland, 2003.

Zambrano, Ana L. "Charles Dickens and Sergei Eisenstein: The Emergence of Cinema." *Style,* 9 (1975), 469–487.

Zander, Peter. "Deutscher Härtetest: Wolfgang Petersen hat 'Troja' verfilmt – und fand in den Sagen Parallelen zu George W. Bush." *Berliner Morgenpost* (May 12, 2004); http://morgenpost.berlin1.de/archiv2004/040512/feuilleton/story677622.html.

Index

This index covers the Introduction and Chapters 1–12. Entries for the city of Troy and for the film *Troy* have been excluded because of their ubiquitous occurrences throughout the book. Names of mythical and fictional characters have been excluded as well. Some of the films and film directors listed here are also dealt with in Chapter 13.